GOD-FLESHED

GOD-FLESHED

A Chronicle of the Comings of Christ

ROY ABRAHAM VARGHESE
WITH RACHEL AND MARY VARGHESE

A Crossroad Book
The Crossroad Publishing Company
New York

The Crossroad Publishing Company
481 Eighth Avenue, New York, NY 10001

Printed in the United States of America

Library of Congress Cataloging-in-Publication Data

Varghese, Roy Abraham.
    God-fleshed : a chronicle of the comings of Christ / Roy Abraham
Varghese ; with Rachel and Mary Varghese.
       p. cm.
    Includes bibliographical references.
    ISBN 0-8245-1893-4
    1. Jesus Christ – Person and offices. I. Varghese, Rachel.
II. Varghese, Mary. III. Title.
BT202 .V26 2001
232 – dc21
                              00-011167

1   2   3   4   5   6   7   8   9   10   06   05   04   03   02   01

For
Rani
Rena
Mohan

flesh of our flesh, blood of our blood.
May the Word-made-Flesh
feed you forever with His Flesh and Blood.

In the beginning was the Word, and the Word was with God, and the Word was God. (John 1:1)

In him dwells the whole fullness of the deity bodily. (Col. 2:9)

And the Word became flesh and made his dwelling among us. (John 1:14)

This man is all that has been, all that is and all that has to be. He controls eternal life and it is for the redemption of mankind he surpasses his immortal sphere and descends to the mortal sphere. He comes to give everyone reward as per their deeds. (*RigVeda* X:90:2, c. 1200–900 B.C.)

This man, the first born, was tied to a yoopa [*wooden sacrificial post*] and the gods and the kings along with the seers performed the sacrifice. (*RigVeda* X:90:7)

Those who meditate and attain this man, believe in heart and chant with their lips, get liberated in this world itself and there is no other way for salvation. (*YajurVeda* XXXI:18; *RigVeda* X:90:16)

King Shaka asked: "May I know, who you are?" With apparent joy that male replied, "Know that I am the Son of God. I am born in the womb of a virgin. 'Eesa Maseeha' is my well known name.'" (*Bhavishya Mahapuraana – Prathisarga Parva,* III, chap. 2, v. 23)

He was pierced for our offenses, crushed for our sins. Upon him was the chastisement that makes us whole, by his stripes we were healed....Like a lamb led to the slaughter or a sheep before the shearers, he was silent and opened not his mouth. (Isa. 53:5, 7)

As the visions during the night continued, I saw one like a son of man coming, on the clouds of heaven; when he reached the Ancient One and was presented before him, he received dominion, glory, and kingship; nations and peoples of every language serve him. His dominion is an everlasting dominion that shall not be taken away; his kingship shall not be destroyed. (Dan. 7:13–14)

Every spirit that acknowledges Jesus Christ come in the flesh belongs to God, and every spirit that does not acknowledge Jesus does not belong to God. (1 John 4:2–3)

Whoever eats my flesh and drinks my blood has eternal life. (John 6:54)

And not as common flesh do we receive it but as truly the life-giving and very flesh of the Word himself. (Council of Ephesus, 431)

Our paschal lamb, Christ, has been sacrificed. Therefore let us celebrate the feast. (1 Cor. 5:7)

Then the angel said to me, "Write this: Blessed are those who have been called to the wedding feast of the Lamb." (Rev. 19:9)

Without bread and cup, the Body and Blood of Christ would not be there. Without the Body and Blood of Christ, the New Testament would not be there. Without the New Testament, forgiveness of sins would not be there.... Forgiveness of sins embraces eternal life and salvation. See, all this the words of the Supper offer and give us, and we embrace it by faith. Ought not the devil, then, hate such a Supper and rouse fanatics against it? (Martin Luther, *Confession,* 338)

In the sacrament of the Lord's Supper, Jesus Christ, true God and true man, is present wholly and entirely in his body and blood, under the signs of bread and wine.... Our traditions have spoken of this presence as "sacramental," "supernatural" and "spiritual." These terms have different connotations in the two traditions, but they have in common a rejection of... an understanding of the sacrament as only commemorative or figurative. (*The Eucharist,* I, 3, Joint Declaration of the Lutheran-Roman Catholic Joint Commission, 1980)

Communion with Christ in the Eucharist presupposes his true presence, effectually signified by the bread and wine which, in this mystery, become his body and blood.... The elements are not mere signs; Christ's body and blood become really present and are really given. (*Final Report of the Anglican-Roman Catholic International Commission,* September 7, 1971)

But if every gram of material contains this tremendous energy, why did it go so long unnoticed? The answer is simple enough: so long as none of the energy is given off externally, it cannot be observed. It is as though a man who is fabulously rich should never spend or give away a cent; no one could tell how rich he was. (Albert Einstein, "E=MC^2," *Out of My Later Years*)

When I steeped myself in prayer, I was transported in spirit to the chapel, where I saw the Lord Jesus, exposed in the monstrance. In place of the monstrance, I saw the glorious face of the Lord, and He said to me, "What you see in reality, these souls see through faith. Oh, how pleasing to Me is their faith! You see, although there appears to be no trace of life in Me, in reality it is present in its fullness in each and every Host. But for Me to be able to act upon a soul, the soul must have faith. O how pleasing to Me is living faith." (Sister Faustina Kowalska)

Contents

Acknowledgments

We wish to express our gratitude to the following individuals for their kind assistance in the creation of this volume:

Anila Varghese   Kazimierz Dadak
Michael Abraham Varghese   Fiorella de Ferrari
Tim Laurel   Ann Ball
Brian Hanlon   Ann McGlone
Bryan Thatcher   Dan Gallo
William R. Farmer   Dudley Plunkett

Msgr. George W. Rost, Rector, Basilica of the Sacred Heart of Jesus, Hanover, Pennsylvania, for the portrait of the Sacred Heart

The Sylvestrine-Benedictine monks of the Monastery of the Holy Face of Jesus, Clifton, New Jersey, for the portrait of the Shroud of Turin

The National Shrine of the Infant Jesus of Prague, Prague, Oklahoma, for the portrait of the Infant Jesus of Prague

The Discalced Carmelite Nuns of Dallas, Texas, for the Portrait of Veronica's Veil.

The Franciscan priests of the Santuario del Miracolo Eucaristico in Lanciano, Italy

Introduction

The third Christian millennium directs our hearts and minds to the past and the future, to the Event that divides history into B.C. and A.D. and its significance for the age ahead of us. *God-Fleshed: A Chronicle of the Comings of Christ* is a study of the claim that the divine Life incarnated Itself two thousand years ago and that humankind itself has since been drawn into the very Life of God ("what came to be through him was life and this life was the light of the human race"; "in him dwells the whole fullness of the deity bodily and you share in this fullness in him"). The Incarnation, we will try to show, did not end with the death of the Word Who "became flesh and made his dwelling among us." On the contrary, all of human history since His death has been alive with His presence and activity. In point of fact, every word He uttered in the accredited narratives of His disciples has continually incarnated itself in humanly inexplicable phenomena and celestial missives that are as poignant as they are profound.

Paradoxically, this dramatic body of data — so compelling in its cross-historical magnitude and enduring mystical power — has been almost entirely ignored by the theologians and New Testament critics who constantly embark on expeditions to recover the Jesus of history in order to reconstruct the Christ of faith. As a result of the endeavors of the sensationalists among them over the last two hundred years, there is now more confusion about the identity of Jesus Christ both in academia and in popular media portrayals than ever before in history since the Arian heresy. Let us hasten to add that this is no indictment of either serious scholarship or honest rational inquiry, both of which are essential prerequisites for truth-judgments. But works that spring from irrational skepticism in the face of hard facts, theories that portray wild speculation as sober history, and fads introduced for their sensationalist shock value are a different matter. Sadly, many of today's headline-grabbing lives of Jesus belong to this category. Although every one of them has had a short life span — what is contemporary is temporary — they have done their damage in creating a thought-climate of confusion and disbelief. Fortunately, in parallel with the turn to theism in much of modern science and philosophy, there has been a significant movement in mainstream New Testament studies of the present day toward a rational grounding of the story and sayings of Jesus. Time after time, we find that the Jesus Who was buried by the critics of one generation rises again in the writings of the scholars of the next.

Nevertheless, a truly comprehensive consideration of Jesus Christ cannot be restricted to a study of the New Testament texts. Texts cannot argue back when they are explained away or ignored or distorted. It is more difficult to explain away events and encounters that continue to occur in contemporary settings. Far more noteworthy (and newsworthy) than the latest sensational theories of the theologians are the innumerable instances of the physical transformation of the Eucharistic elements solemnly consecrated in accordance with the command of Christ; the manifestation of His wounds in holy men and women; and His supernal reaffirmations of His Message of infinite mercy and love to holy men and women throughout Christian history. These and similar phenomena are data that demand an explanation. It is our contention that the classical identification of Jesus with the God of Israel and the postulation of the Eucharist as a vehicle of the divine Life best explain the cascade of spectacular phenomena under review here. These postulates fit the facts better than any competing hypothesis, past or present, but most critics who reject the classical postulates ignore the striking facts they explain. Their counter-hypotheses are almost always based on their own speculation and do not even pretend to address or account for any of the related events that have taken place since the New Testament narratives were first documented.

The Face of God

In reviewing the data, we begin with the primordial source underlying all other affirmations about Jesus, the New Testament narratives. In this review, we start with four hard facts that cannot be denied by any inquirer:

1. There are nearly two billion people today who claim that Jesus Christ is God and that His death is somehow fundamental to human salvation.

2. There is a body of writing, called the New Testament, that presents the life and teaching of Jesus as understood by His followers. In these writings, Jesus claims to be the Messiah of Israel, the Anointed One, Who is identified with Yahweh, the God of Israel.

3. The first followers of Jesus were initially demoralized by His execution but were then totally transformed by an experience that gave them strength and courage to confront the most powerful empire of their time and to give up their lives preaching the Gospel of Jesus. These followers claimed that Jesus appeared to them physically after His death as He had promised.

4. This experience of the Risen Jesus continued and continues to bring millions of people from unbelief to faith in Christ.

In part 1, "Christos," we consider the latest discussions in New Testament scholarship in the light of these hard facts and conclude that:

1. there can be little doubt that Jesus worked miracles;
2. the New Testament texts and the beliefs of the early Christians indicate that Jesus identified Himself with God;
3. there is a historical core to the story of the empty tomb;
4. the transformation of the disciples cannot be explained without accepting their story of the resurrection of Jesus
5. the transformation of millions of other people through the centuries can best be explained by reference to the claim that Jesus Christ was God Incarnate.

We note here that the fundamental flaw in modern New Testament studies and the numerous "searches" for the "historical Jesus" — from Reimarus to the Jesus Seminar — may be described as the "fish out of water" syndrome. There are two ways to study a fish: either as it swims around in its natural habitat or when it is taken out of the water and set on a dry surface. The two ways of studying it will yield radically different results. In the first instance, the fish is alive and acting in its natural mode. In the second, it struggles to survive, then dies, and finally rots. The contention here is that the search for the historical Jesus — especially as practiced in the last two hundred years — belongs to the second category. A historically legitimate study of the New Testament is possible only if it is carried out within the context of the community that gave it birth — and it is in this context that we consider the Jesus of history.

In recognizing the Incarnation of God in Christ, we inevitably encounter the question of the world religions. If Jesus is God and man, what do we make of the hundreds of other religions and belief systems that coexist in the world today? This is a question worthy of an entire library of books, and we cannot hope to address it in any adequate or comprehensive fashion here.

Nevertheless, there is an important perspective on this issue, described in chapter 3, "The Witness of Mythology and the World Religions," that has rarely been brought to light. The religions of the world can be divided into pre- and post-Christian religions. The three most ancient and influential pre-Christian religions were the revelation-centered world-vision of the people of Israel, the belief system derived from the Vedas of India, and the mystery-mythology cults of the Mediterranean. Remarkably, all three of these major religious ensembles in different ways and degrees speak of a god who becomes man and sacrifices himself for the salvation of humanity. While the Israelite prophets spoke of the Messiah who was to be "pierced for our offenses" the Vedic scribes portray Prajapathi, the First-born of the Supreme Spirit Who becomes the Creator of all things and is the Sacrificer at His own Sacrifice on a wooden stake, a Sacrifice borne to save humanity from the bondage of sin. Is it simply a coincidence that the dominant thought-forms of the pre-Christian world were "mentally" prepared for the historical actuality of God becoming man and dying on the Cross for the salvation of humanity? Just as the roads of the Roman Empire ensured the rapid spread of the Christian message and the conceptual tools of Greek thought enabled the clear formulation of Christian doctrine, so the pre-Christian religions prepared the mind, imagination, and psyche of the ancient world for the Incarnation of God in Jesus Christ. Thus the Son of God entered history only after first coming into the world in myth and prophecy.

The Heart of God

The physicist Stephen Hawking concludes his book *A Brief History of Time* with the proclamation that "the ultimate triumph of human reason" would be "to know the mind of God." Although reason on its own is incapable of such a triumph, it can still lead us to the discernment that God has chosen to make His "mind" known through acts in history that reached their climax in the life and teaching of Jesus Christ. But it was not just His Mind that He disclosed to us. His public revelation in the Jesus of first-century Palestine was followed by private revelations to chosen souls in subsequent centuries. The messages that these holy and sincere souls claim to have received from the same Jesus are of interest simply from the standpoint of the insight they give us into the "heart" of God and into how He sees us and our actions. Those who wish "to know the heart of God" have only to read the messages accompanying the two most influential private revelations of Jesus, the Sacred Heart and the Divine Mercy.

Part 2, "Agnus Dei," concerns these and other visions of Jesus experienced in the centuries after the compilation of the New Testament. Christian doctrines are not simply conceptual constructions built from biblical verses or theological theories. They are descriptions of reality, of the way the world is. Consequently, the doctrines have often come to life in actual events in history. Since the time of Christ, the three main kinds of phenomena involving Christian doctrine have been appearances of Mary, visions of Christ, and miracles of the Eucharist. *God-Sent: A History of the Accredited Apparitions of Mary* considered the first of these phenomena, one that is remarkable simply in terms of history and geography: these apparitions have been reported across the world and in every era after Christ. Credible claims of visions of Jesus, however, have in general been restricted to selected souls, and the messages transmitted in these visions focus on the infinite love and mercy of Jesus and the terrible pain that sin inflicts on Him. The third class of phenomena, miracles of the Eucharist, began in the Age of the Apostles and continues to this very day.

Concerning claims of visions of Jesus, detailed in part 2, it must be clarified first that even in an authentic vision, Jesus is not present in His Risen Body, for He clearly taught that He will not come again in a corporeal mode until the end of history. He is present to the mind of the visionary and present mentally rather than physically. This difference in mode does not affect the fact that the messages received are actual messages from Him. Moreover, the application of certain criteria will help us distinguish authentic visions of Jesus from hallucinations. The messages received in the accredited visions are less novel revelations than they are expositions and amplifications of the Gospel teachings akin to the great liturgies. The primary theme is the Passion of Christ: the unconditionality of God's love and mercy and the continuing cost of sin. The messages are important in turning the Passion from a distant memory to a present reality, from theological abstraction to stupefying Fact. Concurrent with the visionary encounter with Jesus is the actual participation in His Passion experienced by victim souls who bear the stigmata. These phenomena again reinforce the centrality of the Passion.

The Incarnation with its culmination in the supreme Act of Redemption was the greatest event in human history. Since the eternal fate of every human person is directly related to this momentous Event, it is hardly something that could be expected to remain in the background. The message of Jesus will not be left to the mercy of historians and theologians. Moreover, the pain and suffering inflicted on a divine Person by His creatures — and borne in His freely offered Sacrifice — is infinite in its magnitude because it was experienced in all its horror by an infinite Person. It is the centrality of the Incarnation and the Passion, then, that make them ever-present realities in all of subsequent history, realities that sometimes manifest themselves both as obscurely and as dramatically as the Incarnation Itself.

The visions and messages of Jesus are of especial importance in the third millennium because we live in an age in which the forces of evil, both within ourselves and without, seem to have overcome all that is good and pure and holy. Weakness of will, darkness of intellect, and hardness of heart seem inevitable and irresistible. Every environment is an occasion of temptation, every thought leaves a new stain on the soul, every impulse is the instrument of another fall that instantly wipes out everything achieved in the past. Given the depth of the darkness that has descended on us, it would be reasonable to expect nothing but wrath and retribution from the All-Holy God of Infinite Justice. But the Jesus Who speaks to us through the great private revelations of the last century comes to us with an entirely different message.

On the one hand, every sin is another wound we inflict on Jesus, another freely chosen step toward self-inflicted punishment in this world and damnation in the next. On the other hand, paradoxically, every time and any number of times we sin and repent, we come closer to Him than we were when we remained smug and self-righteous. The two greatest dangers are self-satisfied pride at one extreme and despair after sin at the other. These conditions are far more repulsive to God than a fall followed by repentance. If this seems too good to be true, let's consider a few representative messages chronicled by St. Faustina Kowalska and Sr. Josefa Menéndez.

St. Faustina

"Proclaim that mercy is the greatest attribute of God. All the works of My hands are crowned with mercy."[1]

"Even if the sins of soul are as dark as night, when the sinner turns to My mercy, he gives Me the greatest praise and is the glory of My passion."[2]

"Let the greatest sinners place their trust in My mercy. They have the right before others to trust in the abyss of My mercy. My daughter, write about My mercy towards tormented souls. Souls that make an appeal to My mercy delight Me. To such souls I grant even more graces than they ask. I cannot punish even the greatest sinner if he makes an appeal to My compassion, but on the contrary, I justify him in My unfathomable and inscrutable mercy."[3]

"The cause of your falls is that you rely too much upon yourself and too little on Me. But let this not sadden you so much. You are dealing with the God of mercy, which your misery cannot exhaust. Remember, I did not allot only a certain number of pardons. My child, know that the greatest obstacles to holiness are discouragement and an exaggerated anxiety."[4]

Sr. Josefa Menéndez

"A soul will profit even after the greatest sins, if she humbles herself."

"My Heart is not so much wounded by sin, as torn with grief that they will not take refuge with Me after it."[5]

"I pursue sinners as justice pursues criminals. But justice seeks them in order to punish, I, in order to forgive."[6]

"I love those who after a first fall come to Me for pardon. I love them still more when they beg pardon for their second sin, and should this happen again, I do not say a million times, but a million million times, I still love them and pardon them, and I will wash in My Blood their last as fully as their first sin."[7]

If it is said that this sounds like wishful thinking, we must remind skeptics that "Do not be afraid" is the theme sounded most often in the verses of Scripture. And it was St. Paul who wrote, "Where sin increased, grace overflowed all the more" (Rom. 5:20) and "God delivered all to disobedience, that he might have mercy upon all" (Rom. 11:32).

Granted, St. Paul also warns us that God "will repay everyone according to his works: eternal life to those who seek glory, honor and immortality through perseverance in good works, but wrath and fury to those who selfishly disobey the truth and obey wickedness" (Rom. 2:6–8).

And this warning is also found in all the private revelations. Despite the promise of mercy and the invitation to repentance, we can still choose to persist in our rejection of God to the very end. Since God's unconditional love respects the freedom of our will, the soul that does not want Him will be separated from Him. Thus St. Faustina reports this anguished message,

"Often a soul wounds Me mortally, and then no one can comfort Me. They use My graces to offend Me. These are souls who despise My graces as well as all the proofs of My love. They do not wish to hear My call, but proceed into the abyss of hell. The loss of these souls plunges Me into deadly sorrow.

God though I am, I cannot help such a soul because it scorns Me; having a free will, it can spurn Me or love Me."[8]

"Before I come as a just Judge, I first open wide the door of My mercy. He who refuses to pass through the door of My mercy must pass through the door of My justice."[9]

But the possibility that we might reject God should not discourage us. Rather it should spur us on to distrust our own capabilities totally on the one hand and trust God totally on the other. We should begin with the awareness that life on earth is going to be a never-ending struggle between good and evil both within and without us. St. Faustina is warned, "My child, life on earth is a struggle indeed." Nevertheless she is also given this assurance, "But fear not, because you are not alone. I am always supporting you, so lean on Me as you struggle, fearing nothing."[10]

The messages of the New Testament, the private revelations in the visions of Jesus, and the advice of the great spiritual masters of the past form one unified whole:

1. God is Holiness Itself and cannot tolerate the slightest sin. He demands not simply the proclamation of faith but faith translated into practice: "Not everyone who says to me, 'Lord, Lord,' will enter the kingdom of heaven, but only the one who does the will of my Father in heaven. Many will say to me on that day, 'Lord, Lord, did we not prophesy in your name? Did we not drive out demons in your name? Did we not do mighty deeds in your name?' Then I will declare to them solemnly, 'I never knew you. Depart from me you evildoers.' Everyone who listens to these words and acts on them will be like a wise man who built his house on rock" (Matt. 7:21–24).

2. The greatest danger to our souls is not falling into sin but resting in pride, pride that is manifested most often in smug self-righteousness. "If we say, 'We are without sin,' we deceive ourselves, and the truth is not in us. If we acknowledge our sins, he is faithful and just and will forgive our sins and cleanse us from every wrongdoing" (John 1:8–9). Sin can bring us to our senses if we recognize its repulsive nature and our slavery to it as well as the need for repentance and constant reliance on God. "The tax collector stood off at a distance and would not even raise his eyes to heaven but beat his breast and prayed, 'O God be merciful to me a sinner.' I tell you, the latter went home justified, not the former" (Luke 18:13–4). Moreover, "There will be more joy in heaven over one sinner who repents than over ninety-nine righteous people who have no need for repentance" (Luke 15:7).

3. Repentance is a lifelong process and growth in holiness depends on our continuing penitence for the sins of the past and constant watchfulness. In their great epistles on good and evil, both St. Paul and St. Peter are conscious of their own past failings and God's solution: St. Paul tells us of the need for repentance and reliance on God's mercy and St. Peter about the need to be "sober and vigilant."

4. True repentance requires great love as well as amendment of our lives, prayer, self-denial, and, of course, constant humility. The repentant woman in the Gospels shows "great love" because "her many sins have been forgiven" (Luke 7:47). "The love of God is this, that we keep his commandments" (1 John 5:3), and "If you do not repent, you will all perish as they did" (Luke 13:3). In addition, "If you live according to the flesh, you will die, but if by the spirit you put to death the deeds of the body, you will live" (Rom. 8:13). "Whoever thinks he is standing secure should take care not to fall" (1 Cor. 10:12).

5. St. Peter lays out a pathway for receiving God's "precious and very great promises" and sharing "in the divine nature": the faithful must persevere in supplementing their "faith with virtue, virtue with knowledge, knowledge with self-control, self-control with endurance, endurance with devotion, devotion with mutual affection, mutual affection with love" (2 Pet. 1:5–7). Anyone who lacks these is "blind and shortsighted, forgetful of the cleansing of his past sins." Rather these actions must "increase in abundance" in you and you should be "all the more eager to make your call and election firm, for in doing so, you will never stumble. For, in this way, entry into the eternal kingdom of our Lord and Savior Jesus Christ will be richly provided to you" (2 Pet. 1:10–11).

Many of the devotions and practices "packaged" with the revelations of the Sacred Heart and the Divine Mercy, for instance the Nine First Fridays and the celebration of Mercy Sunday, are "programs" for implementing this scriptural path to salvation. No one knows better than the God Who is Mercy that we have never needed these weapons and shields as desperately and continually as we do today.

The Life of God

Whereas visions of Jesus were purportedly witnessed by specific individuals at specific points of time and space, Christians have consistently taught that the Eucharist represents a continual coming of Christ across the world. The Eucharist has been defined as "a prayer of thanksgiving and praise over the elements of bread and wine." The term, as we discuss it here, refers not just to the prayer of consecration but also to the New Reality that comes about after the prayer, namely, the very Flesh and Blood of God Incarnate. For the objective observer, we present the following sequence of facts that call for an explanation:

1. At various points in history, the bread and wine consecrated at Mass have verifiably turned into flesh and blood and, more important, have retained the characteristics of flesh and blood sometimes through centuries — a scientifically inexplicable datum.

2. Most such transformations have taken place in response to either disbelief in the presence of Christ in the consecrated elements or sacrilegious acts.

3. The only framework of explanation offered for these events is the Christian claim that the act of consecration at Mass transforms bread and wine into the Body and Blood of Jesus Christ and that, though this is a transformation of reality rather than appearance, on occasion God brings about a transformation of appearance as well to confirm the change of reality.

4. Some Christians in the last four hundred years have denied the doctrine of the transformation but their denials are inconsistent with the teaching of Jesus and St. Paul, the writings of the Fathers, the proclamations of the Councils, and the texts of the ancient liturgies that reflected the faith of the first Christians.

In presenting the Eucharistic story in part 3, "Corpus Christi," we begin with the biblical data. The recent controversies over the existence of a "Bible Code" of secret messages encrypted in the text of the Old Testament have eclipsed the reality of another Code that requires neither computers nor convoluted argumentation for its decryption. A study of biblical texts from Genesis to Revelation and the exposition of these texts by those who were closest to the New Testament writers reveals a Truth that is far more fundamental and far-reaching than anything conceived by those who posited the "Bible Code." The themes that constitute the Code may be illustrated by the parallels shown in the table on the following page.

The institution of the Eucharist at the Last Supper is so central that it is documented in the three Synoptic Gospels and in St. Paul's epistle to the Corinthians. The necessity and significance of the Eucharist is laid out in John 6. Now, when Jesus said, "Take and eat; this is my body," He meant His statement to be taken either symbolically or literally. A study of the earliest liturgies and the early Fathers will show that the first Christians certainly understood Him literally. Of course, interpretation is the issue. But it is simply a superstition to assume that true interpretations of biblical texts emerge out of the blue. In the first place, every text can be interpreted in different (sometimes contradictory) ways. Secondly, fundamental Christian doctrines were defined after centuries of reflection on the biblical message. From a historical standpoint, the only way to crack the Bible Code is to rely on those for whom the Code was a language: the contemporaries and disciples of the Apostles with the liturgies and letters they have bestowed on posterity. Here we find that the Eucharist played a central role in the ancient liturgies and Councils and the writings of the Fathers: a full-blooded, fully fleshed-out Christianity inevitably centered on the Flesh and Blood of Christ. In the same breath that the Councils defined the flesh of Christ as "the flesh of God the Word" (Constantinople III) they also proclaimed that

> when he became united to his Flesh, he made it also to be Life-giving, as also he said to us: Verily, verily, I say unto you, Except ye eat the flesh of the Son of Man and drink his Blood. For we must not think that it is flesh of a man like us (for how can the flesh of man be life-giving by its own nature?) but as having become truly the very own of him who for us both became and was called Son of Man. (Ephesus)

Old Testament	*New Testament*
Abraham, the Father of Israel, offers up his son as a sacrifice	God the Father gives His Only begotten Son for He "so loved the world"
Lamb without blemish offered up in sacrifice	The all-holy Lamb of God (Jesus) offered up in sacrifice
The blood of the lamb preserves the People of God from physical death	The Blood of the Lamb preserves the People of God from spiritual death
Blood of animals offered in sacrifice seals the old covenant	Blood of the Lamb offered in sacrifice seals the new covenant
The Feast of Passover is a commemoration of the first Passover and is to be celebrated by the sacrifice of a lamb and the complete consumption of its flesh	The Lord's Supper is a commemoration of the Last Paschal Meal and is to be celebrated by the unbloody offering of the Lamb and the consumption of Its Flesh
Bread from heaven preserves the people of Israel in the desert	The Daily Bread from the Father in Heaven gives strength and deliverance from evil. Jesus is born in Bethlehem, which means "House of Bread."
God is literally present among His People in the Ark of the Covenant, which also contains the heavenly manna	God is literally present among His People in the Body and Blood of the Lord, which consummates the New Covenant and which retains the appearance of bread and wine
Desecration of the Ark of the Covenant results in sickness and death	Unworthy reception of the Lord's Body and Blood results in sickness and death
Prophecy of a pure sacrifice offered in all nations from the rising of the sun to its setting	The Lord's Supper is to be celebrated by Jews and Gentiles until the Second Coming of the Lord
The High Priest makes atonement for his sins and the sins of his people by entering and offering blood once a year in the Holy of Holies, which is patterned on Heaven	The eternal High Priest makes atonement once for all for the sins of His People by shedding His own blood and then enters Heaven itself, where He serves as a Minister of the Sanctuary and commences a ministry of intercession for those who approach Him

It must be remarked here that Jesus' command that we eat His Body and drink His Blood is unique in recorded religious history (here we are talking of history not mythology; the witness of mythology will be considered presently). No prophet of Israel, no Hindu, Buddhist, Taoist, or Confucian sage had ever asked his followers to consume him. But this is exactly what Jesus commanded, adding that only those who followed this command would receive eternal life.

He was Life and to receive this Life, to share in the divine Life, one would have to eat His Flesh.

But what does it mean to say that Jesus is present in the Eucharist? Here modern science may be helpful at least in giving us a viable model. *The change that takes place at the consecration of the Eucharistic elements is the transformation of lifeless matter into a vehicle of the divine Life.* Hence every instance of the genesis of life — from the cellular level to the creation of the conscious self — is a distant image of the Eucharistic Event. The thesis developed here is that *the drama of the manifestation of progressively higher forms of life in the world, which began with the creation of matter out of nothing and continued with the elevation of matter into various forms of life, reaches its climax with a transformation as dramatic as the initial creation out of nothing: namely, the elevation of matter into a vehicle for the highest form of life, the divine Life that underlies all of creation.* The infinite Energy of the Eucharist is a spiritual energy, and it can be experienced only by the soul (assuming, of course, that it has not defaced its "communication link" to the Energy Source). The invisibility of spiritual energy is analogous to the hiddenness of material energy. About the latter, Albert Einstein remarked, "But if every gram of material contains this tremendous energy, why did it go so long unnoticed? The answer is simple enough: so long as none of the energy is given off externally, it cannot be observed. It is as though a man who is fabulously rich should never spend or give away a cent; no one could tell how rich he was."

The Eucharist becomes present to us at the Sacrifice of the Mass. On the basis of Scripture and the understanding of Scripture given us by the Fathers and Councils of the Church, we speak of the Mass as a participation in Calvary, the Last Supper, and the heavenly intercession that Jesus continues to make on our behalf before the Father. At the Paschal Meal, Jesus announced His intention to lay down His life in atonement for sin — and called on His followers to eat His Flesh and drink His Blood as a memorial of this Event. At Calvary, He executes His intention. And, finally, in Heaven, He continues to intercede for us before the Father (Hebrews, Revelation).

Each offering gives meaning to the next: the offering made at the Last Supper shows the purpose of the Passion, and the Passion makes possible the intercession in Heaven. The Mass in turn brings all three offerings before us here and now. It is by no means a repetition or a new offering: it is simply a manifestation in earthly terms of the one continuous Act of Offering in Heaven made by the Son before the Father. Moreover, a thousand Masses do not diminish the definitive nature of the actual historical sacrifice on Calvary, just as a thousand performances of a symphony by Beethoven do not signify that there was no original composition.

Concurrent with the witness to the Eucharist in Scripture, theology, and liturgy, there is also a historical witness to the Eucharist that comes to us in the great miracles of the Eucharist. For our purposes here, we define a miracle of the Eucharist as (1) any phenomenon involving a naturally inexplicable transformation in the physical and observable appearance of the consecrated Host or the consecrated "wine," and/or (2) a singularity in which the Host or the "wine" is observed to transcend a law of nature (for instance, the law of gravity).

Eucharistic miracles have been classified under the following categories:

- Transformation of the Host into flesh
- Appearance of blood on the Host
- Transformation of the consecrated "wine" into blood
- Preservation of Hosts over centuries
- Hosts that transcend gravity or other laws of nature
- Visions of Jesus witnessed by the congregation during the consecration of the Host
- Lifetime subsistence on the Host

Simply from the standpoint of "hard facts," claims of the major Eucharistic miracles cannot be ignored or dismissed for the following reasons:

- They cannot be hallucinations since the subjects of some of these miracles — Hosts that have turned to flesh — are even today available for tangible observation.
- The continued preservation of the Host or of the flesh or the blood as the case may be over a period sometimes of centuries is not explicable from a scientific standpoint.
- In cases where it is claimed that the Host turned to flesh, scientific analysis in the main instances has shown that the object in question is human flesh. How this flesh could retain its original characteristics over hundreds of years despite exposure to physical, biological, and atmospheric contaminants is inexplicable on a purely natural level.
- In cases where the miracle is a claim of the consecrated wine turning to blood, again scientific analysis has confirmed that we are dealing with human blood. It is well known that blood loses its chemical properties within an hour of being shed and blood from a dead body decays almost immediately.

These phenomena are not restricted to ancient or medieval times. Reliable reports of the conversion of Hosts into flesh and blood continue to emerge even in the present day, and in certain cases these conversions have been accurately recorded. Four categories of Eucharistic miracles are considered here:

1. Ancient Eucharistic Miracles with Continuous Contemporary Evidence
2. Modern Eucharistic Miracles with Continuous Contemporary Evidence
3. Hosts That Transcended the Laws of Nature
4. Visions of Jesus during the Mass.

On the "negative" side, we also consider the belief of satanists in the Real Presence of Jesus in the Eucharist.

The Glory of God

The conclusion, "Alpha and Omega," is a consideration of the end of the world, but "end" in the sense of its purpose, not its terminus. The true end, the consummation and crowning glory of the material creation, was the Incarnation of the Son of God. Only when the Word became Flesh could our flesh participate in the Life of the Word. The event that made the ultimate union of the Divine and the human possible was material and spiritual: He had to shed His Blood and give up His Body. It is this same Body and Blood that we now receive at His great wedding feast, for the vehicle through which the God-Fleshed gives us His Life is Itself material. Both the Resurrection of Christ and the transmission of divine Life through the Eucharist are the initial manifestations of the ultimate transformation of the world, the coming to be of a new heaven and a new earth.

The subtitle of this book, *A Chronicle of the Comings of Christ,* bears on the four senses in which we can speak of the coming of Christ (which is also the structural sequence of the book): the incarnation of God in Christ in first-century Palestine ("Christos"); the accredited visions of Jesus in subsequent history ("Agnus Dei"); the daily miracle of the Eucharist ("Corpus Christi"); and the coming in glory at the end of time ("Alpha and Omega"). It should, nevertheless, be clarified that the Christian Faith knows of only two definitive Comings of Christ: the Incarnation itself and the Second Coming at the end of history. We speak of visions as "comings" only in an analogous sense: Jesus does not appear to these selected souls in His Risen Body. And although He is truly present in the Eucharist, it is a Presence that brings us before His glorified Body in Heaven: and in this sense the Mass truly takes us to Heaven. All that we know of Jesus through visions and the Eucharist, then, serves simply to consolidate and amplify what we knew from the Gospels while preparing our minds and hearts for the Final Coming.

PART ONE

CHRISTOS

What do we know about Jesus? If you start just with history, we know that in today's world nearly two billion people claim that Jesus is God and man, that He rose from the dead and that He will come again in glory. Another datum of evidence is the New Testament, a collection of writings that includes four Gospels with different accounts of the life, death, and resurrection of Jesus, as well as the letters of Paul, which include valuable traditions about Jesus. Then we have the doctrines about Jesus decisively laid out in the teachings of the Councils of the Church that began with the Council of Jerusalem. Additionally, we have (1) the writings of the early Church Fathers from Asia and Europe who expounded specific teachings about Jesus, (2) the ancient liturgies of the Church that implicitly "propounded" the beliefs about Jesus held by the first Christian communities, and (3) the conversion experiences of millions of people across the world and throughout history who accepted Jesus as Lord and Savior. Finally, many holy men and women through the centuries have claimed to have had visions of Jesus. Some of them further affirmed that they received specific messages from Him, and others were privileged to participate in His suffering often by visibly bearing the kinds of wounds He bore on the cross.

Although this book is largely concerned with the post–New Testament visions and messages of Christ and with the great Eucharistic miracles, its starting points are the veracity of the Gospel accounts of Jesus and the truth of the teachings about Jesus found in the Fathers, Councils, and liturgies of the Christian Church. What do the Gospel accounts show us? They show us a Person Who claimed to be both God and man and was thus regarded by His followers ("Before Abraham came to be, I AM" (John 8:58); " 'Are you the Messiah, the Son of the Blessed One?' Then Jesus answered, 'I am' " (Mark 14:61); "In him dwells the whole fullness of the deity *bodily*" (Col. 2:9); Who performed fundamental miracles of nature (restoring sight, bringing a dead person back to life); Whose life mirrored Isaiah's prophetic saga of the Suffering Servant; and Who was morally irreproachable. A key question in this context was whether or not Jesus would — as He claimed — be raised to life after being put to death by His enemies.

Here we turn to history. We know without doubt that Christianity has spread to every corner of the world, that it began its genesis in first-century Israel, and that its initial "evangelists" were the Jewish followers of Christ. What needs explanation is the transformation of these evangelists from cowering fisherfolk and peasantry who had just witnessed the murder of their Master into death-defying, world-traveling messengers of the Good News. What made them, men who had never left the safety of home, take on the most powerful empire of their time and sacrifice their lives in distant lands? To the very last, in the face of horrible deaths at the hands of savages, they held firm and bore witness to one truth: Christ had risen from the dead. No other explanation for the change in the disciples — and of the changed lives of millions throughout history — is plausible without reference to the actual historical resurrection of Jesus Christ from the dead. This is one of those "obvious facts" that cannot be explained away without the mental equivalents of blindfolds and earplugs.

Having said all this, we must acknowledge that it is all but impossible to address the issue of who Jesus is in isolation from the contemporary conversation in New Testament studies. Two questions dominate this arena: What do we know about Jesus from the available textual evidence and what can be concluded from this evidence as to His identity? To a third party, two other questions might seem even more fundamental: Should New Testament studies and the speculation of scholars play a role in reaching a conclusion on the identity of Jesus and, if so, to what extent? What other sources of information are available in addressing the question of His identity?

Over the last two decades, the present author has engaged in discussions and projects — including the organization of three international conferences and the production of an anthology entitled *Crisis in Christology* — centering on precisely these questions. Contributors included such acclaimed New Testament scholars as Peter Stuhlmacher and Martin Hengel of Tübingen, N. T. Wright of Oxford, C. F. D. Moule and Brian Hebblethwaite of Cambridge, Wolfhart Pannenberg, known for his work on the Resurrection, William R. Farmer, editor of the *International Bible Commentary,* and Benjamin Meyer, author of *The Aims of Jesus.* Although their input was invaluable, the opinions expressed here are the sole responsibility of the author, and it is likely that at least some of them will disagree with the conclusions of this study. Moreover, Professor William Farmer, the editor also of *Crisis in Christology* and the author of numerous works on the New Testament narratives, kindly reviewed this section of the book, at the request of the author, and his critical analysis has helped preserve it from at least a few obvious pitfalls. Nonetheless Professor Farmer by no means endorses the views expressed here and, of course, any errors that survived his erudite scrutiny must be attributed entirely to the author.

Chapter 1

The Search for
the Jesus of History

This is not the place for an exhaustive study of the current state of New Testament scholarship. Our concern rather is to consider the intersection of these academic pursuits with both logical principles and extra-textual evidence available to all. Below first is a chronology of the so-called "search for the historical Jesus." (N. T. Wright's *Who Was Jesus?* presents a more detailed study of these movements and individuals.)

1694–1768   HERMANN S. REIMARUS. Originator of the Quest for the Historical Jesus. Jesus seen as a Jewish revolutionary Whose mission failed and Whose body was stolen by the disciples who then concocted various stories about Him. The miracle stories were mere fictions. Reimarus was a Deist, and his writings must be seen against the background of the anti-supernaturalism of the Enlightenment that had begun to take root in Europe. He was the first to draw a distinction between the historical Jesus on one side and the Jesus of the Gospels and the Christ of faith on the other. It has been said that Reimarus substituted dogmatic orthodoxy with dogmatic skepticism.

1808–1874   DAVID F. STRAUSS. In his *Life of Jesus, Critically Examined,* Strauss claimed that what "was once sacred history for the believer is, for the enlightened portion of our contemporaries, only fable." Most of the stories in the Gospels, especially the miracles, he said, were "myths." The depiction of Jesus as the miracle-working Son of God was simply mythological. The philosopher Friedrich Nietzche gave up Christian belief after

29

reading Strauss's book in 1864. He remarked that "if you give up Christ, you give up God also" and was later to postulate the dictum that "God is dead." Nietzche's work influenced, among others, Adolf Hitler.

1841   BRUNO BAUER. In three volumes Bauer sought to show that Jesus never existed. Although this view had some influence for two generations after him in German universities, it is not taken seriously today even by prominent atheists. Marx and Engels made the nonexistence of Jesus a dogma of Marxism. Rudolf Bultmann, the most influential skeptical scholar of the last century, wrote: "Of course the doubt as to whether Jesus really existed is not worth refutation. No sane person can doubt that Jesus stands as founder behind the historical community whose first distinct stage is represented by the oldest Palestinian community."[1]

1823–1892   ERNEST RENAN. Renan held that Jesus was a moral teacher Whose mission failed and Whose teachings have been misrepresented by a repressive church. (He is reminiscent of Crossan and Funk in our own day.)

1832–1910   H. J. HOLTZMANN. Holtzmann solidified the idea that Mark was the first of the Gospels to be written (Marcan priority), along with another missing document of sayings of Jesus called "Q" (from the German "Quelle" for "source"), and that the other Gospels are based on Mark. In his view Mark and Q were more historical than theological and mythological. He considered Jesus to be simply a teacher of timeless ethical truths.

1863–1914   JOHANNES WEISS. Weiss saw Jesus' teachings about the Kingdom of God in the context of Jewish eschatology and a belief in the impending end of the world.

1875–1965   ALBERT SCHWEITZER, author of *The Quest of the Historical Jesus,* disputed both traditional teachings about Jesus and the liberal orthodoxies of his day. He understood Jesus and his teaching in terms of contemporary Jewish apocalyptic belief systems. Jesus saw himself as the Messiah announcing the Kingdom of God — namely the end of the world — whose death was required to bring about the Kingdom. But the world did not end after he died, and the only way in which Jesus lives on is in his radical message.

1910s   REV. R. J. CAMPBELL. In his New Theology, Campbell proclaimed that "Jesus was God but so are we" and that humanity and divinity were two sides of one great consciousness.

1884–1976   RUDOLF BULTMANN / FORM CRITICAL SCHOOL. Bultmann believed that the Gospels do not give us a reliable portrait of Jesus. His focus was on the faith of the early Church as reflected in the "Jesus stories." In his view the stories and sayings of Jesus were transmitted in oral pericopes; when reduced to writing these reflected the beliefs of second- and third-generation churches and of the individual writer and not the historical record. In *Jesus and the Word*, he said, "In my opinion we can sum up what can be known of the life and personality of Jesus as simply nothing."[2] Bultmann's program for New Testament studies was one of demythologization: any account of the supernatural was simply a mythological mode adopted by the early Christians in communicating their faith.

1950s–1960s   NEW QUEST FOR THE HISTORICAL JESUS. Here the focus is on "sayings" of Jesus as opposed to His deeds. The debate is on the criteria that could establish the authenticity of the sayings. Popular criteria for judging authenticity include: embarrassment (a saying that would embarrass the early Church); discontinuity (sayings and actions not obviously connected to Judaism or the early Church); multiple attestation (sayings and actions found in more than one source); coherence (words and actions that fit in with other words and actions that are accepted as historical); rejection and execution (sayings or actions that may have been responsible for His crucifixion).

1955   R. B. BRAITHWAITE / LOGICAL POSITIVISM. According to this approach, stories and sayings of Jesus are simply expressions of the emotion of agape and are meant to inspire us. There is no divine reality and so these stories have no authority beyond their emotive power.

1960s   "DEATH OF GOD." Atheism is the truth and should be the foundation of Christian theology, according to this movement. All supernatural claims and references are meaningless.

1977   "MYTH OF GOD INCARNATE." Seven British theologians published a work with this title (edited by John Hick) in which they claimed that the idea that Jesus is God Incarnate or the Second Person of the Trinity is simply "a mythological or poetic way of expressing his significance for us." Jesus is seen as the "Man of Universal Destiny"; the belief that He is God Incarnate is forcefully rejected.

1990s   THE JESUS SEMINAR. This group has revived the focus on the sayings of Jesus. Various theologians vote on various levels of probability regarding the authenticity of the sayings. In one of their books, *The Five Gospels,* the majority voted that 82 percent of the sayings are inauthentic. John Dominic Crossan and Burton Mack see Jesus as a Cynic Philosopher Who rejected conventional beliefs and values. Crossan pointedly rejects claims that Jesus rose from the dead. Mack views the Gospels as "imaginative creations" and not "historical accounts"; Mark's Gospel simply created a myth of Jesus' life. Crossan relies as much on the Gospels of Peter and Thomas as he does on the canonical Gospels.

Although much intellectual energy has been devoted to the ongoing search for the historical Jesus, there are still major obstacles haunting the whole enterprise:

1. No Consensus on the Formation of the Gospels: There is the lack of anything approaching a consensus among the hundreds of scholars engaged in the search. The standard procedure, writes N. T. Wright, is to isolate three different stages in the production of the Gospels: first the oral traditions that preceded the Gospels, then the coagulation of these traditions into definite literary sources, and finally the formation of the Gospels from these sources.[3] Concerning the first stage, there are numerous mutually incompatible theories claiming to explain how the traditions were formed and what they were; there is no consensus on any one of these theories. As to the second stage, there is vigorous disagreement about the initial literary sources. A majority of scholars say Mark was the first Gospel along with the missing "Q"; Matthew and Luke were later Gospels written using these two sources. An influential minority, however, has brought new evidence to bear to support the traditional view that Matthew was indeed the first Gospel. In yet another twist to the debate, some scholars who hold to Marcan priority say that the current Mark actually came after Matthew but that there was a now-missing proto-Mark that preceded Matthew. The Jerusalem School for the Study of the Synoptic Gospels believes that Luke was the first Gospel. On the third stage, again there is no agreement as to when, where, and why each of the Gospels was written.

2. No New Historical Information in the New Lives of Jesus: There is the absence of any new historical information about Jesus after well over two centuries of intense, almost obsessive, study of the New Testament texts. Of course there are numerous hypotheses and volumes of speculation — but these are invariably the objects of fierce dispute and the victims of rapid demise as the attention span of academia turns to the attractions of the next season. Also, hypotheses and speculation are not the same thing as fact. About this phenomenon, the Harvard scholar Helmut Koester remarks, "The vast variety of interpretations of the historical Jesus that the current quest has proposed is bewildering."[4] In a similar vein, another New Testament scholar, James D. G. Dunn said,

The new quest of the historical Jesus which began in reaction against Bultmann's dehistoricizing of Jesus' significance, has itself broken down in a confused welter of unanswered methodological questions.... The consequence being that many scholars in effect despair of knowing anything with confidence regarding the historical Jesus.[5]

Michael Cahill concludes that "since Bultmann, progress has been made in the area of the world of Jesus, but not a jot of firm knowledge of the individual historical person of Jesus has been garnered."[6] Cahill is indignant about the dishonesty of those who pass off speculation as fact:

> Numerous lives of Jesus are being published in our day.... This air of confidence is remarkable because the works produced are riddled with hypotheses and speculation to a degree that appears to give the lie to the initial confidence. The reader has but to note the differing range of presuppositions and methods of the authors to wonder at the scholarly basis for the confidence. The reader will also observe the high frequency of terms such as "maybe," "possibly," "probably," "likely," and should begin to wonder if readers can be expected to share the self-assurance of the authors' initial decision to attempt a life of Jesus.[7]

Moreover, according to Cahill,

> A feature of the recent lives of Jesus phenomenon is the degree to which works marked by tentative hypothesis and tortuous scholarly analysis of obscure material have been marketed for a more general public.... When flimsy hypotheses masquerade as exciting new hard scientific discoveries it can be difficult for the lay person to tell the difference. A scholar who decides to go public with a hypothesis owes it to the public to label the product clearly "hypothesis on hold." Dogmatic claims are not to be made about hypothetical constructs. This is to traffic in ignorance and emotionalism.[8]

3. The Jesus Seminar: The Jesus Seminar, the most notorious of today's quests for the historical Jesus, has been taken to task precisely for making dogmatic claims about hypothetical constructs. In a penetrating analysis of this enterprise, N. T. Wright notes the following:

- The Seminar is not taken seriously by mainstream scholarship: "There is nobody currently teaching at Harvard, Yale, Princeton, Duke, McGill or Stanford.... Where is the rest of the guild?... They are conspicuous by their absence." Although the Seminar claims that their version of the Bible is "the Scholar's Version," Wright points out that at best they represent "*some* scholars" from "a very narrow band."[9]

- The Seminar allows only two options: fundamentalism or skepticism. Although the Seminar selects the second option, they ignore the fact that many mainstream scholars adopt neither point of view. Moreover, a serious discussion of the issues relating to the identity of Jesus requires some sophistication in philosophical matters — something that is again conspicuous by its absence.

- The legitimacy of any democracy depends on the possibility of an honest vote. The Seminar's primary claim to fame was its methodology of voting on the various issues. But it seems obvious today that the Seminar reached its conclusions through dubious elections — thus fundamentally undermining its credibility. The authenticity of a saying of Jesus is determined by color codes on which the participants vote (red for what He said, black for what He did not, and pink and gray in between). But, as Wright notes, "the Jesus Seminar could print a text in pink or gray, even though the great majority of the Seminar voted red or black."[10] Citing one example, he writes, "I confess I cannot understand how, if a majority in each case thought the saying authentic or probably authentic, the 'weighted average' turned out to be 'probably inauthentic.' "[11]

- "The one thing this book [*The Five Gospels*] cannot offer is an answer to the question on its front cover (*What Did Jesus Really Say?*). All it can do is report, in a manner that will often mislead the ordinary reader, what some scholars think Jesus may have said."[12]

- Wright finds the three guiding principles of the Seminar to be misguided. "First, the Seminar in fact presupposes a particular portrait of Jesus. Second, the Seminar adopts a particular, and highly misleading, position about eschatology and apocalyptic, particularly about the Kingdom of God; this too was presupposed. Third, the Seminar assumes a particular picture of the early church, especially its interest and transmission of material about Jesus. In each case there is every reason to reject the principle in question."[13]

- "In order to sustain their home-made view of Jesus, the authors of this book [*The Five Gospels*] and presumably a fair number at least of Fellows of the Jesus Seminar have had to invent, as well, an entire picture of the early church out of not much more than thin air. Sometimes they have borrowed other people's inventions, but they, too, are based on little or nothing. . . . Of course, once scholars are allowed to invent whole communities at will, anything is possible. Any jigsaw puzzle can be solved if we are allowed to create new pieces for it at a whim. But we should not imagine that historical scholarship built on this principle is of any great value."[14]

Recent archaeological studies indicate that the City of Sepphoris near Nazareth was culturally Jewish during the time of Jesus and became a Hellenistic center only one to two centuries later.[15] This finding significantly undermines the thesis that Jesus was an exponent of Greek philosophy, a favorite idea of the Seminar, espoused in particular by John Dominic Crossan.

For considerations such as those cited here, the theologian Howard Clark Kee writes that, "One can hope that the publications of the Jesus Seminar and others developing along comparable lines will be recognized as what they are — peripheral, prejudicial pronouncements — rather than being taken as a substantive development in responsible scholarly study of the historical Jesus."[16]

4. Self-Portraits and Ideological Agendas: Many of the critics observe that the Gospels are not to be taken as objective history, that they are rather reflections of the faith of their writers. This criticism is ironic because the same can be said about the critics themselves and their writings. The nineteenth-century German portraits of Jesus as a charismatic preacher often bore striking resemblances to nineteenth-century German theologians. The late twentieth-century portraits of Jesus as a Cynic Philosopher/Zealot/Activist with a do-it-yourself spirituality and a program of social protest seem to be little better than self-portraits of many modern movements. The most radical critics tend to be more concerned with advancing an agenda than with engaging in serious scholarship. In an analysis of their methods, William Loewe writes,

> The Jesus Seminar is waging a public campaign with missionary zeal; its strategy is of course a familiar one. Research on the historical Jesus originated as a child of the Enlightenment, and from the outset it has been scholarship with an agenda. Whether the goal be to undermine the Christian Church, as it was for H. S. Reimarus, or to sweep away the accumulated debris of traditional belief and practice in order to concoct a version of Christianity more palatable to modern sensibilities, as it was for Adolf von Harnack, the strategy in either case consists in an appeal to one's reconstruction of the historical Jesus as the real Jesus whom one can then play off against Jesus as the Christian Church confesses and proclaims him. Such is the position being offered diligently for public consumption by the Jesus Seminar.[17]

5. The "Real" Jesus: But the historical Jesus of the theologians cannot be identified with the "real" Jesus simply because there is no single reconstruction that is generally accepted. "As a matter of fact," writes Loewe,

> the historical reconstructions offered by Reimarus and Harnack as identical with "the real Jesus" have themselves fallen victim to the progress of research on the historical Jesus, while the various reconstructions proferred by members of the Jesus Seminar differ significantly among themselves and remain methodologically problematic. Hence the claim, common to both the "old quest" and the Jesus Seminar, that "the historical Jesus" is simply to be identified with 'the real Jesus' is naïve.[18]

Forward into the Past

Despite the shortcomings listed above, New Testament scholarship has made some positive contributions to our understanding of the historical dimension of Christianity. Some critics have sought to brush aside the surface credibility of the Gospel narratives by offering highly speculative accounts of what they claim actually took place. But a significant body of mainstream New Testament scholars has helped lay the groundwork for a more incisive approach to these texts. In his *Jesus and Judaism,* the then Oxford scholar E. P. Sanders noted, "The dominant view today seems to be that we can know pretty well what Jesus was out to accomplish, that we can know a lot about what he said, and that those two things make sense within the world of 1st century Judaism."[19] The great Tübingen New Testament scholar Peter Stuhlmacher says, "As a Western Scripture scholar, I am inclined to doubt these [Gospel] stories, but as a historian I am obliged to take them as reliable. The biblical texts as they stand are the best hypotheses we have until now to explain what really happened."[20] Contemporary archaeology has confirmed the existence of at least three key figures in the Gospel narratives: Pontius Pilate (through the discovery in 1961 of a Latin inscription in Caesarea Maritima that read "Pontius Pilatus, Prefect of Judea"), the High Priest Caiaphas (through the discovery of an ossuary with the bones of "Joseph son of Caiaphas"), and the Jewish ruler Herod Antipas (through the discovery of remnants of his building projects in Sepphoris).[21]

Moreover, the German researcher Michael Hesemann, relying on the studies of Israeli archaeological experts, Greek and Latin scholars, and carbon-14 dating of the fragment, has now confirmed that the relic of the True Cross of Jesus with the inscription INRI kept in the Basilica of the Holy Cross of Jerusalem in Rome can reliably be dated to first-century Palestine; experts have also said that the relic comes from the wood of an olive tree.

In *The Aims of Jesus,* B. F. Meyer has made a major contribution to a historically grounded understanding of the mission of Jesus, drawing attention to three overriding themes in this context:

[Jesus'] identification of himself and his disciples as eschatological antitypes of Israel, her kings and prophets; his allusions to divinely appointed eschatological "measures" (of time, of evil, of revelation) being filled to the brim; and his pointing, as to signs of the time, to the enactment, in his own activities, of God's promises of salvation for the end-time. These three facets of the consciousness of Jesus exhibit a point of convergence: a full awareness of being charged with the climactic and final mission to Israel as promised and previewed in the scriptures.

He notes that we can independently establish this same conclusion

by a cumulative and convergent argument drawing on five data in the Gospel narratives, the historicity of which has won almost universal agreement. These are: Jesus' proclamation that the reign of God was at hand; the fact that Jesus spoke and acted "with authority"; that he was widely known as and was a wonderworker; that he "cleansed" — or mounted a demonstration at — the Jerusalem temple; and that he died crucified, condemned by the Romans as "the king of the Jews."[22]

About the gradual manner in which Jesus revealed Himself, he writes, "The paucity of messianic self-revelation" was a result neither of "simple ignorance nor any supposed sense of personal ordinariness" but of

an economy of revelation that withheld the secret of his person and destiny out of realism and wisdom respecting his listeners.... The disciples were neither swift nor deft in construing the intentions and paradoxical self-disclosures of Jesus. The conditions of the possibility of accurate comprehension were not given except with the so-called Easter experience. But what this [Easter] experience generated in the disciples was not the celebration of new, previously unknown messianic and soteriological themes. *All* had been previously adumbrated by Jesus.[23]

The noted New Testament scholar William R. Farmer has helped highlight the cardinal importance of Isaiah — particularly its portrait of the Suffering Servant — in understanding the mission of Jesus and the faith of the first Christians. As Farmer shows in *The Gospel of Jesus* (Louisville: Westminster John Knox, 1994), Isaiah introduces us to such fundamental concepts of the New Testament as the very term "gospel" or "good news," the idea that God's salvation is for all nations and tongues, and the promise that God's Servant would be a light for all nations who would die for the sins of all ("the Lord laid upon him the guilt of us all"). Moreover, key texts in the Gospel narratives are direct quotes, clear parallels, or prophetic fulfillments of passages in Isaiah. In the present author's view, it is this Isaiah paradigm that helps unlock the true meaning of the mission of Jesus while also making sense of experiential encounters with Jesus ranging from the moving visions of the Sacred Heart and the Divine Mercy to the everyday "personal" relationship with the Lord offered to all. Conversely, a failure to recognize the role of Isaiah leads scholars to many of the cul-de-sacs of sensationalist skepticism.

A renewed acknowledgment of the miracles of Jesus was one of the positive developments of the last two decades of the twentieth century. Even such Jesus Seminar skeptics as Robert Funk and Marcus Borg accept some of the healings and exorcisms of Jesus. Funk comments that His reputation as a healer makes it probable that He did engage in healing. "Behind this picture of Jesus as healer and exorcist," writes Borg, "I affirm a historical core.... More healing stories are told about Jesus than about any other figure in the Jewish tradition."[24] The fact that exorcisms were attributed not just to Jesus but to His followers suggests to scholars that Jesus did perform exorcisms. Josephus, the first-century Jewish historian, wrote that Jesus was "a doer of startling deeds." As to the claims of Jesus bringing the dead back to life, it is striking that the town of Bethany was renamed as el-Azariyeh, "the place of Lazarus," by the Arabs.

In contrast to the older Bultmannian view that the miracle stories belong to mythology, scholars today consider them from the standpoint of their historical basis. "The miracle stories," writes Craig A. Evans,

> are now treated seriously and are widely accepted by Jesus scholars as deriving from Jesus' ministry. Major studies on the historical Jesus discuss the miracles, whether in general terms or in reference to specific miracles, with little or no discussion of myth or the philosophical issues at one time thought to be necessary for any assessment of the miracle traditions in the Gospels. Several specialized studies have appeared in recent years, which conclude that Jesus did perform miracles.[25]

Evans cites seven criteria that support the historicity of the miracle stories:

1. *Multiple Attestation.* The miracle tradition is found in the various Gospels and in Paul.

2. *Dissimilarity.* In working His miracles Jesus does not come across either as a Jewish holy man or a Hellenistic wonder worker. The cure is effected when He speaks the word and He performs the miracle in His own name.

3. *Embarrassment.* Some of the miracle stories (for instance, the charge that Jesus was working miracles through Beelzebul or the fact that He did not work miracles in His own country) would have been embarrassing to the early Church and so it is unlikely they would have invented them.

4. *Context and Expectation.* The Messiah was not expected to heal or to exorcise demons, and so the tradition of miracle stories was not required to establish Jesus as Messiah. Moreover, Jesus refused to show a sign when asked to do so.

5. *Effect.* Critics agree that Jesus attracted large crowds. According to many scholars, the crowds first came to hear Him because of His healings and exorcisms.

6. *Coherence.* The miracles are taken for granted in many of the sayings of Jesus that even the skeptical accept as authentic, for instance, Jesus' responses on Beelzebul and Satan.

7. *Principles of Embellishment.* The miracles stories do not have the obvious embellishments found in legends about some Jewish holy men and in the apocryphal gospels.[26]

The Resurrection

If the miracles are important in understanding the identity of Jesus, there is one miracle in particular that is of the utmost importance: His resurrection from the dead. The evidence for the Resurrection has remained compelling from the first years of Christianity through the darkest days of the skeptical onslaught on the veracity of the New Testament. Today, a number of renowned scholars accept at least the existence of various pieces of data that are inexplicable without recourse to the Resurrection. Two of the most persuasive defenders of the Resurrection in the last four decades have been the German theologian Wolfhart Pannenberg, who moved from atheism to faith through his rational investigation of the Resurrection, and the Jewish scholar Pinchas Lapide.

The three foundations of the Resurrection hypothesis are the existence of the empty tomb, the reports of the appearance of Jesus to His disciples and others, and the origin of the Christian Church. On a theological level, the Resurrection was understood by the first Christians in the context of Isaiah's prophecy of the Suffering Servant, who was raised up and exalted by God.

It must be said first that the Resurrection claims are very ancient and therefore unlikely to have been the product of legend. 1 Corinthians 15:3–8 and Luke 24:34 are two of the most ancient creeds of the Church, and both affirm the Resurrection; the appearances recorded in Matthew are also ancient in origin. In Corinthians, Paul writes,

For I handed on to you as of first importance what I also received: that
Christ died for our sins in accordance with the scriptures; that he appeared
to Kephas, then to the Twelve. After that, he appeared to more than five
hundred brothers at once, most of whom are still living, though some have
fallen asleep. After that he appeared to James, then to all the apostles. Last
of all, as to one born abnormally, he appeared to me.

(The terms "handed on" and "what I also received" are rabbinic terms referring
to a sacred tradition; hence the conclusion that these verses come from a creed.)
In Luke we see, "The Lord has truly been raised and has appeared to Simon."
More details about the appearances are given in the Acts of the Apostles, showing
the significance of the Resurrection for the early Church.

The Empty Tomb

On the empty tomb, the following pieces of evidence are weighty:

1. Jesus was buried. This is confirmed by 1 Corinthians 15, by the multiple
attestation of the Gospel accounts, and by the fact that there were no other
stories about what happened to Jesus' body.

2. The tomb was guarded. Even the early Jewish critics did not deny that the
tomb was guarded. They simply claimed that the guards fell asleep.

3. There is a historical core to the various stories about the discovery of the
empty tomb. Although the various Gospels describe the sequence of discovery
differently, there are some common threads: Joseph of Arimathea buried Jesus,
the empty tomb was discovered by women followers who went to visit it, and
angels were seen outside the tomb. Concerning the discrepancies, N. T. Wright
notes, "This is what eyewitness testimony looks and sounds like. And in such
cases the surface discrepancies do not mean that nothing happened; rather, they
mean that the witnesses have not been in collusion."[27]

4. The fact that women were the first witnesses indicates that the story was
not fabricated. Jewish law did not accept the testimony of women. Nevertheless,
all the accounts state that the first witnesses to the empty tomb were women. If
these accounts were legendary, it is more than likely that men would have been
presented as the initial witnesses.

5. The Jews did not deny the empty tomb. The earliest enemies of Christianity could have put an end to the religion by displaying the body of Jesus. But
in actual fact, the Jews admitted that the tomb was empty and tried to explain
this away by charging that the disciples had stolen the body. It is unlikely, however, that the demoralized disciples would be willing to give up their lives by
perpetrating such a fraud.

6. The Gospel accounts of the discovery of the empty tomb do not contain
any of the fanciful details found in the apocryphal gospels. Moreover, there is
no description of what happened when the Resurrection actually took place.

7. Wolfhart Pannenberg noted that

one of the strongest points in favor of a positive judgment here is what
we know about the early disputes between Christians and Jews about the

Resurrection. The Jews accepted that the tomb was empty. The dispute, however, was about how this is to be explained. The Jews said the disciples had removed the body. But they did not question the fact that the tomb was empty. That, I think, is a very remarkable point. And then, of course, my main reason is a general reflection, given the concreteness of the Jewish understanding of a resurrection from the dead. It would hardly be conceivable that the earliest Christian congregation could have assembled in Jerusalem of all places, where Jesus had died and was buried, if His tomb was intact.[28]

Appearances

The second foundation for belief in the Resurrection of Jesus is the evidence that He appeared to His disciples and many of the faithful. In one of the earliest New Testament documents (1 Corinthians), St. Paul affirms that Jesus appeared to him, to Peter, to the apostles, and to five hundred brothers. This epistle was written when many of those who had seen the Risen Christ were still alive, and so it is unlikely that Paul would have concocted a story that could easily have been contradicted. The Gospels talk of Jesus appearing to Mary Magdalene and various other women, to ten of the Apostles when Thomas was absent, and later to all eleven of them and to the disciples on the road to Emmaus.

Granted that there are multiple claims of appearances, the question is whether the appearances did in fact occur. The legend hypothesis is implausible because 1 Corinthians 15 is dated very early. Another hypothesis is that the witnesses were simply hallucinating. But, as the great Resurrection scholar William Lane Craig has shown, this hypothesis does not hold water for various reasons: hallucinations are individual in nature and are experienced only by one person, but the appearances of the Risen Lord were witnessed by hundreds; those who hallucinate usually expect to see the object of their hallucination, but the terrified disciples had no expectation of seeing their Master again after His crucifixion and burial; hallucinations are sometimes induced by drugs or mental illness, but the appearances were witnessed by a wide range of people with different personalities and backgrounds over an extended period of time.

It has also been alleged that the disciples were lying. This objection is simply implausible because the Apostles staked their lives on the claim that they had seen the risen Christ. Almost all of them died horrible deaths — but they went to their deaths proclaiming the risen Lord. It is hardly reasonable to suggest that they were willing to die for a lie. But it was not just a question of them staking their lives on the appearances. The fact that these orthodox Jews felt compelled to change the Sabbath from Saturday to Sunday, the day associated with Jesus' rising from the dead, is momentous testimony to their belief that He appeared to them. And instead of celebrating the Passover once a year, they now celebrated the Eucharist in its place each Sunday. Also, at least some of those who saw Christ were initially skeptics, in particular, Saul of Tarsus. He had no reason to "invent" the Resurrection since it contradicted his previous beliefs.

About the idea that the appearances were the result of autosuggestion, Pinchas Lapide writes

> In none of the cases where rabbinic literature speaks of such visions [springing from autosuggestion] did it result in an essential change in the life of the resuscitated or of those who had experienced the visions. Only the vision remains, which was retold in believing wonderment and sometimes also embellished, but it did not have any noticeable consequences. It is different with the disciples of Jesus on that Easter Sunday. Despite all the legendary embellishments, in the oldest records there remains a recognizable historical kernel which cannot simply be demythologized. When this scared, frightened band of the Apostles which was just about to throw away everything in order to flee in despair to Galilee; when these peasants, shepherds, and fishermen, who betrayed and denied their master and then failed him miserably, suddenly could be changed overnight into a confident mission society, convinced of salvation and able to work with much more success after Easter than before Easter, then no vision or hallucination is sufficient to explain such a revolutionary transformation. For a sect or school or an order, perhaps a single vision would have been sufficient — but not for a world religion which was able to conquer the Occident thanks to the Easter faith.... If the defeated and depressed group of disciples overnight could change into a victorious movement of faith, based only on autosuggestion or self-deception — without a fundamental faith experience — then this would be a much greater miracle than the resurrection itself.[29]

Origin of Christianity

These considerations bring us to the third foundation for belief in the Resurrection, which is the origin of Christianity itself. The explosion of the Christian movement in first-century Palestine can be explained only by reference to the Resurrection. From the very beginning, as even Bultmann acknowledged, the message that Jesus had risen from the dead lay at the heart of the Christian Gospel. Affirmation that Jesus was the Messiah would have been impossible if He had not been resurrected because, for all practical purposes, His mission would be considered a failure if it ended with the cross. Moreover, the claim that Jesus had risen from the grave is not something that could have been extrapolated from any popular belief system. Although some Jews believed in the idea of resurrection, such a resurrection is one that involved the entire human race and that took place at the end of history. Jesus' resurrection, however, involved one individual, and it took place within the historical process.

After reviewing reductionist rejections of the Resurrection in theologians like Rudolf Bultmann, Lapide writes,

> Most of these and similar conceptions strike me as all too abstract and scholarly to explain the fact that the solid hillbillies from Galilee who, for the very real reason of the crucifixion of their master, were saddened to

death, were changed within a short period of time into a jubilant community of believers. Such a post-Easter change, which was no less real than
sudden and unexpected, certainly needed a concrete foundation which can
by no means exclude the possibility of any physical resurrection.[30]

Writing as a devout Jew, Lapide concludes,

I cannot rid myself of the impression that some modern Christian theologians are ashamed of the material facticity of the resurrection. Their varying
attempts at dehistoricizing the Easter experience which give the lie to the
four evangelists are simply not understandable to me in any other way. Indeed, the four authors of the Gospels definitely compete with one another
in illustrating the tangible, substantial dimension of this resurrection explicitly. Often it seems as if renowned New Testament scholars in our days
want to insert a kind of ideological or dogmatic curtain between the pre-
Easter and the risen Jesus in order to protect the latter against any kind of
contamination by earthly three-dimensionality. However, for the first Christians who thought, believed, and hoped in a Jewish manner, the immediate
historicity was not only a part of that happening but the indispensable
precondition for the recognition of its significance for salvation.[31]

Surveying the three foundations listed here, William Lane Craig concludes:
"One might ask, 'Well, then how do skeptical scholars explain the facts of the
resurrection appearances, the empty tomb, and the origin of the Christian faith?'
The fact of the matter is they *don't*. Modern scholarship recognizes no plausible
explanatory alternative to the resurrection of Jesus."[32]

Chapter 2

The Identity of Jesus

If there are good grounds to accept both the miracles of Jesus and his resurrection from the dead, we are still left with the question of who Jesus was. Some of the Jesus Seminar participants say that the title "Son of God" is as metaphorical as the epithet "Lamb of God." The contributors to *The Myth of God Incarnate* contend that the whole idea of Incarnation is mythological. These varied responses raise three issues: Who did Jesus believe Himself to be? What did His followers believe about Him? Are the traditional teachings about His identity coherent?

It can be said first that Jesus does not use the terminology of the great Councils of the Church in describing Himself (although all that He says about His identity makes sense in the light of the Conciliar proclamations). On the other hand, all that He said and did indicated to His listeners that He was not only more than just a man but that He was in some sense uniquely identified with Israel's God. Consequently, the New Testament writers end up with a portrait of Jesus that made sense only within the framework of Trinitarian doctrine.

Jesus' identification of Himself with the God of Israel may be seen in numerous passages (cited by R. T. France among others):

- He forgives sins (Mark 2:1–12) — something only God can do.

- He gives rest to those who embrace His yoke (Matt. 11:28–30) — Judaism saw this as a function of the divine Wisdom.

- He had the right to cleanse God's temple (Mark 11:27–33).

- His words have eternal validity (Mark 13:31) — like God's (Isa. 40:8).

- His words had greater authority than the Old Testament (Matt. 5:31–32), Abraham (John 8:53), and Jacob (John 4:12).

- He was the Lord of the Sabbath (Mark 2:28).

43

- He decides the eternal destiny of every person and His decision is based on the state of their relationship with Him (Matt. 7:21–23; Mark 8:34–38).

- He is the ultimate judge; He is king of an everlasting kingdom (Matt. 25:31ff.).

- To accept or reject Him is to accept or reject God (Matt. 10:40).

- He is the Good Shepherd Who seeks and saves the lost (Luke 19:10) — like God Who is shown as a Shepherd in Ezekiel 34.

- He is the stone on which people stumble (Luke 20:18) — an image for God in Isaiah 8.

- He compares John the Baptist (Mark 9:12) to Elijah, who prepares the way for the coming of God in judgment (Mal. 3:1).

- His depiction of Himself as Judge (Matt. 24:31) is comparable to the depiction of God as Judge in the Old Testament (e.g., Dan. 7:9).

- He portrays Himself as shepherd, bridegroom, and sower in His parables — roles assigned to God in the Old Testament.

The titles "Messiah," "Son of Man," and "Son of God" applied to Jesus in the New Testament are of obvious importance in understanding Who He was. We must first, of course, understand what is meant by these titles.

"Messiah" is Hebrew and "Christ" Greek for "the Anointed One." The charge that Jesus never saw Himself as Messiah (first made by William Wrede) cannot be seriously entertained. The accounts of Jesus' Baptism and Temptation show that He has a messianic role to play as does the Transfiguration with the two messianic figures Moses and Elijah. Simon Peter's confession that Jesus is the Messiah at Caesarea Philippi (Mark 8:27–31; Matt. 16:13–21) is an explicit affirmation of His messianic role because Jesus commends Peter for stating this truth. Jesus' triumphant entry into Jerusalem, recorded in all the Gospels, is again messianic in its relation to Old Testament prophecy. Most important, the main charge against Jesus at His trial was His claim to be the Messiah, a claim He did not deny and which led to His condemnation: "Again the high priest asked him and said to him, 'Are you the Messiah, the Son of the Blessed One?' Then Jesus answered, 'I am'" (Mark 14:61–62).

One of the greatest contemporary authorities on Jesus' messianic claims, the Tübingen theologian Martin Hengel, writes,

> With his messianic claim, Jesus the Jew may appear alien, indeed vexing, since his "mythical" characteristics obscure our ethically determined, demythologized picture of him. But the real Jesus was very different. He lived in the language and imagination of the Old Testament and its Jewish-Galilean environment, and he conducted himself with the — in the truest sense of the word — "apocalyptic" (the word comes from "to reveal") right to usher in God's reign over Israel (and all nations), and, as the "Anointed of God," to fulfill the promises made to the fathers and the prophets. His death — which he consciously affirmed — placed the seal of confirmation

on this right. That Jesus conducted himself in this manner, I hold to be provable by the methods of historical-critical research.[1]

The title "Son of Man" is the one Jesus applied to Himself most often. In the Old Testament it is used to refer both to "man" (Ps. 8:5) and, more commonly, to a heavenly figure (Dan. 7:13) who will judge all people at the end of time. Jesus uses the title both to emphasize His authority (Mark 2:10; Luke 12:19) and His humility (Mark 10:45).

"Son of God" is the title by which a voice from Heaven refers to Jesus at His baptism and transfiguration, and He is addressed thus by Peter (Matt. 16:16), demons, and a centurion. Although the Old Testament has different understandings of this title, where it refers to Israel and to her king, in the Gospels the meaning of this title is especially evident in the special relationship between Jesus and His Father: "No one knows the Son except the Father, and no one knows the Father except the Son" (Matt. 11:27).

The theologian Jean Galot has shown that Jesus' use of the term *Abba,* which means "Papa" or "Daddy," to refer to God is unique in religious literature and indicates an equality of nature. In fact, throughout the Gospels, He refers to God only as "Father" except on the single occasion when he quotes from Psalm 22. "The term *Abba,*" writes Galot

> had never been introduced into Jewish religious language. Only rarely was God invoked even as Father, since we know of no such anterior instance in Palestinian Judaism.... To invoke God by calling him *Abba* was something totally unheard-of.... It would never have been used in the language of prayer because of the Jews' sense of reverence for God's transcendence. The disciples must have been shocked when they heard Jesus utter this word. If Mark reported it, we must concede that Jesus really spoke it, for no one else would have had the audacity to do so.[2]

The implications for the identity of Jesus are monumental:

> Fatherhood implies a relationship of generation and a similarity of nature. Jesus certainly never gave a formal definition of Abba. And yet if the Father had not been endowed with fatherhood in the most complete and real sense, the invocation would not have been completely true. In fact, the word Abba contains a whole theology, the theology that led the Council of Nicea to proclaim that the Son is consubstantial with the Father.... As when he identified himself with the covenant or as the Bridegroom, there was in his use of Abba an implicit affirmation of his divine identity. For, as we have already emphasized, this divine identity was not detached from the human reality of Jesus. Rather, it was perfectly incarnated. Indeed, Abba expressed a human experience of divine sonship. There is no more human word than "papa" or "daddy." Here it became a divine name. This was perhaps the most remarkable expression of the Incarnation.[3]

With reference to the messianic titles, Peter Stuhlmacher writes,

Without seeing and recognizing that the earthly Jesus had already claimed to be the messianic "Son of Man" whom God had sent to Israel, there is no way to historically understand either Jesus' work or the passion story. The apostles did not simply attach to Jesus certain characteristics and ways of behavior subsequent to Easter which he never had on earth (nor claimed to have); on the contrary, the post-resurrection confession of the Christian Church in Jesus as Son of God and Messiah confirms and recognizes who Jesus historically wanted to be and who he was and remains for faith....

Our attempt to trace the development of faith in Christ can be significantly advanced by following the transmitted texts closely and being aware of the fact that, in view of Jesus' striking deeds and his astonishing words among his contemporaries, the question must have arisen: Who is this man? What authority — or also: what demon (cf. Mark 3:22–30) — does he have? The assumption that Jesus never answered nor had anything to say to this question (an assumption which modern critical scholarship has to make) is very unlikely and makes Jesus into a walking historical riddle. The texts, in any case, depict him in another (historically believable) way.[4]

N. T. Wright has shown that Jesus saw Himself as sharing the throne with Israel's God, as being the One through Whom God would achieve decisive victory:

The language was deeply coded, but the symbolic action was not. He was coming to Zion, doing what YHWH had promised to do. He explained his action with riddles all pointing in the same direction.... This also accounts for his sovereign attitude to Torah; his speaking on behalf of Wisdom; his announcement of forgiveness of sins. By themselves, none of these would be conclusive.... But predicate them of the same young man who is then on his way to Jerusalem to confront the powers that be with the message, and the action, of the kingdom of God, and who tells stories as he does so that are best interpreted as stories of YHWH returning to Zion, and you have reached, I believe, the deep heart of Jesus' own sense of vocation. He believed himself called to do and be what, in the scriptures, only Israel's God did and was.[5]

In contrast to this profound and subtle portrait of Jesus, the Jesus Seminar leaves us with little that is historically or theologically reliable. Wright notes that the Seminar's contribution

is, for the most part, a shallow and one-dimensional portrait, developed through anachronistic parallels (the laconic cowboy) and ignoring the actual first-century context. Its attractive and indeed sometimes compelling features, of Jesus as the subversive sage, challenging the status quo with teasing epigrams and parables, have been achieved at the huge cost of screening out a whole range of material which several of the leading Jesus-scholars around the world, in major, serious and contemporary works of historical reconstruction, would regard as absolutely central. By far the most important of these is the material often designated "apocalyptic"; and, within that, Jesus' announcement of the kingdom of God.[6]

The identification of Jesus with the God of Israel in the Gospels, writes R. H. Stein, is amplified in the rest of the New Testament. Jesus is:

- the Lord of creation (Col. 1:16–17; Phil. 2:9–11; 1 Cor. 15:27);
- identified with Yahweh of the Old Testament (Rom. 10:9–13 and Joel 2:32; 2 Thess. 1:7–10; 1 Cor. 5:5 with Isa. 2:10–19, etc.);
- recognized as having always existed (2 Cor. 8:9; Phil. 2:6);
- the "form" (Phil. 2:6) and "image" of God (Col. 1:15);
- referred to as "God" in Rom. 9:5, 2 Thess. 1:12; Titus 2:13; Heb. 1:5–8; 1 John 5:20; John 1:1);
- the one in Whom "dwells the whole fullness of the deity bodily" (Col. 2:9).

Martin Hengel notes that Paul uses the title *Christos* on 270 occasions.

The portrait of Jesus presented in the Gospels and the New Testament — He was the sinless Messiah Who by His Self-Sacrifice on the Cross saves us from our sins, the Son of God Who rose from the dead, the King and Judge Who will determine our salvation — entailed a twin affirmation: Jesus was the divine Savior just as surely as He was a man. Now this twin affirmation has always been as controversial as it is mysterious. But it is an affirmation that tries to explain the facts as we have them. How so?

The Oxford logician Michael Dummett points out that if we have no reason to dismiss the credibility of the New Testament narratives and if we review what we know about Christ from the New Testament and the acts of His Apostles, the next step is to compare the thesis of the Incarnation of God in Christ with competing hypotheses. If the thesis of the Incarnation explains the facts in the New Testament and if there are no other plausible counter-hypotheses, then the act of accepting the Incarnation is an act of judgment, not of blind faith. Judgments to be valid must have a rational ground. A truly extraordinary set of facts may legitimately have a truly extraordinary explanation.

Hard Facts

It seems reasonable that we make our act of judgment on the basis of the following hard facts:

1. A tiny group of first-century Jewish fishermen and peasants left their homelands and purposefully traveled across the world preaching the message that their crucified leader rose from the dead and exhorted them to bring all nations to salvation through faith in Him. These disciples almost all suffered terrible deaths preaching His message of repentance and mercy. In a relatively short period of time they were transformed from cowering wretches

to triumphant warriors, a transformation so radical that neither delusion nor deception can sufficiently explain it.

2. The accounts of their leader found in the Gospels they wrote show a man who identified Himself with God, Who spoke and acted as Yahweh of Israel.

3. The other books of the New Testament show that its writers indeed believed their leader to be not just the Messiah, but God in human flesh. The portrait of the community shown in the New Testament is a portrait of a community suffused with hope and love and marching to the beat of a supernatural drummer.

4. Millions of people through the centuries claim to experience the presence of the Risen Lord and proclaim Him as their Lord and God.

5. The earliest preachers and teachers of the Christian community and its ancient liturgies and Councils consistently affirmed the New Testament portrait of Jesus as very God and very Man and their own experience of Him as Savior and Lord.

The striking declaration that Jesus Christ is God Incarnate makes sense of these "hard facts" just as a denial of this declaration flies in the face of these facts. "The Christological dogma of the Council of Chalcedon," wrote Walter Kasper in his classic work *Jesus the Christ,*

> constitutes, in the language and in the context of the problem at that time, an extremely precise version of what, according to the New Testament, we encounter in Jesus' history and what befell him: namely, in Jesus Christ, God himself has entered into a human history, and meets us there in a fully and completely human way. The dogmatic profession of faith that Jesus Christ in one person is true God and true man, must therefore be regarded as a valid and permanently binding interpretation of Scripture.[7]

Nevertheless, the doctrine of the Incarnation is unutterably mysterious and will always remain so. But it is a mystery of excess of light, not of darkness. "It is obvious," continues Kasper, "that both ontological and psychological investigation of the mystery of God's incarnation of Jesus Christ, come up against an insuperable limit of thought, speech and sympathetic insight.... The limit is, as it were, the obverse, the negative of something extremely positive, not darkness but excess of light, dazzling to our eyes."[8]

Mysterious though it is, the doctrine of the Incarnation is not contradictory in itself. In *The Logic of God Incarnate,* Thomas Morris addresses a severe challenge: how can two kinds of being so radically distinct from each other as Creator and creature be united in one individual? The whole problem lies in how we understand the Divine and the human, in particular the latter. Morris considers the definition of what is essential to humanity. He distinguishes what is common to humanity from what is essential. It may be common for humans to be sinful, but this does not make it an essential property of humanity. Likewise, he distinguishes being fully human from being merely human. We are both fully human and merely human. But it is at least possible for a divine being to take on a human nature whereby it is fully human but not merely human. Thus Jesus Christ was fully human because He had all the properties essential to being human, but He also possessed properties above the human, divine properties. The renowned philosopher Bernard Lonergan noted the consequences of the affirmation that in Jesus there was one divine Person Who had two natures: "You can't be a human person and be a divine Person. It's one Person Who has a human nature and a divine nature, a human consciousness and a divine consciousness. If you were both a man and a dog, you know yourself as a man by your human consciousness and you know yourself as a dog by your dog consciousness. Except it couldn't happen to you. You need an infinite Subject to have this."[9]

The doctrine of the Incarnation was affirmed because it made sense of the facts experienced by both the disciples and almost all subsequent Christians. Brian Hebblethwaite, a participant in the Myth of God Incarnate debates, specifies several other reasons for the importance of the doctrine: in this doctrine we see God revealing Himself to us in the most intimate possible fashion so that in the life, teaching, death, and resurrection of Jesus we know what God is like, as also His will for us; a correlate of this doctrine is the doctrine of the Trinity, the doctrine that within God there is an everlasting relationship of love; without this doctrine, Christians would have to deny their experience of the Risen Christ being present today in their lives and in the Church; most important, through the Passion and Death of Jesus Christ, we encounter God's direct participation in redeeming us from our sins and overcoming evil.[10]

We have spoken up to this point about the conclusions of New Testament scholars and to a limited extent about the "hard facts" of history. There is another approach to the New Testament texts, however, that needs at least to be considered by those who are trying to determine the identity of Jesus. In "The Uninventable Glory of God as the Deepest Reason for Our Faith in Jesus Christ," the noted phenomenologist philosopher Josef Seifert uses the Gospel narratives themselves as the datum that draws us to a recognition of the divinity of Christ. While acknowledging that faith is a gift of grace, Seifert also sees it as the supreme act of human reason. Faith requires belief in the trustworthiness of Jesus, of His Apostles, His Church, and His Bible; it is belief *in* Jesus, in the sense of loving surrender, and belief *that* what He says is true. But neither the moral goodness nor the miracles of Christ are sufficient grounds for accepting His divinity. "The ultimate ground for our unwavering faith in Christ," writes Seifert,

> is our awareness that the uninventable eternal glory of God, His necessary sacred holiness, is encountered in an incarnate/visible form in Jesus Christ. The glory of God that we glimpse, if only barely, in philosophy shines most clearly through the incarnate Word of God, in His miracles and the inner holiness and glory of His words, in the divine beauty of His mercy (Prodigal Son, Mary Magdalen) as well as His horror of sin: the irreducible and unique glory of God manifests itself in the newborn Savior announced to

the shepherds, the Sermon on the Mount, the forgiveness of the adulteress, the piercing of the Heart of Jesus on the cross for our sins and the gloriously risen Christ. . . .

This glory is a spiritual splendor that can only proceed from the inner holiness of God and that presupposes the uninventable inner perfection and truth of the divine nature. The divine glory and uninventable holiness of charity that permeates the words and miracles, the life and death of Christ, not only justify faith but elevate it beyond probable opinion to an inner certainty and absolute, unconditioned Yes. A similitude of this glory is visible in true followers, the saints, as well as in the doctrines of Jesus and His Church (the inner truth and unity and beauty of the doctrines reveal the glory of God). The most reliable approach to Scripture scholarship, in this context, would be to delve into the glory of God in Christ and into the inner spiritual meaning of the scriptural texts in their "divine form."[11]

Other scholars have noted the need to explore the Gospel narratives with alternate tools. William Thompson has written that

perhaps we can draw a distinction between the historical dimension of our faith and of Jesus Christ, and the historian's attempt, whether professional or scholarly or non-professional, to appropriate the former. Scientific, historical methods are only one of several ways in which Christians can appropriate the historical dimension of our faith. Meditating on Holy Scripture, the spiritual traditions of meditating on the mysteries of Jesus, the celebration of Jesus' mysteries in the liturgy through sacrament and word, some literary-narrative approaches to Scripture — these, too, are appropriate and in varying ways sometimes more appropriate to an historical appropriation of Jesus the Christ.[12]

Yet another dimension to the whole discussion here is the traditional doctrine that the books of the Bible are divinely inspired. Both Jesus and the first Christians upheld the Jewish conviction that the books of the Old Testament were written under the inspiration of God and were therefore authoritative and true. As the Apostles and Evangelists produced their own corpus of writings on the life and teachings of Jesus, they were aware, as were their followers, that these works were also divinely inspired. In his presidential address to the Society of Biblical Literature, D. Moody Smith noted:

In the case of the earliest Christian Gospels we observed already that the initial and fundamental impulse for their composition came with the proclamation of Jesus as the fulfillment of scripture. The use of the Gospels alongside the older, Jewish scriptures in worship, certainly as early as the mid-second century, probably much earlier, was likely a continuation of the use to which the earlier Gospel traditions had already been put. Matthew and Luke particularly, if in different ways, adopted biblical genres and styles as they also continued the biblical story. . . . If I have made a case for anything it is this: that the intention to write scripture should not be excluded from a consideration of the purpose as well as the result of the composition of the Gospels.[13]

The early Fathers, Councils, and liturgies treated these writings with great reverence since they constituted the Word of God. Even those who dissented against orthodox teachings accepted the authoritative status of Scripture; their only quarrel was one of interpretation. Rarely, if ever, is the dimension of divine inspiration discussed in the writings of modern critics. But it cannot be denied that this dimension is historically an essential part of the Christian package. Thus, for those who accept the teaching of Christ, the Bible can be read at different levels: as a work of history to be subjected to historical analysis, as a work of literature to be aesthetically analyzed, and as a Work of God to be reverentially pondered.

The Fish Out of Water Syndrome

Earlier we characterized the fundamental flaw in modern New Testament studies and the numerous "searches" for the "historical Jesus" as the "fish out of water" syndrome. There are, it was pointed out, two ways to study a fish: either as it swims around in its natural habitat or after it is taken out of the water and set on a dry surface. The results will vary depending on the mode we adopt, whether it is the one in which the fish is alive and acting in its natural environment or the one in which it struggles to survive, then dies, and finally rots. We have contended that the search for the historical Jesus over the last two hundred years belongs to the second category.

A historically legitimate study of the New Testament, it must be stressed, is possible only if it is carried out within the context of the community that gave it birth. And that community is not a community created out of the speculation of today's scholars — in which case we're back where we started, with simply the texts of the New Testament. To know what the community believed we must consider the ancient liturgies, the Councils, the Fathers, the Creeds. It is pointless to apply dissimilarity criteria twenty centuries later, to determine what Jesus said, while ignoring the extra-biblical testimony on this issue of those who lived in the first century. If the Passion Narratives and the Words of Institution of the Eucharist lay at the center of Christian worship from the beginning, how can a scholar who lives two thousand years later simply declare arbitrarily that there is no historical basis for these accounts?

We can vote all we want on what we think are the authentic sayings of Jesus using our own constantly changing criteria for determining what is authentic. But no one can claim with any credibility to be certain that Jesus did not make a particular statement, because that judgment is based on a criterion that may or may not be true. If we want to ascertain what Jesus said, we should look at what His first followers believed as reflected in their writings and prayers. The writings of the early Church Fathers and the texts of the earliest liturgies give us much greater insight into the historical basis of the biblical accounts than do the imaginative re-creations of contemporary critics. As to the identity of Jesus, why would a critic today have greater authority than the earliest generations of Christians? There is no new piece of evidence or knowledge that has changed the state of play. The early Councils gave us a clear portrait of Jesus Christ after considering various alternatives. Modern theologians who reject the classical teachings about Christ have to embrace one of these ancient alternatives packaged in contemporary jargon. In embracing such an alternative, they have no arguments that were not already advanced — and rejected — hundreds of years ago.

Commenting on the train of thought outlined here, Professor Farmer observes, "So the main question for the historian to answer is not, did Jesus say or do this, but rather, how are we to understand a particular text in the New Testament as a text that was formulated for use in the Church at a particular time and place. Once the historian can answer this question he will be in a good position to make inferences about the historical Jesus, but not before. The Jesus Seminar wants to short-circuit this whole enterprise and do the impossible: i.e., decide what Jesus did and said without reference to the Church He instituted, in which Church the traditions about what He did and said were handed down to the Evangelists."

In sum, we have the following pieces of hard evidence as it relates to the New Testament narratives:

- the sayings and deeds of Jesus described in the canonical Gospels;

- the amplification of these same sayings and deeds in the first liturgies;

- the application of the teachings of Jesus to doctrine and life in the writings of the early Fathers and in other ancient Christian documents;

- the confirmation of the New Testament claims about the identity of Jesus in the proclamations of the Councils and Creeds.

If we want to know who Jesus is and what He taught and did, we should at least consider all four of these sources, for then we would be studying the fish in its natural habitat. A study of the historical Jesus that relies only on criteria about the New Testament texts constructed by critics who lived centuries later is both anachronistic and logically circular. Depending on the narrowness of the criteria deployed, it is a study of a fish that is dying, dead, or rotting.

The Search for the Christ of Faith

If New Testament studies in the last two hundred years may be characterized as the search for the historical Jesus, the Ecumenical Councils of the first eight centuries of Christendom may be characterized as the search for the Christ of Faith. The Councils were called to study and explain both the data of Scripture and the data of the experience shared by Christians. In defining the conclusions reached from their study of the data, the Councils specifically rejected conclusions that they considered alien and inauthentic. In the Acts of the proceedings of the Councils, the Council Fathers made clear references to their conviction that their definitions were protected from error by divine guidance. This conviction was shared by the Christian community at large for at least one and a half millennia.

The central datum under discussion in the Councils was the identity of Jesus. The teachings that Jesus was God and man and that God was a Trinity of Divine Persons were reaffirmed in every Council with growing precision because it was felt that only this double doctrine could do justice to the data. Each new articulation of these doctrinal foundations laid to rest a succession of competing hypotheses labeled as heresies because they were foreign to the lived experience of the followers of Jesus. In point of fact, almost every possible alternate interpretation of the identity of Jesus was floated in the first centuries of Christianity and banished after intense debate. So much so, the supposedly novel and radical approaches to the identity of Christ periodically proposed today are at best reincarnations or resuscitations of ancient doctrinal deviations. These deviations are objectionable today for the same reason they were objectionable over a thousand years ago: they cannot adequately explain the data given us in the New Testament or in Christian experience. A survey of the teachings of the Councils will help us understand what is at stake.

325   NICAEA I. *Doctrines taught:* Jesus Christ is of the same substance (*homoousios*) as God. The Nicene Creed was developed to teach this and other truths of the Christian Faith (see below p. 54). *Doctrines condemned:* Arianism: the Son is a creature and neither preexistent nor of the same substance as God.

381   CONSTANTINOPLE I. *Doctrines taught:* The Holy Spirit is consubstantial with the Father and the Son. The Nicene Creed confirmed and further refined. *Doctrines condemned:* Semi-Arians: the Son is like the Father but not in essence. Pneumatomachians: The Holy Spirit is a creation of God but not God. Eunomians: Arians who believed in a form of polytheism (three deities). Eudoxians: Arians. Sabellians: Denial of three divine Persons, the view that Father, Son, and Holy Spirit are simply three modes of one divine Person. Apollinarians: Christ had no human soul or mind.

431   EPHESUS. *Doctrines taught:* There is only one Person in Christ, a divine Person, although He has two natures, divine and human. Mary is therefore Theotokos, the Mother of God (see below p. 54). *Doctrines condemned:* Nestorianism: There are two persons in Christ, one human and one divine.

451   CHALCEDON. *Doctrines taught:* Jesus is truly God and truly Man, and the two natures exist in Him "without confusion, without change, without division, without separation." In His divinity, Christ is "consubstantial with the Father" and in His humanity He is "consubstantial with us in manhood." *Doctrines condemned:* Eutychianism/Monophysitism: Christ has only one nature, a divine nature, although He took on human flesh.

553   CONSTANTINOPLE II. *Doctrines taught:* Ratification of previous Councils, particularly of Chalcedon (see below p. 55). *Doctrines condemned:* Teachings of Arius, Eunomius, Macedonius, Apollinaris, Nestorius, Eutyches, and of *The Three Chapters,* a volume of suspected heresies.

680   CONSTANTINOPLE III. *Doctrines taught:* Ratification of the previous five Councils and affirmation that there is a human and a divine will in Christ (see below p. 56). *Doctrines condemned:* Monothelitism, the view that there was only one will in Christ.

787   NICAEA II. *Doctrines taught:* Ratification of the previous Councils and a defense of the practice of venerating sacred images. *Doctrines condemned:* Iconoclasm, the view that the veneration of sacred images is equivalent to idolatry.

Nicaea I: The Creed

We believe in one God, the Father Almighty, maker of all things visible and invisible; and in one Lord Jesus Christ, the Son of God, the only begotten of his Father, of the substance of the Father, God of God, Light of Light, very God of very God, begotten not made, being of one substance with the Father. By whom all things were made, both which be in heaven and in earth. Who for us men and for our salvation came down [from heaven] and was incarnate and was made man. He suffered and the third day he rose again, and ascended into heaven. And he shall come again to judge both the quick and the dead. And [we believe] in the Holy Ghost. And whosoever shall say that there was a time when the Son of God was not or that before he was begotten he was not, or that he was made of things that were not, or that he is of a different substance or essence [from the Father] or that he is a creature, or subject to change or conversion — all that so say, the Catholic and Apostolic Church anathematizes them.

St. Athanasius's exposition of homoousios:

That the Son is not only like to the Father, but that, as his image, he is the same as the Father; that he is of the Father; and that the resemblance of the Son to the Father, and his immutability, are different from ours: for in us they are something acquired, and arise from our fulfilling the divine commands. Moreover, they wished to indicate by this that his generation is different from that of human nature; that the Son is not only like to the Father, but inseparable from the substance of the Father, that he and the Father are one and the same, as the Son himself said: "The Logos is always in the Father, and, the Father always in the Logos," as the sun and its splendour are inseparable.

Ephesus

If anyone shall not confess that the Word of God the Father is united hypostatically to flesh, and that with that flesh of his own, he is one only Christ both God and man at the same time: let him be anathema.

If anyone asserts that, at the union of the Logos with the flesh, the divine Essence moved from one place to another; or says that the flesh is capable of receiving the divine nature, and that it has been partially united with the flesh; or ascribes to the flesh, by reason of its reception of God, an extension to the infinite and boundless, and says that God and man are one and the same in nature: let him be anathema.

If anyone shall after the [hypostatic] union divide the hypostases in the one Christ, joining them by that connection alone, which happens according to worthiness, or even authority and power, and not rather by a coming together, which is made by natural union: let him be anathema.

If anyone says that Christ, who is also Emmanuel, is One, not [merely] in consequence of connection, but [also] in nature, and does not acknowledge the connection of the two natures, that of the Logos and of the assumed manhood, in one Son, as still continuing without mingling: let him be anathema.

Theodore [of Mopsuestia, and in this he was followed by Nestorius,] (and here is his fundamental error,) not merely maintained the existence of two natures in Christ, but of two persons, as, he says himself, no subsistence can be thought of as perfect without personality. As however, he did not ignore the fact that the consciousness of the Church rejected such a double personality in Christ, he endeavoured to get rid of the difficulty, and he repeatedly says expressly: "The two natures united together make only one Person, as man and wife are only one flesh.... If we consider the natures in their distinction, we should define the nature of the Logos as perfect and complete, and so also his Person, and again the nature and the person of the man as perfect and complete. If, on the other hand, we have regard to the union, we say it is one Person." The very illustration of the union of man and wife shows that Theodore did not suppose a true union of the two natures in Christ, but that his notion was rather that of an external connection of the two.... As a temple and the statue set up within it are one whole merely in outward appearance, so the Godhead and manhood in Christ appear only from without in their actuality as one Person, while they remain essentially two Persons.

If anyone shall divide between two persons or subsistences those expressions which are contained in the Evangelical and Apostolical writings, or which have been said concerning Christ by the Saints, or by himself, and shall apply some to him as to a man separate from the Word of God, and shall apply others to the only Word of God the Father, on the ground that they are fit to be applied to God: let him be anathema.

Constantinople II

If anyone uses the expression "of two natures," confessing that a union was made of the Godhead and of the humanity, or the expression "the one nature made flesh of God the Word," and shall not so understand those expressions as the holy Fathers have taught, to wit: that of the divine and human nature there was made an hypostatic union, whereof is one Christ; but from these expressions shall try to introduce one nature or substance [made by a mixture] of the Godhead and manhood of Christ: let him be anathema. For in teaching that the only begotten

Word was united hypostatically [to humanity] we do not mean to say that there was made a mutual confusion of natures, but rather each [nature] remaining what it was, we understand that the Word was united to the flesh. Wherefore there is one Christ, both God and man, consubstantial with the Father as touching his Godhead, and consubstantial with us as touching his manhood. Therefore they are equally condemned and anathematized by the Church of God, who divide or part the mystery of the divine dispensation of Christ, or who introduce confusion into that mystery.

If anyone shall take the expression, Christ ought to be worshipped in his two natures, in the sense that he wishes to introduce thus two adorations, the one in special relation to God the Word and the other as pertaining to the man; or if anyone to get rid of the flesh, [that is of the humanity of Christ,] or to mix together the divinity and the humanity, shall speak monstrously of one only nature or essence of the united (natures), and so worship Christ, and does not venerate, by one adoration, God the Word made man, together with his flesh, as the Holy Church has taught from the beginning: let him be anathema.

If anyone does not confess that our Lord Jesus Christ who was crucified in the flesh is true God and the Lord of Glory and one of the Holy Trinity: let him be anathema.

Constantinople III

Our Lord Jesus Christ must be confessed to be very God and very man, one of the holy and consubstantial and life-giving Trinity, perfect in Deity and perfect in humanity, very God and very man, of a reasonable soul and human body subsisting; consubstantial with the Father as touching his Godhead and consubstantial with us as touching his manhood; in all things like unto us, sin only excepted; begotten of his Father before all ages according to his Godhead, but in these last days for us men and for our salvation made man of the Holy Ghost and of the Virgin Mary, strictly and properly the Mother of God according to the flesh; one and the same Christ our Lord the only begotten Son of two natures inconfusedly, unchangeably, inseparably, indivisibly to be recognized, the peculiarities of neither nature being lost by the union but rather the proprieties of each nature being preserved, concurring in one Person and in one subsistence, not parted or divided into two persons but one and the same only begotten Son of God, the Word, our Lord Jesus Christ, according as the Prophets of old have taught us and as our Lord Jesus Christ himself hath instructed us, and the Creed of the holy Fathers hath delivered to us; defining all this we likewise declare that in him are two natural wills and two natural operations indivisibly, inconvertibly, inseparably, inconfusedly, according to the teaching of the holy Fathers. And these two natural wills are not contrary the one to the other (God forbid!) as the impious heretics assert, but his human will follows and that not as resisting and reluctant, but rather as subject to his divine and omnipotent will. For it was right that the flesh should be moved but subject to the divine will, according to the most wise Athanasius. For as his flesh is called and is the flesh of God the Word, so also the natural will of his flesh is called and is the proper will of God the Word, as he himself says: "I came down from heaven, not that I might do mine own will but the will of the Father which sent me!" where he calls his own will the will of his flesh, inasmuch as his flesh was also his own.

For as his most holy and immaculate animated flesh was not destroyed because it was deified but continued in its own state and nature, so also his human will, although deified, was not suppressed, but was rather preserved according to the saying of Gregory Theologus: "His will [i.e., the Saviour's] is not contrary to God but altogether deified."

We glorify two natural operations indivisibly, immutably, inconfusedly, inseparably in the same our Lord Jesus Christ our true God, that is to say a divine operation and a human operation, according to the divine preacher Leo, who most distinctly asserts as follows: "For each form does in communion with the other what pertains properly to it, the Word, namely, doing that which pertains to the Word, and the flesh that which pertains to the flesh."

For we will not admit one natural operation in God and in the creature, as we will not exalt into the divine essence what is created, nor will we bring down the glory of the divine nature to the place suited to the creature.

We recognize the miracles and the sufferings as of one and the same [Person], but of one or of the other nature of which he is and in which he exists, as Cyril admirably says. Preserving therefore the inconfusedness and indivisibility, we make briefly this whole confession, believing our Lord Jesus Christ to be one of the Trinity and after the incarnation our true God, we say that his two natures shone forth in his one subsistence in which he both performed the miracles and endured the sufferings through the whole of his economic conversation, and that not in appearance only but in very deed, and this by reason of the difference of nature which must be recognized in the same Person, for although joined together yet each nature wills and does the things proper to it and that indivisibly and inconfusedly. Wherefore we confess two wills and two operations, concurring most fitly in him for the salvation of the human race.

•

This portrait of Jesus Christ painted by the great Ecumenical Councils is the result (often in the face of severe persecution) of centuries of exploration of the Gospels and the experience of Jesus shared by those who knew Him best. In its exhaustive exposition of the identity of Jesus it has bestowed on posterity a coherent and systematic body of teaching that cannot be ignored by those who seek an explanation of all the data relating to Him. If we abandon the teachings of the Councils, we are inescapably led to the counter-hypotheses that have historically proven to be inadequate and ultimately short-lived explanations. If we seek the truth about the identity of Jesus we should at least consider the answer given by those who have pursued this quest from the first days of Christianity. Against Arians, Apollinarians, Nestorians, Monophysites, and Monthelites, whether ancient or modern, the holiest men and women of Christendom affirm that Jesus Christ is "very God and very man, one of the holy and consubstantial and life-giving Trinity, perfect in Deity and perfect in humanity."

Chapter 3

The Witness of Mythology and the World Religions: A New Paradigm

The Incarnation did not take place in a religious vacuum. Then as now there were numerous bodies of religious belief and practice. The question that we face is how the existence of mythologies and religions espousing alternative worldviews can be "reconciled" with the claim that Jesus Christ is the definitive revelation of God in history.

All too often this question is addressed in inappropriate and irrelevant contexts, either in polemical encounters where religions are pitched as products in a competitive marketplace or in lowest common denominator dialogues where differences are ignored or explained away.

Another approach is proposed here. We start with the assumption that an investigation of the historical data leads us to affirm both the facticity of the resurrection of Jesus Christ from the dead and the truth that He is God Incarnate. If the historical data can at least support these affirmations, then we are in a position to consider religious history from the standpoint of the Incarnation.

The myths and religions of the world can be divided into pre- and post-Christian belief systems, those which preceded the coming of Christ and those which emerged after. Our focus here is on the pre-Christian systems rather than the post-Christian religions because the latter were largely defined and established in conscious opposition to the fundamental Christian claim of the Incarnation. If this fundamental claim can be shown to be viable, then the burden of proof shifts to those who deny it.

Pre-Christian mythologies and religions, on the other hand, are not necessarily antagonistic or incompatible in claims or content. On the contrary, it is possible to see a preparation for and a prefiguration of the Incarnation in the three most ancient world-visions, the Judaic Scriptures, the mystery religions of East and West, and the Vedas and Puraanas of Hinduism. Although there is a danger of reading too much of the present into the texts of the past, it is nevertheless possible to discern at least a few clear correlations between what was seen in a glass darkly in those texts and that which took place, so to speak, in the broad daylight of history in the New Testament.

The parallels and links between events, concepts, and individuals in the Old and New Testaments are described in some detail in different parts of this book. In this section we will consider similar correlations in ancient mythology and (very briefly) the Hindu texts. At the outset it must be admitted that the citations that follow are not comprehensive or systematic accounts of the belief systems in which they were formed. This is not a treatise of comparative religion. Our objective here is simply to identify ideas and concepts that mysteriously emerged in different corners of the world centuries before they found historical fulfillment in the life of Jesus.

First, let us consider the themes found in some of the great mythologies of the past. A recent book, *The Jesus Mysteries*,[1] draws attention to many of the themes in ancient myths that reappear in the New Testament:

- Osiris, the legendary Egyptian god, became a man, died, and then rose again. This sequence of events was celebrated annually as early as forty-five hundred years ago. Pythagoras observed these rituals in the seventh century B.C. and helped create a similar mystery religion in Greece centered on Dionysius, the wine god. Other Mediterranean cultures adapted this story of the dying and resurrecting god-man to their own deities, Attis in Asia Minor, Adonis in Syria, Mithras in Persia.

- Many of these god-men are called "sons of god" and some of them have virgin mothers.

- Baptism as a rite to wash away sin is found in many of the mystery religions.

- The god-men performed miracles ranging from the transformation of water into wine to healing the sick.

- Bread and wine are consumed as part of the initiation ritual.

- Osiris-Dionysius are unjustly put to death.

- Osiris-Dionysius-Mithras rise from the dead and go to heaven.

A major difference between the pagan myths and the Christian accounts centers on their historical status: the myths have no historical basis whatsoever whereas Christianity is indomitably historical. C. S. Lewis points out that:

> the heart of Christianity is a myth which is also a fact. The old myth of the Dying God, *without ceasing to be myth*, comes down from the heaven of legend and imagination to the earth of history. It *happens* — at a particular date, in a particular place, followed by definable historical consequences.

> We pass from a Balder or an Osiris, dying nobody knows when or where, to a historical Person crucified (it is all in order) *under Pontius Pilate.*[2]

Curiously, *The Jesus Mysteries* makes the extraordinary claim that the early Christians "created" Christianity by hijacking these pagan myths and perpetrating a massive cover-up. Although the book brings some interesting parallels to light, *Publishers Weekly* rightly describes it as "a disappointing, sensationalist polemic." The authors ignore the roots of the Christian story both in Judaism and the historical process. Most important, there is the hard fact of the post-Resurrection transformation of the Apostles — an event without parallel in the mystery religions and fundamental to the rise of Christianity. St. Peter draws specific attention to this element: "We did not follow cleverly devised myths when we made known to you the power and coming of our Lord Jesus Christ, but we had been eyewitnesses to his majesty" (2 Pet. 1:16). The authors also seem unaware that great scholars have been aware of the pagan parallels for centuries and have adroitly addressed the fascinating connection between pagan mythology and Christian fact.

Questions about the remarkable resemblance between the myths and the story narrated in the New Testament are inevitable. How did these myths originate? Why are there significant common themes in the myths of cultural groups that were geographically spread apart? And why the resemblance to the New Testament narratives? Three answers are possible to these questions:

1. The myths can be explained entirely in terms of anthropology, psychology, and sociology.

2. They are deceptions of the Devil that function as counterfeit Christianities.

3. They were "implanted" by God from the beginning to prepare the human psyche and mind (weakened though these were by Original Sin) for the coming of Christ.

If the Christian revelation is true, and if we believe that God seeks to bring everyone to knowledge of the truth, then the third possibility seems to be the most plausible one. Two classic contributions to a greater understanding of the relation between Christianity and the mystery religions are *Greek Myths and Christian Mystery* by Hugo Rahner and *The Mystery of Christian Worship* by Odo Casel. A few excerpts from these works will be of value here. While Rahner highlights the differences between Christianity and the mystery religions (a valuable corrective to the theses of *The Jesus Mysteries*), Casel focuses on Christianity as a fulfillment of the themes found in the mysteries.

"Christianity," writes Rahner, "is a mystery of revelation, a mystery of ethical demands, and a mystery of redemption. It is these three aspects that bring it into such sharp contrast with the piety of the Hellenistic mystery cults."[3] Regarding the first, he writes,

> Christian revelation is not myth but history and its precipitate is the visible Church; its character is to be seen in the clear and concrete quality of what

is written in the New Testament, in the unambiguous and definable content of the apostolic tradition, in the fixedness of the essential pattern imposed upon the sacraments. The God of the Christian mystery is not a thing fashioned out of the thoughts and longings, however sublime, of pious and searching Hellenistic souls, nor is he the God of learned men or even of the mystics.[4]

He is the God of Abraham, Isaac, and Jacob. On the moral dimension, Rahner notes:

The piety of the cults is at best only the tragic and earth-bound effort towards moral, and often only towards ritual, purification: it is the effort of the soul to mount upward by its own power. There is no such upward mounting in Christianity; there is only the descent of God and the outpouring of divine grace which brings about our transformation in the love of Christ.[5]

With regard to redemption,

The salvation proclaimed by all the cults was a salvation essentially conceived in terms of the natural order and in that form transposed into the other world. In the words of Boulanger, "The idea that God should die and rise again in order to lead his faithful to everlasting life is unrepresented in any Hellenistic religion. . . . " And as with sin, so, in the Christian mystery, the newly granted life lies wholly outside the natural order; it is "life everlasting," "a new birth" and "a seeing of God," and there is not a shred of evidence to suggest that the piety of the cults knew of anything of the kind.[6]

Rahner points to one unexpected reason for the similarity between the cults and Christianity:

Now for the final cause of similarity between Christianity and the cults. That cause is nothing less than the growing influence of Christianity to which in late antiquity the cults themselves began to be subject, a development to which recent scholarship has become increasingly alive. . . . The world of the cults is still a rich one, but it is in decay, and it is a victorious Christianity that confronts it. Yet it is precisely this period of the fourth century that is documented better than any other in regard to the mystery cults, a fact which is itself evidence of their very wide diffusion. It is therefore surely not unreasonable to suppose that — given the growing authority of the Christian Church — Christian practices should have had some sort of influence on what was still a popular institution and that it should have had an effect on the form the disintegrating cults began to assume.[7]

Despite his critical comments, Rahner does not deny that there could be some divine guidance in the themes celebrated in the mystery religions. In the religious development of humanity, he writes, there is also a contact directed from above: a divinely fashioned plan is discernible in human religious evolution, especially among the peoples of later antiquity. The story of that evolution is not merely one of crisis in the sense of the Epistle to the Romans; it is also the story of a pedagogy towards Christ. "Nevertheless God left not himself without testimony," says that same Paul (Acts 14:16). The ancient mystery cults are the altar bearing the inscription: "To the Unknown God."[8]

While acknowledging the limitations of the mystery religions, Casel also recognizes the positive role they played in preparing the world for the coming of Christ:

> The Indo-germanic peoples in their striving for deeper union with God had gradually fashioned richer and more refined forms of worship. These, particularly in the Hellenistic age, ... entered a period of fruitful mixing of Greek and Near Eastern ideas, and led to the mystery cults. This synthesis, which in many respects was to give its language and form to the coming Christianity ... developed the ritual-form mystery to its classical height. Its fundamental idea was participation in the lives of the gods, who in some way or other had appeared in human form, and taken part in the pain and happiness of mortal men....
>
> The ancient mysteries ... remained the prisoners of unredeemed nature, in the slavery of the "world's elements" as St. Paul says of a Jewish-hellenistic cult; they did not lead to the supernatural life of the true God. They were only a shadow, in contrast to the Christian mysteries; but they were a longing, "a shadow of things to come"; the body whose shadow they cast was "the body of Christ" which showed itself beforehand in the types of the Old Testament too.... They made it possible to give a body to the new and unconceived elements of the New Testament's revelation. When St. Paul speaks of the "things wrapped in silence for the ages" or of the "hidden mystery," everyone in the ancient world knew immediately what this was: the familiar language of the mysteries, its purpose to make clearer to them, that as these mysteries were surrounded by a terrible majesty which claimed reverence, so, too, God's saving design came out of the hidden depths of his vast silences; and that these silences were now revealed.[9]

Christianity fulfilled all that was good and true in the mystery religions:

> The symbolic, strength-giving rites of the mysteries were real for the ancients; when the church of Christ entered the world she did not end, but rather fulfilled their way of thinking.... It was symbolism which was sanctified and divinized when the Logos appeared in human flesh, and "we saw the glory of God in the face of Christ." It cannot seem strange to us, then, when at his going away, Christ leaves the mysteries as signs of his divine presence, or when John, deepest of the evangelists, in his "Spirit-informed" gospel, makes so much of them. On the other hand, it is also an historical truth that the Hellenes sometimes found it easier to grasp and to grasp

more deeply the truth of the gospel than did the Jews with their purely Semitic, imageless, legal thinking. The Christianity of the ancient world appears to us as the fulfillment and glorification of what Greco-Roman antiquity was.[10]

The climax of this story of fulfillment was the sacrifice of Christ.

What the ancient world longed for but only attained in so shadowy and imperfect a form is now fulfilled by Christ's coming in grace, fulfilled in an over-powering fashion; it is so wonderful than men have had no inkling of it. This is the point where divine love and divine life come down upon the poor earth, take a share in the poverty of mankind, overcome sin which has once more brought chaos into the world, create the sacrificial deed to conquer worlds by the death of an incarnate God, restore the oneness of God and man, heal and glorify the creature. Out of the blood of the dying God-man and the glory of his transforming light eternal salvation flows, divine life for those who belong to him. All of this was at work in the new alliance, the ecclesia, in the vast simplicity of her Spirit-informed rites filled with symbolism and reality beyond the scope of worlds.... The best of the ancient world did service to Christendom. The service was extremely desirable; in Christianity the mystery-type gained a wholly new meaning. The sacrificial service of the old alliance was done away with, or better, fulfilled with the sacrifice of Christ.[11]

The theologian Eric Mascall considers the same issues with particular attention to the relationship between Christian liturgy and the mystery religions:

The historical status of such figures as Mithras or Osiris is, to say the least, highly ambiguous, nor was it of the least importance to the religion of their devotees. In contrast, the central fact of the Christian faith was the crucifixion of Jesus of Nazareth under Pontius Pilate, and the Church staked its very existence upon the assertion that this particular Jew had risen from the dead.... It is, of course, possible to find here and there in Christian liturgical forms traces of thought and language which may be derived from mystery-religions. There is nothing that need disquiet us in this. Christianity is the fulfillment of the mystery-religions, as it is of all human aspirations and intuitions, however imperfect and distorted these may be. What was, however, essential was that the Church and its liturgy should remain firmly rooted in the flesh and blood of Jesus the Messiah.... What the Church is doing when it celebrates the liturgy is not offering a mystical experience to the initiates of an ecstatic cult, but fulfilling the command of the incarnate Lord to do as his *anamnesis* what he did at the Last Supper, for the gathering into unity of the people of God.[12]

About this primordial preparation in ancient mythology, Leon McKenzie writes:

To say that some early Christians responded favorably to the heralding of the risen Jesus because their minds and imaginations were forestructured previously by exposure to pagan myths of rebirth and renewal is to raise the important issue of divine providence. Providentially, it is maintained, just as Roman roads were appropriated by Christian missionaries and the Greek language used for spreading of the Christian message throughout the Mediterranean world, so also was human consciousness made ready by pagan resurrection myths for the message of the risen Jesus....

Without the experience of pagan resurrection myths, many individuals at the beginning of the Christian era might not have been equipped psychically and spiritually for the reception of the good news of Jesus' bodily resurrection.

The stories of Atis, Adonis, Hyacinth, Osiris, and other dying and reviving gods can be understood in the great scheme of things only by recognizing the celebration of these myths prior to the Christian message as anticipating, in a highly ambiguous but undeniable manner, the resurrection of Jesus. Pagan revival myths, it can be effectively argued, do not explain the resurrection of Jesus as "just another myth." On the contrary, for the Christian faithful (and perhaps even those who are not Christian but whose hearts are open to the Christian message) the resurrection of Jesus ultimately explains the meaning of pagan myths. Myths of dying and reviving gods were conscious expressions of the resurrection archetype within the collective unconscious.... The recitation of the myths of Attis, Adonis and other heroes, and the ritual enactments of these myths, prepared the minds and imaginations of millions of people for the Christian message. While elements of these myths departed from the truth and were sometimes morally disreputable, the core meaning of the myths served the cause of Jesus Christ. When pagan resurrection myths were celebrated they point obscurely to the future key event, the resurrection of Jesus, that served to validate whatever degree of truth borne by the myths.[13]

From the mystery religions of East and West, we turn to Hinduism, a mother-religion of the ancient world (both Buddhism and Jainism sprang from this religion). It is not without significance that tradition indicates that Jesus sent several of His Apostles to minister to the Gentiles with their mystery religions and one to address the Hindus in India. There is an ancient community of Christians in India whose entire identity as a community centers on the claim that their ancestors were converted by St. Thomas. If indeed St. Thomas was behind the conversion of this community — it is a historical fact that there was a community of Jews in India from ancient times — then there is some ground for holding that Hinduism in some sense would be prepared for the coming of Christ. Curiously, there is an ancient legend that one of the Three Wise Men was a Hindu scholar named Viswamitra from Benares who, on his return, proclaimed the birth of the Redeemer of the Vedic writings.

Here we review passages from some of the religious texts of Hinduism that appear to foreshadow the coming of Christ.[14]

The four holiest texts in Hinduism are the Vedas: RigVeda, YajurVeda, Sama-

Veda, and AtharvaVeda. Of these four, the RigVeda, believed to have been written between 1200 and 900 B.C., is considered the most authoritative. The tenth and last volume of the RigVeda centers on Prajapathi, a majestic personage who is thought to be a prefiguration of Jesus Christ (the Prajapathi of the Vedas is not to be confused with the prajapathis of later legends such as are found in the Puraanas). The connection between Prajapathi and Jesus Christ has been drawn by both Hindu and Christian scholars. Prajapathi is the First-Born from Paramatma, the Glorious Self, who is equal to Paramatma and is the Creator, Protector, and Sustainer of all things. He is also the Nishkalanka Purusha, the sinless one, half mortal and half immortal, who comes down to earth and offers himself as a sacrifice bound on a stake to save the human race from the bondage of sin. He is mysteriously the sacrificer at his own sacrifice. The Vedas say that "for salvation there is no other Path except this Prajapathi who sacrificed himself for the redemption of the human race; he who knows him shall escape the pangs of death" (YajurVeda XXXI).

Prajapathi

In the beginning only the Lord almighty and his supreme spirit existed, and from the supreme spirit of the God proceeded 'Hiranyagarbha' (Prajapathi) in the form of light. As soon as [he was] born, he the first born son of God, alone, was the Lord of all that is. He established the earth and the heaven. Let us offer sacrifice to that God. (RigVeda X:121:1).

After creating the sky, waters, and the earth, the supreme spirit of the Lord almighty thought, "I created the worlds. Now to provide for and to save these worlds I have to create a savior." Thinking thus he gave birth to a man from himself. (Ithareya Upanishad 1:1:3)

This man is all that has been, all that is and all that has to be. He controls eternal life and it is for the redemption of mankind he surpasses his immortal sphere and descends to the mortal sphere. He comes to give everyone reward as per their deeds. (RigVeda X:90:2)

This man, the first born, was tied to a yoopa [wooden sacrificial post] and the gods and the kings along with the seers performed the sacrifice. (RigVeda X:90:7)

The Sacrificer is Prajapathi at his own sacrifice. (*Sacred Books of the East,* 12:160)

Those who meditate and attain this man, believe in heart and chant with their lips, get liberated in this world itself and there is no other way for salvation. (YajurVeda XXXI:18; RigVeda X:90:16)

The Sacrificial Rituals

Prajapathi is sacrificed on a wooden stake.

1. The sacrificial victim is to be crowned with a crown made of thorny vines (Sathapadha Brahmana).

2. His hands and legs are to be bound to a yoopa causing bloodshed (RigVeda X:90:7, 15; Bruhadaranyakopanishad III:9:28).

3. None of his bones are to be broken (Ithareya Brahmanam 2:6).

4. Before death he should be given a drink of somarasa [sour wine made out of a herb called somalatha] (YajurVeda XXXI).

5. After death his clothes are to be divided among the offerors (Ithareya Brahmanam).

Easa Maseeha

Another set of Hindu holy books are the Puraanas. A Hindu leader, Sri Chandrasekharendra Saraswati, calls the Puraanas the "magnifying glass" of the Vedas. There are a total of eighteen Puraanas by Maharshi Vedavyasa written between 700 and 600 B.C.. The Bhavishya Mahapuraana concerns the future and includes passages on Adam, Eve, Noah, Moses, and other Old Testament figures (similar parallels are also found in the Vedas). The most notable section in this book is a prophecy of Jesus Christ:

> [King Shakapathi, the ruler of Huna Desh, meets a young man clad in white.] King Shaka asked: "May I know, who you are?" With apparent joy that male replied, "Know that I am the Son of God. I am born in the womb of a virgin. 'Eesa Maseeha' is my well known name." (Bhavishya Mahapuraana — Prathisarga Parva, III, chap. 2, v. 23)

Many volumes have been written on the relationship between Hinduism and Christianity and there are numerous other areas of Hindu thought (the concepts of sacrifice, the moral order, the Absolute, for instance) that are relevant to this discussion. But our objective here is simply to point out that along with Judaism and the mystery religions, Hinduism too can be seen as part of the primordial preparation for the coming of the only begotten Son of God Who sacrificed Himself for the salvation of humanity.

The new paradigm proposed here is that the three major religious worldvisions of the pre-Christian era constituted, in different fashions and different degrees, a prophetic and mythological witness to the coming of the Son of God. It could hardly have been otherwise. "The resurrection of Jesus," writes McKenzie,

> would be unacceptable to many of us, however, if it was not redolent of ancient structures of imagination and thinking. The same God who raised Jesus from the dead is the God who created the ancient structures of imagination and thinking. Primal meaning structures are what make human beings authentically human. To reject these meaning structures or archetypes is to begin to deny not only our continuity with the past but the common experiences of our race concerning the great theme of death and resurrection that is written in the everyday processes of the natural world.[15]

Although we have treated the truth of the Incarnation as our starting point, this position has been abandoned by a number of modern theologians. They are committed to the thesis that all religions are true, which is to say none of them are true. John Hick, who abandoned traditional Christianity to propound the view that God is at the center of the universe of different religions, now says that even "God" is too divisive a concept and prefers to put the "Real" at the center. Gavin D'Costa sees three problems with the position of Hick and other so-called pluralists: pluralists see religious language merely as expressions of attitude or intentions but not as statements describing reality in any sense; they do not take other religions seriously because they fail "to take the sheer plurality of their conflicting claims seriously"; since they do not want to make a choice even between theism and nontheism, they are ultimately left with agnosticism.[16] Terrence Merrigan makes this same point:

> The great appeal of pluralist theology is its claim to take the world's religious traditions seriously in their distinctiveness....It can be argued that pluralist theology issues in a radical contradiction of its own basic premise. That is to say, it begins by insisting that it takes each religion seriously in its particularity and ends by treating them all in terms of its own universalist vision. In other words, within pluralist theology, salvation history does not ultimately possess any particular content. It cannot yield any distinctive doctrine of God (since it cannot legitimately invoke any particular tradition).[17]

The survey here indicates that the great pre-Christian religions in different degrees prepared humanity for the Incarnation of God in Christ. The affirmation of the Incarnation in the sense defined by the Councils is fundamental to Christianity and this insight is to be maintained especially in interreligious dialogues. Bertram Stubenrauch notes:

> Even where we find notions of some kind of incarnation present [in non-Christian systems], such concepts are devoid of that drama which is called the Cross. They recognise neither the resolute freedom of God nor the soteriological power of human free will. Judaism, for instance, recognizes a kind of incarnation, namely, the mercy of Jahweh on high which, reaching down into the depths, seeks out the needy. It is an incarnation of the divine glance. God refuses to turn his face away from earthly misery. He shows himself to be involved even to the extent that he and man...can so "exchange roles" as to be fused into a common destiny. Nevertheless, the divine mercy remains without any creaturely substratum. The same holds true to a much greater degree for the mercy of Mohammed's God. Hinduism, likewise, acknowledges various incarnations: the divine, shining through thousands of facets, appears in many human forms. But none of these incarnations are definitive, because creation likewise is not definitive. Incarnation is just appearance; it remains provisional, because earthly existence itself is only an illusion and exists only provisionally. By way of contrast, New Testament Christology contains an implication of incomparable significance in its understanding of the incarnation: God uses Himself

in his own lasting definition of man. . . . The incarnate Logos will always remain man, true God and true creature at the same time.[18]

The Incarnation as Christians have understood, affirmed, and articulated this doctrine is the claim that in Jesus Christ the Ultimate Reality, the Absolute, united Itself with a human nature and entered human history at a specific place and a specific time. This Event was not a partial or transient or mythological manifestation or symbol of the Infinite. Rather, the fundamental truth underlying this doctrine is the recognition that in Jesus "dwells the whole fullness of the deity bodily."

PART TWO

AGNUS DEI

Chapter 4

"Saul, Saul, why are you persecuting me?": Accredited Visions and Messages of Jesus in History

The history of the post-Ascension visions of Christ begins in the New Testament and continues from the first century.

In the Acts of the Apostles, we read about the vision of Saul (who later became the Apostle Paul):

> On his journey, as he was nearing Damascus, a light from the sky suddenly flashed around him. He fell to the ground and heard a voice saying to him, "Saul, Saul, why are you persecuting me?" He said, "Who are you, sir?" The reply came, "I am Jesus, whom you are persecuting. Now get up and go into the city and you will be told what you must do." The men who were traveling with him stood speechless, for they heard the voice but could see no one. Saul got up from the ground, but when he opened his eyes he could see nothing; so they led him by the hand and brought him to Damascus. For three days he was unable to see, and he neither ate nor drank.... Ananias went and entered the house; laying his hands on him, he said, "Saul, my brother, the Lord has sent me, Jesus, who appeared to you on the way by which you came, that you may regain your sight and be filled with the holy Spirit." Immediately things like scales fell from his eyes and he regained his sight. He got up and was baptized. (9:3–9, 17–18)

In the Book of Revelation, we see Jesus again in the first of John's visions:

> A sharp two-edged sword came out of his mouth, and his face shone like the sun at its brightest. When I caught sight of him, I fell down at his feet as though dead. He touched me with his right hand and said, "Do not be afraid. I am the first and the last, the one who lives. Once I was dead, but now I am alive forever and ever. I hold the keys to death and the netherworld." (Rev. 1:16–18)

These visions of Jesus were to continue into the Apostolic Age, one famous instance being Peter's encounter with Jesus as he attempted to leave Rome, and thereafter into Christian history. Many of the "movers and shakers" of the Christian world — from St. Augustine to St. Francis of Assisi — were privileged to encounter their Lord early in their apostolates.

Now, before considering the chronology of these visions and the content of the messages associated with some of them, we have to consider the nature of the visionary experience: were the recipients seeing Jesus in His Risen Body or was it a message sent directly from Him through a "vehicle" that He instituted (e.g., an image of Him imprinted in the subject's mind)? The second option in no way suggests that the message was not actually from Jesus. Many direct messages from God in the Bible were delivered by angels, but the manner of their delivery did not undermine the claim that the messages had a divine origin. Likewise, the actual mechanism utilized in the delivery of a message from Jesus has no bearing on the question of whether it actually comes from Him.

Criteria

The possibility that a vision of Jesus is not an apparition of Him in His Risen Body is the preferred option for various reasons:

1. Until the General Judgment of the human race, only two individuals "possess" their glorified Risen Bodies, Jesus, Who ascended to Heaven, and Mary, who was assumed body and soul into Heaven. From the ancient exposition of Scripture in the writings of the Fathers and also from the teaching of those like St. Teresa of Avila who had visions of Jesus, we are given to understand that after His Ascension Jesus will not come to this world again in His Risen Body until His Second Coming at the end of history (the only possible exception being the appearance to Paul, an event through which he was anointed an Apostle). Jesus ascended to Heaven so that the Holy Spirit could now be present in the world both spiritually and through apparitions of His Spouse, the Virgin Mary, in her Risen Body.

2. The only "apparition" of Christ, in the sense of the presence of a three-dimensional person in his or her glorified body, that we can affirm without hesitation is the presence of Jesus in the Eucharist. But here the Presence is not one in which Jesus comes down to the Eucharistic elements but one whereby — through the instrumentality of the Holy Spirit — these are

"taken up" into Him as He reigns in glory in Heaven. These elements become the Bread *from* Heaven and reception of the Eucharist is, in a mysterious but real sense, a participation in the life of Heaven.

3. It is surely significant that most of the accredited visions of Jesus have been individual — not shared by numerous witnesses, as were the apparitions of Mary. The messages of these visions tend to be intimate conversations between two hearts and are principally concerned with reflection on the Passion of Jesus and on His infinite Love and Mercy. Moreover, many of these visions involved a participation in central events in the earthly life of Jesus and were, therefore, clearly not apparitions in the sense of a current event involving His Risen Body.

If the great visions of Christ were not apparitions of Him in His Risen Body, how should they be characterized? St. Augustine categorized supernatural visions under three headings: corporeal, imaginative, and intellectual. A corporeal vision is one in which our sensory organs are presented with a reality, as happens when one witnesses the apparition of a Risen Body. An imaginative vision is the supernatural presentation of a reality to our imagination, the example here being an image of Jesus that He Himself brings about in the mind of the recipient. An intellectual vision is the presentation and apprehension of a sublime reality by the intellect, for example, some great insight into the mystery of the Trinity. Authentic visions falling under each one of these three categories are brought about by some external agency and are not actions initiated by our own minds.

The route taken in an imaginative vision is one that reaches the subject's physiological and mental processes without going through the sensory organs. An image and a message are directly presented to our minds without the involvement of our senses. Three critical questions arise here: (1) Who is the image and message coming from? (2) What medium is used to produce the image/message of the Person being perceived? (3) Who produces the image and the message? The answers, with respect to an authentic vision of Jesus, are the following: (1) The image and the message come from Jesus. (2) These are produced by a direct supernatural action on the mind of the subject. (3) The direct supernatural action, although initiated and directed by Jesus, may actually be executed by an angel or even the Holy Spirit. Whatever the route taken, the end-product is an authentic message from Jesus Himself.

It should be emphasized here that in describing a vision as an image directly produced in the mind we are not suggesting that Jesus is not present in and through that image. There are at least two different modes in which He could be present: in His Risen Body or through an image of Himself. In authentic visions of Jesus, He is presented to us mentally rather than physically (for reasons outlined above). This difference in mode does not affect the fact that the messages received are actual messages from Him. An entirely inadequate analogy would be the difference between a conversation with a person sitting in the room with us and a conversation carried on with that person via a live video transmission. In both cases, it is the same person with whom we are engaged in conversation although the mode of presence is different. This analogy is only intended to make the point that the mode of presence is not material to the question of the source of the communication. But the analogy does not apply to the nature of the vision itself: in other words, the manner in which the image of Jesus is presented or the way in which the visionary participates in certain events in the life of Jesus remain mysteries.

But how are we to determine the authenticity of a vision of Jesus? How can an authentic vision be distinguished from a hallucination induced by a pathological state or a deception of the Devil? It must be noted first that the idea of a vision of Jesus is neither novel nor heterodox. From the early days of Christianity, some of the holiest and wisest men and women have reported such visions and these visions were accepted as genuine by the Church as a whole. Despite the anti-supernaturalism of some of the Reformers, Martin Luther stated that he does not "detract from the gifts of others, if God by chance reveals something to someone beyond Scripture through dreams, through visions, and through angels."[1]

In the case of an apparition of Mary, authenticity is determined by various criteria including some piece of tangible evidence left behind as a lasting sign (like the *tilma* of Guadalupe). Visions of Jesus, however, are not "material" in the same sense, and the criteria used in evaluating their authenticity include these:

1. the sanity and sanctity of the person who receives the vision;
2. the sublimity of the message and its consistency with orthodox doctrine;
3. the effect of the vision and message in the lives of the faithful;
4. the approval given by ecclesiastical authorities after an appropriate investigation (important for ruling out obvious instances of fraud and lack of mental balance);
5. the occurrence of miracles (suggested by theologians like Karl Rahner as further confirmation of the authenticity of a vision).

The visions and messages of Jesus considered here for the most part meet the first four criteria. Concerning the fifth, we can say that the most famous visions of Jesus were witnessed by individuals who have since been beatified or canonized. Both processes require miracles that can be reliably attributed to the intercession of the person being beatified or canonized. By extension, the earthly confirmation of celestial status is at least strongly suggestive of the integrity of this person who claims to have had a vision of Jesus.

On the following page is a chronology of the visions of Jesus given in E. C. Brewer's *Dictionary of Miracles*.[2]

Theme: The Passion as a Portrait of Infinite Love and Mercy

The messages of Jesus in His visions are not new in the sense of being different from what He has already taught in the Gospels. In fact, these messages may be construed as expositions and amplifications of the Gospel teachings much like the great liturgies.

Witness	Period	Vision
Pope Alexander I	118	Jesus as an infant
Forty Christians in prison	320	Jesus commends them for courage in facing death
St. Philomena	320	Infant Jesus
St. Porphory	353–420	Jesus on the cross
St. Gregory the Great	540–604	Jesus as a beggar
St. Jerome	347–419	Instructed by Jesus to spend more time on Scripture
St. Hubert of Brittany	c. 714	Jesus as a beggar
St. Wulsin of Sherbourne	tenth century	Jesus reigning in Heaven
Emperor St. Henry	1014	Jesus celebrating Mass in St. Mary Major
Hildegard of Bingen	1098–1179	Wrote of heavenly vision shown by Jesus
Mechtild of Magdeburg	1207–1282	Jesus' messages about God's love
St. Francis of Assisi	1221	Jesus gives him roses to commend his actions
St. Lutgard	1246	Jesus appears to bring her to faith, shows His Heart
St. Rosa of Viterbo	1235–1252	Jesus on the cross
St. Antony of Padua	1195–1231	Seen with the Infant Jesus
St. Gertrude the Great	1256–1302	Infant Jesus; Jesus in glory; stigmata
St. Hyacinth of Kiev	1257	Jesus crowning the Virgin Mary
Bl. Angela of Foligno	1309	Visions of Jesus and messages
St. Mechtilde of Heldelf	1293	Vision of Jesus during Mass
St. Bridget of Sweden	c. 1312	Jesus crucified
St. Clara	1346	Jesus on the throne
St. Catherine of Siena	1347–1380	Jesus as King; Jesus crucified
St. Vincent Ferrer	1396	Healed by Jesus
Julian of Norwich	1450	Suffering of Jesus
St. Columba	1477–1501	Jesus crucified
St. Catherine dei Ricci	1522–1590	Suffering of Jesus; stigmata
St. Angela of Brescia	1535	Set up Ursuline Order after vision of Jesus
St. Teresa of Avila	1515–1582	Various visions of Jesus
St. Ignatius of Loyola	c. 1537	Jesus crucified
St. Rose of Lima	1586–1617	Jesus as a child; stigmata
St. Margaret Mary Alacoque	1648–1690	Sacred Heart of Jesus
Sr. Mary of St. Peter	1816–1848	Messages from Jesus on the Holy Face
Sr. Conchita of Mexico	1862–1937	Messages from Jesus; victim-soul
Sr. Mary of the Divine Heart	1863–1948	Visions of the Sacred Heart
Sr. Josefa Menéndez	1890–1920	Messages from Jesus; victim-soul
Sr. Mary of the Trinity	1901–1942	Messages from Jesus; victim-soul
St. Consolata Betrone	1903–1946	Messages from Jesus; victim-soul
St. Faustina Kowalska	1905–1938	Divine Mercy

The unifying theme in all the visions of Jesus is the stunning nature of the tragedy of the Cross — a tragedy that immediately calls to mind both the infinite love of God and the deadliness of sin. The Incarnation with its culmination in the supreme Act of Redemption, it was observed, was the greatest event in human history. The Book of Revelation informs us that "from the foundation of the world" there is a book of life with the names of all those who are saved, a book that belongs "to the Lamb who was slain" (Rev. 13:8). Not only is the heartrending and life-giving death of Jesus an Event that is mystically present in all of subsequent history, but it somehow reaches back in time to the very foundation of the world. As for the future that is eternity, even here the monstrosity of the Crucifixion leaves its mark, for the glorified King and Savior appears as "a Lamb that seemed to have been slain" (Rev. 5:6).

The primordial sin against God by the first humans, no matter how slight it may have been, erected an infinite barrier between Him and His creation — a barrier that could be brought down only by the infinite Sacrifice of a divine

Person united to a human nature. Likewise the pain and suffering inflicted on this Person by His creatures as He sacrificed Himself is infinite in its magnitude because it was experienced in all its horror by an infinite Person. One instant of suffering for the Son of God is incomparably more intense than any suffering undergone by any human person.

The Passion of Christ haunts history as inescapably and perennially as Original Sin. Just as every sin after Original Sin cemented and consolidated the barrier between God and humanity, every sin after the Passion and Death of Christ committed by those who accept Him is another nail driven into His Flesh. If we think of the agony that a parent undergoes in observing the voluntary spiritual and moral self-destruction of a son or daughter, we get a glimmer of the agony undergone by the Son of God as He experienced in human flesh — suffering in mind and spirit — the self-immolation of those who were both His creation and His brothers and sisters.

The suffering for the sins of humanity that He took on Himself was for sins past, present, and future: "Through his suffering, my servant shall justify many, and their guilt he shall bear. He shall take away the sins of many, and win pardon for their offenses" (Isa. 53:11–12). This is not to say that everyone will automatically be saved — only those who accept the divine invitation, an invitation offered to all, will benefit fully from the merits of the Passion. When He asks Saul, "Why are you persecuting me?" we are given to understand that this persecution of Christians personally afflicts Him. In fact, those who reject the Faith they had once accepted, apostate Christians, "are recrucifying the Son of God for themselves" (Heb. 6:6). This does not mean, of course, that Jesus suffers in Heaven. Rather His suffering at Calvary "included" the suffering caused by all of our subsequent acts against God just as truly as the redemption acquired at Calvary was "included" in the divine Plan before "the foundation of the world."

The Passion is the central theme of the messages in the visions of Jesus: through the lives we lead, we can either be persecutors inflicting the Passion or participants in the Passion uniting ourselves to Christ and His mission: "I rejoice in my sufferings for your sake, and in my flesh I am filling up what is lacking in the afflictions of Christ on behalf of his body, which is the church" (Col. 1:24). We see all our thoughts and actions, our choices and intentions, in this new and somber light of the Passion. Only those who are willing to participate in the Passion by dying to themselves can enjoy its fruits in the Resurrection.

The Passion is important above all because it reveals to us most fully and permanently the infinite love and mercy of God. The prayer taught in the Divine Mercy revelation is basically a reminder of the Passion: "For the sake of His sorrowful passion, have mercy on us and on the whole world."

The messages in the visions are messages from a Lover Who has been betrayed. "How could you do this to Me?" asks the Lamb as we lead Him to the slaughter with every sin. Love is vulnerable, and infinite love is infinitely vulnerable. Infinite love is also infinitely merciful. Intent though we are on hurling ourselves to destruction, the Lover Whom we have murdered offers to us the very Life we have taken from Him.

Just as there is a progression in our understanding of the public revelation — chronicled in the Councils and Creeds — there is also a sequential buildup in the themes that emerge from private revelation. While the first progression is called the development of doctrine, the second might be called the development of devotion. Neither development deviates from the original body of revealed data and each one complements the other.

Chapter 5

The Sacred Heart

In every age in history, God raises up holy and fearless men and women who testify to truths and mysteries that seem obviously to have a supernatural source. In the following three chapters we will consider the lives and writings of mystics who have encountered Jesus and whose encounters have changed the course of history and the life of both the Church and the world.

Overview

The most influential and theologically significant series of visions of Jesus in Christian history was undoubtedly St. Margaret Mary Alacoque's encounter with the Sacred Heart of Jesus. Although these visions and messages occurred in France in the seventeenth century, their theological core goes back to the Old and New Testaments, the writings of the Fathers, and the messages associated with many of the accredited visions of Jesus both before and after. The portrait of Jesus presented in this encounter is a portrait that dramatically focuses our minds on the Jesus of the Gospels. The visions are significant also in being directed to the world and the Church at large and in the emphasis they place on the urgency and fruitfulness of devotion to the Sacred Heart.

Martyrdom is not instantiated just in the physical sacrifice of one's life — although it is clearly the most dramatic form of it. A martyrdom of the spirit in which one willingly and continually suffers slights and humiliations without resentment or reprisal and physical debilitation with praise and gratitude is just as commendable. This was the martyrdom to which St. Margaret Mary was called. She was not a traveling knight of faith like St. Francis of Assisi, an organizational genius like St. Ignatius of Loyola, or a mystic like St. John of the Cross. She was an unknown nun in an obscure convent who led a life of humiliation, grief, and physical and mental suffering, all of which she joyfully, even eagerly, accepted.

She was born on July 22, 1647. Her father died while she was very young, and this left her and her mother in poverty and at the mercy of unkind relatives. While still a child, she resolved that she would accept all her suffering as a participation in the Passion of Christ and vowed to lead a life of perfect chastity. Although approached with numerous offers of marriage (which her mother encouraged her to accept for the sake of financial stability), Margaret Mary entered the Order of the Visitation in Paray-le-Monial in June 1671. Early in her training as a nun, she was already aware that Jesus was speaking to her, and in 1673 she was led to accept St. Francis of Assisi as her model. On December 27, 1675, she received the first great vision of the Sacred Heart. Asked by her superiors to describe her experience, she wrote,

The following is all that I am able to tell you to satisfy the orders of my Superiors:

On the Feast of St. John the Evangelist, having received from my divine Saviour a favor almost similar to that which this Beloved Disciple received on the evening of the Last Supper, the divine Heart was represented to me as a throne all of a fire with flames radiating its light on every side.

It appeared more brilliant than the sun, and transparent like crystal. The wound which He received on the Cross appeared clearly. There was a crown of thorns around the Sacred Heart and It was surmounted by a cross. My divine Saviour gave me to understand that these instruments of His Passion signified that the immense love which He had for men was the cause of all the sufferings and all the humiliations which He willed to suffer for us; that from the first moment of His Incarnation, all these torments and all this contempt were present to Him, and that it was at this first moment that the Cross was, so to speak, planted in His Sacred Heart, which then, in testimony of Its love for us, accepted all the humiliations, poverty and sorrows which His sacred Humanity was to suffer during the whole course of which His love was to expose Him to the end of the ages of the altar in the most holy and august Sacrament.

He then gave me to understand that the great desire which He had of being perfectly loved by men had caused Him to form this design of manifesting to them His Heart and of opening to them all the treasures of love, mercy, grace, sanctification and salvation which It contains, in order that all those who would be willing to render to It and procure for It all the love and honor in their power, would be enriched in profusion with these divine treasures of which this Sacred Heart is the source; and He assured me that He takes a singular pleasure in being honored under the figure of this Heart of flesh, the image of which He wishes to be exposed in public, in order, He added, to touch the unfeeling hearts of men. He promised me that He would pour out in abundance into the hearts of all those who would honor It, all the gifts with which It is filled, and that everywhere this image would be exposed in order to be specially honored, it would draw down all kinds of blessings; that, in addition, to favor in a special manner the Christians of these last ages by proposing to them an object and a means which are at the same time so suitable to make men love Him and love Him solidly.

After that my divine Saviour spoke to me (as far as I know) these words: "That is, My child, the design for which I have chosen you; for this have I conferred on you so many graces, taking special care of you from the cradle. The reason why I made Myself your Master and Director was in order to dispose you to receive all these great graces, among which you are to regard as the most precious that by which I reveal to you and give you the greatest of all treasures by showing and at the same time giving to you My Heart." Then prostrating myself with my face pressed to the earth, it was impossible for me to express my sentiment in any other manner than by my silence, which I soon interrupted by my tears and sighs.

From that time, the graces of my sovereign Master became more abundant. The result of these greater graces was that not being able to contain the sentiments of the ardent love which I felt for Jesus Christ, I tried to diffuse them by my words every time that occasion offered, thinking that others, receiving the same graces as I had received, would have the same sentiments. But I was dissuaded from doing so both by Father Claude de la Colombière and by the great opposition with which I met.[1]

About her conversation with Jesus, she writes,

"My divine Heart," he told me, "is so passionately fond of the human race, and of you in particular, that it cannot keep back the pent-up flames of its burning charity any longer. They must burst out through you and reveal my Heart to the world, so as to enrich mankind with my precious treasures. I'm letting you see them now; and they include all the graces of sanctification needed to snatch men from very brink of hell. You are the one I have chosen for this great scheme — you're so utterly unworthy and ignorant, it will be all *my* work."

Next, he asked for my heart. I begged him to take it; he did, and placed it in his own divine Heart. He let me see it there — a tiny atom being completely burned up in that fiery furnace. Then, lifting it out — now a little heart-shaped flame — he put it back where he had found it. "There, my well-beloved," I heard him saying, "that's a precious proof of my love for you, hiding in your side a little spark from its hottest flames. That will be your heart from now on; it will burn you up — to your very last breath; its intense heat will never diminish — only over your bleeding; so deeply, it will bring you more humiliation and suffering than relief. That is why I insist that you ask for this treatment in all simplicity; you will then be doing what you are told, as well as finding satisfaction in shedding your blood on the cross of humiliation. As a proof that the great grace I have just given you is not an illusion, but the basis of all those which I have still in store for you . . . although I've closed the wound in your side, you will always feel the pain of it. And how have you been describing yourself up to the present: my slave? Well, now I'm giving you a new name: the beloved disciple of my Sacred Heart."[2]

In 1674, she received two more visions:

The Blessed Sacrament was exposed, and I was experiencing an unusually complete state of recollection, my sense and faculties utterly withdrawn from their surroundings, when Jesus Christ, my kind Master, appeared to me. He was a blaze of glory—his five wounds shining like five suns, flames issuing from all parts of his human form, especially from his divine breast which was like a furnace, and which he opened to disclose his utterly affectionate and lovable heart, the living source of all those flames. It was at this moment that he revealed to me the indescribable wonders of his pure love for mankind: the extravagance to which he'd been led for those who had nothing for him but ingratitude and indifference. "This hurts me more," he told me, "than everything I suffered in my passion. Even a little love from them in return — and I should regard all that I have done for them as next to nothing, and look for a way of doing still more. But no; all my eager efforts for their welfare meet with nothing but coldness and dislike. Do me the kindness, then — you, at least — of making up for all their ingratitude, as far as you can." When I pointed out my capacities, he replied: "Here you are! This will make good your deficiencies, every one of them!" His divine Heart opening as he spoke, such a scorching flame shot forth as I was sure would devour me. It went right through me; and when I could bear it no longer I begged to take pity on my weakness. "I shall be your support," he told me; "Don't be afraid. Simply focus all your attention on my voice — on what I am asking of you so as to fit you for the fulfillment of my plans. First of all, you are to receive me in the holy Eucharist as often as obedience allows. Accept any mortification or humiliation that may result, as a token of my love. Besides this, you are to receive Communion on the first Friday of each month. Then, every Thursday night, I shall give you a share in that fatal sadness which I allowed myself to feel in the garden of olives; death couldn't be so hard as the agonized state to which this sadness will reduce you. You are to get up between eleven o'clock and midnight, to keep me company in humble prayer to my Father, exactly as I spent that night in agony. Lie face downwards with me for an hour — not only to allay God's anger by asking mercy for sinners, but also to soothe in some way the heartache I felt when my apostles deserted me, when I had to reproach them for being unable to watch with me even for an hour. And, during this hour, you are to do what I show you. But listen, child! Don't believe lightly in every inspiration, and don't be too sure of it — Satan is furiously bent on deceiving you. So don't do anything without the approval of those who are guiding you. As long as you have the sanction of obedience, he can never delude you; he is completely powerless over those who obey."[3]

Her accounts of the visions were met with both belief and skepticism. Some of her superiors dismissed them as illusions and ordered her not to continue any of the practices recommended in the visions. Although this was painful, she obeyed them without hesitation. She finally received a sympathetic hearing when a priest named Claude de la Colombière became her spiritual director.

The greatest of the visions occurred in June 1675:

"You can give Me no greater return than by doing what I have so many times commanded you to do. Behold this Heart which has so loved men as to spare Itself nothing, even to exhausting and consuming Itself, to testify to them Its love, and in return I receive nothing but ingratitude from the greatest part of men by the contempt, irreverence, sacrileges, and coldness which they have for Me in this Sacrament for My love; but what is still more painful is that it is hearts consecrated to Me that treat Me thus. For this reason I ask that the First Friday after the Octave of Corpus Christi be set apart for a particular feast to honor My Heart; I ask that reparation of honor be made to My Heart, that Communion be received on that day to repair the indignities which It has received during the time It has been exposed on the altars; and I promise you that My Heart will expand Itself and pour out in abundance the influences of Its love on those who will render It this honor."[4]

The ten years that followed were years of obscurity and continuing humiliation, but by 1686 the messages she transmitted won greater acceptance in her community. From that time until her death in 1690, she engaged in a crusade of letters to promote the devotion. Although she was not to see the fruits of her efforts in her lifetime, the Sacred Heart revelation ended up having a greater impact on both the official liturgy and popular piety than any other vision of Jesus. It became the subject of papal encyclicals and feasts and devotions of the Church (First Friday Masses, the Feast of the Sacred Heart). Margaret Mary herself was canonized a saint on May 13, 1920.

Biblical and Historical Background

In his monumental work on the history of the Sacred Heart, *Heart of the Redeemer,* Timothy O'Donnell shows that the theme of the Heart of God is prominent in the Old Testament and applied to Christ in the New.[5] The theologian Karl Rahner regarded the "heart" as a primal concept in the Bible: "It falls into the category of words for the whole man; that is, it signifies a human reality predicable of the whole man as a person of body and spirit."[6]

Some of the greatest passages in the Old Testament center on the heart:

You shall love the Lord, your God, with all your heart.... Take to heart these words. (Deut. 6:5)

I will place my law within them and write it upon their hearts. (Jer. 31:35).

The Heart of God is a prominent theme:

He regretted that he had made man on the earth and his heart was grieved. (Gen. 6:6).

The Lord had sought out a man after his own heart. (1 Sam. 13:14).

The anger of the Lord will not abate until he has done and fulfilled what he has determined in his heart. (Jer. 31:24).

More than thirty other direct references to the Heart of God in the Old Testament are listed in *The Heart of Christ and the Heart of Man* by Malatesta and Solano (Rome: Pontifical Gregorian University, 1978). In addition, many of the prophecies of the Messiah, in particular the messianic psalms, center on the theme of the heart. Psalm 69:21 is a prominent instance: "Insult has broken my heart." This verse is followed by the prophecy of the events at the crucifixion: "They put gall in my food; for my thirst they gave me vinegar" (v. 22).

The New Testament again highlights the importance of the heart:

> "Blessed are the clean of heart." (Matt. 5:8)

> "For where your treasure is, there also will your heart be." (Luke 12:34)

Jesus also refers to His own Heart:

> "My heart is moved with pity for the crowd." (Matt. 15:32)

> "Take my yoke upon you and learn from me, for I am meek and humble of heart." (Matt. 11:29)

The effect of Christ on us is also referenced to the heart:

> "Were not our hearts burning while he spoke to us on the way and opened the scriptures to us?" (Luke 24:32)

> God sent the spirit of his Son into your hearts. (Gal. 4:6)

St. John's Gospel, above all, is the Gospel of the Heart of Jesus — and it is surely no coincidence that the first revelation of the Sacred Heart to Margaret Mary took place on the Feast of St. John the Evangelist. For the beloved disciple, who witnessed the physical piercing of the Heart of His Savior, this traumatic event was universal and transhistorical in magnitude although the starting point was necessarily material.

> But when they came to Jesus and saw that he was already dead, they did not break his legs, but one soldier thrust a lance into his side, and immediately blood and water flowed out. An eyewitness has testified, and his testimony is true; he knows that he is speaking the truth. (John 19:33–35)

This last sentence with its emphasis on the truth of the testimony signifies the importance of the event. All that John writes about the "living water" from the side of Christ necessary for our salvation has this event as the reference point. A striking instance is John 7:37–39:

> On the last and greatest day of the feast, Jesus stood up and exclaimed, "Let anyone who thirsts come to me and drink. Whoever believes in me, as Scripture says: 'Rivers of living water will flow from within him.'" He said this with reference to the Spirit that those who came to believe in him were to receive. There was, of course, no Spirit yet because Jesus had not yet been glorified.

The Old Testament citation here has been translated with reference to the heart: "For it is written in Scripture: 'Streams of living water shall flow from my heart'"

(Hugo Rahner) and "Out of his heart shall flow rivers of living water"(RSV). The glorification of Jesus takes place at the crucifixion, and it is then that the living water comes forth from His Heart both literally and spiritually. As O'Donnell illustrates, the sanctifying water that comes from the Heart of Christ is a significant theme in the Fathers:

> Origen: "Flowing over the whole earth, he sanctifies all who believe in him. This is what the prophet heralded with the words, 'Streams flow from his heart.' "[7]

> Irenaeus (writing about a deacon named Sanctus): "He himself remained unbending and unyielding, strong in his confession of faith, refreshed and strengthened by the heavenly spring of living water which comes forth from the Heart of Christ."[8]

> St. Justin Martyr: "We Christians are the true Israel which springs from Christ, for we are drawn out of his heart as out of a rock."[9]

> St. Cyprian: "The Lord cries out that whoever thirsts should come and drink the rivers of living water which have flowed from his bosom."[10]

> St. Ambrose: "Drink of Christ, for the streams of living water flow from his bosom."[11]

A devotion centered on the Sacred Heart of Jesus then begins in Scripture and is developed in the ancient writings of the Fathers. The tradition of Jesus showing His Heart to inspire faith and love also takes its starting point in Scripture, for doubting Thomas came to belief after he put his hands into the wounded side of Jesus: "Then he said to Thomas, 'Put your finger here and see my hands, and bring your hand and put it into my side, and do not be unbelieving, but believe' " (John 20:27).

Beyond the scriptural passages themselves, we must consider the Jesus Who is revealed in the Gospels. He is a Man who is grief-stricken by the death of His friend Lazarus, angered by those who defiled His Father's House, moved with compassion by the sight of the hungering multitudes. His parables of the Good Shepherd, the Prodigal Son, and the Good Samaritan show that He is preeminently a Man of the Heart. The Jesus Who is so obviously human in His feelings is the same Jesus Who will reign forever — and it should not surprise us then that the Jesus Who appeared to St. Margaret Mary sounds exactly like the Jesus of the Gospels.

Visions of Jesus centered on the Sacred Heart include those of St. Lutgard, Mechtild of Magdeburg, St. Gertrude the Great, Bl. Angela of Foligno, St. Catherine of Siena, and St. Rose of Lima. But the doctrine and devotion of the Sacred Heart reached its climax in the visions of St. Margaret Mary.

The Promises of the Sacred Heart

In His messages to Margaret Mary, Jesus asked for certain devotions and actions and also made various promises to those who followed these practices. The most famous promise was the assurance that those who received Holy Communion on the First Fridays of nine consecutive months in reparation for the sins committed against God would be granted the grace of final perseverance necessary for salvation. About these and the other Sacred Heart promises, Karl Rahner writes,

> Taken in their entirety, these promises affirm and offer no more than our Lord himself promised in the Gospel to absolute faith (Mt. 17:20–21; Mk. 16:17f; Jn 14:12f.). What is new in these promises is therefore not their content, but the circumstances of their fulfillment, the fact that what has already been promised in substance in the Gospels is now attached precisely to devotion to the Sacred Heart. To anyone with a proper grasp of the devotion, who practices it in the deep and unconditional faith that it demands, this "new" element in the promises will offer no special problem. Taken as a whole, these promises should be interpreted in the same way as those made in the Gospel to the prayer of faith. In neither case are we dealing with a technique or recipe for gaining a hold over God and the unconditioned sovereignty of his inscrutable will. The promises are made to man only in the measure in which he surrenders himself in unreserved faith and unquestioning love to the will of God, which is absolute, and for us unfathomable, love.[12]

Excerpts from the promises and messages of the Sacred Heart are quoted below:

Promises to the Nations

Our Divine Lord desires, it seems to me, to enter with pomp and magnificence into the houses of princes and kings, in order to be honored there as much as He was outraged, despised and humiliated in His Passion, and to receive as much pleasure at seeing the great ones of this world abased and humiliated before Him as He felt bitterness at seeing Himself annihilated at their feet.

Promises to Families

Our Divine Lord assured me that He takes a singular pleasure in being honored under the figure of His Heart of flesh, the image of which He wishes to be exposed in public in order to touch the unfeeling heart of men. He promised that He would pour out in abundance into the hearts of all those who would honor His Heart all the gifts with which It is filled, and that everywhere this image is exposed and honored, it would draw down all kinds of blessings.[13]

Promises to Communities

He promised that He would pour out the sweet unction of His ardent charity on all those communities in which this divine image would be honored; that He would turn away from them the thunderbolts of the just anger of God, and that He would restore them to His grace, if they should have the misfortune to fall into sin.

Promises to Individuals

He promised to pour out into the hearts of all those who honor the image of His Heart all the gifts which It contains. He promised also to imprint His love on the hearts of all those who would wear this image on their persons, and that He would destroy in them all disordered movements.

Protection against the Devil

Let us renew often our consecration to the Heart of Jesus, and let us live that consecration faithfully. The Sacred Heart takes a singular pleasure in it. The devil has a most intense fear of the devotion to this loving Heart, because of the salvation of the multitude of souls which It effects in favor of those who consecrate themselves completely to the Sacred Heart for the purpose of loving It, honoring It, and glorifying It.

Protection against Mortal Sin

I cannot believe that those consecrated to the Heart of Jesus will fall under the domination of Satan through mortal sin, if having consecrated themselves to the Heart of Jesus, they endeavor to honor It, love It, and glorify It, by conforming themselves in all things to Its holy maxims.[14]

Toward Perfection

There is no surer means of attaining perfection than to be consecrated to the Heart of Jesus. If, therefore, we wish to attain that perfection which the adorable Heart of Jesus desires of us, we must make an entire sacrifice of ourselves, and of everything that depends on us, to the Sacred Heart and live entirely for It.

Toward Peace

Establish your dwelling in the amiable Heart of Jesus, and you will find unalterable peace, strength to carry out all your good desires, and a protection against voluntary faults.

Key to Open the Sacred Heart

Our Lord gave me to understand that He wishes to be known, loved and adored by men, and for that end He would give them many graces, provided they consecrated themselves to the devotion and love of His Sacred Heart.

Pledge of Salvation

There is no surer means of salvation than to consecrate oneself to the Divine Heart of Our Lord Jesus Christ. The loving Heart of Jesus will not allow any of those consecrated to It to perish, so great is His desire that His Sacred Heart be known, loved and honored by His creatures. In the Sacred Heart they will find assistance during their life in all their necessities; It will be their secure place of refuge at the hour of their death, into which they will be received and protected from their enemies.

Conversion of Sinners

My Divine Master revealed to me that it was His ardent desire to be known, loved and honored by men, and His eager desire to draw them back from the road to perdition, along which Satan is driving them in countless numbers, that induced Him to manifest His Heart to men with all the treasures of love, mercy, grace, sanctification and salvation that It contains, in order to have a means of satisfying Its desire to pour out on them abundantly Its mercies and Its graces. It is by this means that the Sacred Heart of our loving Jesus wishes to save many souls from eternal perdition. . . . This Divine Heart is like a fortress or a secure place of refuge for all poor sinners who wish to take shelter in It from the Justice of Almighty God, the thunderbolts of whose wrath, like an impetuous torrent, would overwhelm sinners and their sins, on account of the enormous number committed at the present time.[15]

Remedy against Tepidity

Our Lord wishes through this devotion to His Divine Heart to rekindle the charity that has grown cold and has almost been extinguished in the hearts of the greater part of Christians; He wishes to give men a new means of loving God by His Sacred Heart, as much as He desires and merits, and of making reparation for their ingratitude.

If we are cowardly, cold, impure, imperfect, the Sacred Heart is an ardent furnace in which we must purify and perfect ourselves like gold in the crucible. It will purify all that is imperfect in our actions; it will sanctify those that are good.

Promises for the Just

There is no shorter way of attaining perfection than to render to the Divine Heart all the homage, love, honor and praise in our power.

I do not know of any other exercise in the spiritual life more calculated to raise a soul in a short time to the height of perfection, and make it taste the true sweetness that is to be found in the service of God; if it were known how pleasing this devotion is to Jesus Christ, there is no Christian, however little his love for our amiable Saviour, who would not begin to practice it immediately.

The names of beginners are written on the adorable Heart of Jesus only with ink. This signifies the initial grace given us to combat and conquer our imperfections, especially our proud self-love, which insinuates itself everywhere, sullying and disfiguring our holiest actions. These black letters should be purified in the furnace of the love of the Divine Heart from all that is earthly and human and from all self-seeking.

These black letters will gradually brighten in the crucible of Divine Love, and become like silver, which signifies purity of heart. But when in the process of purification all the black letters are changed into letters of silver, we must not stop there, we must continue until they are changed into gold.

It is love that will change them into gold. Charity is the divine gold that will write our names on the Heart of Jesus in letters never to be effaced. We shall then become like holocaust, consumed completely in the ardent flames of the loving Heart of Jesus.[16]

The Great Promise

This promise appears in a letter written in May 1688 by St. Margaret Mary to Mother Saumaise: "On a Friday during Holy Communion, He said these words to His unworthy slave, if I mistake not: 'I promise you in the excessive mercy of My Heart that Its all-powerful love will grant to all those who receive Holy Communion on nine first Fridays of the month consecutively, the grace of final repentance; they will not die under My displeasure or without receiving their Sacraments, My Divine Heart making Itself their assured refuge at the last moment.' "[17]

["With regard to this promise it may be remarked: (1) that Our Lord required Communion to be received on a particular day chosen by Him; (2) that the nine Fridays must be consecutive; (3) that they must be made in honor of His Sacred Heart, which means that those who make the nine Fridays must practice the devotion and must have a great love for our Lord; (4) that Our Lord does not say that those who make the nine Fridays will be dispensed from any of their obligations or from exercising the vigilance necessary to lead a good life and overcome temptation; rather He implicitly promises abundant graces to those who make the Nine Fridays to help them to carry out these obligations and persevere to the end; (5) that perseverance in receiving Holy Communion for nine consecutive First Fridays helps the faithful to acquire the habit of frequent Communion, which Our Lord eagerly desires; and (6) finally, that the practice of the Nine Fridays is very pleasing to Our Lord since He promises such a great reward, and that all Catholics should endeavor to make the Nine Fridays."]

Protection at the Hour of Death

The Divine Heart of Jesus again gave me to understand and assured me that the pleasure which He takes in being known, loved and honored by His creatures is so great that He promised me that none of those who practice this amiable devotion and are devoted to His adorable Heart will ever perish.[18]

For Families

Our Divine Lord assured me that He takes such pleasure in being known, loved and honored by His creatures, that He promises: (1) that people in the world will find through this amiable devotion all the helps necessary for their state of life, that is to say; (2) peace in their families: He promised me that He will unite families that are divided. Our Divine Lord wishes us to have great charity for our neighbor; He wishes us to pray to Him for special effects of this devotion to unite hearts divided and to bring peace to souls; (3) consolation in their afflictions; (4) solace in their labors: He promised that He would protect and assist families that were in any necessity, if they addressed themselves to Him with confidence;

(5) the blessing of Heaven on all their enterprises; (6) that in His Sacred Heart they would find refuge during their life and especially at the hour of their death.

Promises for Apostles of the Sacred Heart

1. My Divine Master showed me the names of several persons written in letters of gold on His Sacred Heart, names of which He will never allow to be effaced. These are names of the persons who have labored the most to make His Sacred Heart known and loved.

2. The Sacred Heart of Jesus has such a great desire to be known, loved and honored by men; He wishes so ardently to establish the empire of His love in all hearts by destroying in them the empire of Satan, that He promises great recompenses to all those who devote themselves with their whole hearts to establishing the reign of His Sacred Heart according to the lights and graces which He gives them.

3. Oh! What happiness for us and for all who contribute in making the loving Heart of Jesus known and glorified! For they will draw down upon themselves the friendship and eternal blessings of this unique Love of our hearts. The Blessed Virgin will be their special protectress, she will assist them in attaining to the perfect life.

4. The loving Heart of Jesus has made known to me that He will take care to sanctify and glorify us before His Heavenly Father in the measure in which we exert ourselves to procure glory for Him and to increase the reign of His love in the hearts of men.

5. The zeal with which you labor to make the Sacred Heart of Jesus known and loved will gain for you in an ever increasing degree the crowning gift of the pure love of God.

6. Oh! What happiness for those who contribute to making the adorable Heart of Jesus known, loved and glorified! By what means they will secure a powerful Protector for their native land.

7. My divine Saviour assured me that those who labor for the salvation of souls will have the art of touching the hardest hearts and will obtain marvelous success, if they themselves are animated with a tender devotion to His Divine Heart.

He will penetrate the most unfeeling hearts by the words of His preachers and faithful friends. He will so pour out the sweet unction of His ardent charity with such strong and powerful graces on their words that He will make them like a flaming sword which will cause the most frozen hearts to melt in His love. The words of these apostles will be like two-edged swords, which will penetrate the most hardened hearts and make the holy fountain of penance spring up in them, purifying and sanctifying the most obstinate sinners and rendering them susceptible to the love of this Divine Heart. By this means the most criminal souls will be led on the salutary penance.

8. The adorable Heart of Jesus wishes to establish the reign of His pure love in all hearts. Happy are those whom He will employ to aid Him to establish His reign! But He did not tell me that His friends would have nothing to suffer, for He wishes them to make their greatest happiness consist in tasting its bitterness.

9. The apostles of the Sacred Heart will obtain the grace of final perseverance and of a holy death.

10. Happy are those whom the Sacred Heart of Jesus will employ in establishing His reign. For it seems to me that It is like a king who thinks only of recompensing His friends while He gains victories and triumphs over His enemies. When this Heart reigns victoriously on Its throne, It will be Itself their eternal recompense.

Thirty-Three Acts of Adoration

One Friday, during holy Mass, I felt a great desire to honor the sufferings of my crucified Spouse. He told me lovingly that He desired me, every Friday, to adore Him thirty-three times upon the Cross, the throne of His mercy. I was to prostrate myself humbly at His feet, and try to remain there in the dispositions of the Eternal Father together with the sufferings of His divine Son, to beg of Him the conversion of all hardened and faithless hearts who resist the impulse of His grace. He told me, moreover, that at the hour of death He will be favorable to those who have been faithful to this practice.

These thirty-three acts of adoration of our Lord on the Cross may be made anywhere on Fridays, and even while attending to one's ordinary work. They require no special attitude, formula or vocal prayer. A simple look of love and contrition coming from the depths of our hearts and sent up to our crucified Lord is sufficient to express our adoration and our gratitude to Him. It is also an appeal to the Blessed Virgin to intercede with the Heavenly Father for the conversion of sinners.

The efficacy of this devotion is proved by the consoling conversions which it obtains and by the holy deaths which are its fruit. We venture to say that it becomes a source of graces to all those who practice it, for never in vain does one approach Jesus Christ Crucified.[19]

St. Margaret Mary's Prayer of Consecration to the Sacred Heart of Jesus

O Sacred Heart of my Lord and Saviour Jesus Christ, to Thee I consecrate and offer up my person and my life, my actions, trials and sufferings, that my entire being may henceforth only be employed in loving, honoring and glorifying Thee. This is my irrevocable will, to belong entirely to Thee, and to do all for Thy love, renouncing with my whole heart all that can displease Thee.

I take Thee, O Sacred Heart, for the sole object of my love, the protection of my life, the pledge of my salvation, the remedy of my frailty and inconstancy, the reparation for all the defects of my life, and my secure refuge at the hour of my death. Be Thou, O most merciful Heart, my justification before God Thy Father, and screen me from His anger which I have so justly merited. I fear all from my own weakness and malice, and placing my entire confidence in Thee, O Heart of Love, I hope all from Thine infinite goodness. Annihilate in me all that can displease Thy heart that I may never forget Thee or be separated from Thee. I beseech Thee through Thine infinite goodness, grant that my name be engraved on Thee, for in this I place all my happiness and all my glory, to live and to die as one of Thy devoted servants. Amen.[20]

Excerpts from Other Messages

[Margaret Mary:] But my Lord, to whom dost Thou address Thyself? To a wretched slave, to a poor sinner who by her unworthiness would be capable of hindering Thy designs. Thou hast so many generous souls to execute Thy commands! "Poor innocent that you are, do you not know that I make use of the weak to confound the strong? That it is usually on the lowliest and the poor in spirit that I show My power with greatest effect, in order that they may attribute nothing to themselves."[21]

My divine Master once gave me the following lesson: "Learn that I am a holy Master, and One that teaches holiness, I am pure, and cannot endure the slightest stain. Therefore thou must act in My presence with simplicity of heart and with an upright and pure intention. Know that I cannot endure the least want of straightforwardness, and I shall make thee understand that, if the excess of My love has led Me to constitute Myself thy Master, in order to teach and fashion thee after My manner and according to My designs, nevertheless I cannot bear tepid and cowardly souls. If I am gentle in bearing with thy weakness, I shall not be less severe and exact in correcting and punishing thy infidelities."[22]

"Listen, My daughter, believe not lightly and trust not every spirit, for Satan is enraged and will seek to deceive thee. Therefore, do nothing without the approval of those who guide thee; if thou art thus under the authority of obedience, his efforts against thee will be in vain, for he has no power over the obedient" (II, 73).[23]

"Not only do I desire that thou shouldst do what thy Superiors command, but also that thou shouldst do nothing of all that I order thee without their consent. I love obedience, and without it no one can please Me."[24]

"Learn that the more thou retirest into thy nothingness, the more My greatness stoops to find thee."[25]

"I have chosen thee as an abyss of unworthiness and ignorance for the accomplishment of this great design, so that everything may be done by Me."[26]

"Behold the wound in My Side where thou art to make thy dwelling now and forever. There wilt thou be able to preserve the robe of innocence with which I have clothed thy soul, so that thou mayest henceforth live the life of a Man-God, living as no longer living, that I may live perfectly in thee.... To do this, if thou dost not wish to outrage My omnipotence and grievously offend Me, thy powers and senses must remain buried in Me...seeking nothing apart from Me, since I wish to be all things to thee."[27]

"I, Who govern thee, am He to Whom thou must be wholly abandoned, without any care or thought of thyself, since My help will only fail thee when My Heart fails in power."

"I will give thee to read in the Book of Life which contains the science of love." And revealing to me His Sacred Heart, He made me read in It the following words: "My love reigns in suffering, it triumphs in humility and rejoices in unity."[28]

"I wish thy heart to serve Me as a refuge wherein I may withdraw and take My delight when sinners persecute and drive Me from theirs."[29]

One day, as I was yearning to receive our Lord, I said to Him: Teach me what Thou wouldst have me to say to thee.: "Nothing but these words: 'My God, my only Good and my All, Thou art wholly mine, and I am wholly Thine.' They will preserve thee from all kinds of temptations, will supply for all the acts thou wouldst make, and serve as preparation for all thy actions."[30]

Chapter 6

The Divine Mercy

If St. Margaret Mary is the Disciple of the Sacred Heart, the Apostle of Divine Mercy is St. Faustina Kowalska. The revelation of God's infinite Mercy, personified in the Passion, and its applications in our daily lives and spiritual growth are the central themes of St. Faustina's encounter with Jesus.

Like Margaret Mary, Faustina too consecrated her life to God as a member of a religious order. She was born on August 25, 1905, in the province of Lodz, Poland, the third in a family of ten children. The family was poor, and Faustina (whose baptismal name was Helena) had to work as a domestic from her earliest years. At the age of seven, she felt the call of God to a life of total consecration. When she was seventeen, she told her parents that she wished to enter a convent. Although they strongly opposed the idea, Faustina joined the Congregation of the Sisters of Our Lady of Divine Mercy in 1925. In April 1927 she went through her own "dark night of the soul" but a year later, on Good Friday, she experienced the flame of Divine Love. Although she led an austere life and was constantly afflicted by ailments, she was the recipient of visions and revelations of Jesus and of such gifts as prophecy, the reading of souls, the hidden stigmata, and mystical participation in the Passion of Christ. She died of tuberculosis on October 5, 1938, at the age of thirty-three, the age at which Jesus (according to Scripture) is said to have died. In 1965, the archbishop of Krakow, Karol Wojtyla, initiated the process of examining the life and virtue of St. Faustina in order to determine her possible canonization as saint. On April 30, 2000, Pope John Paul II, the former Archbishop Wojtyla, canonized her a saint.

One of the first and perhaps foremost students of the message of Divine Mercy, Professor Ignacy Rozycki, has identified five central components to this message, and these are documented in the introduction to Faustina's *Diary: Divine Mercy in My Soul:* (1) The Image of the Merciful Jesus; (2) The Feast of the Divine Mercy; (3) The Chaplet of the Divine Mercy; (4) The Hour of Mercy; (5) The Spreading of Devotion to the Divine Mercy.[1] These themes are described in more detail below with specific reference to the messages of Jesus to St. Faustina. Each message is followed by a number that follows the numbering sequence in her *Diary.*

The Image of the Merciful Jesus

In a vision on February 22, 1931, Jesus appeared in a white robe with red and white rays streaming from His Heart and with one hand raised in blessing and the other placed on His Heart. The words "Jesus, I trust in you" were inscribed at the bottom of the picture. The red rays symbolized the blood that flowed out after He was pierced with a spear and the white symbolized the water that also gushed out.

In the evening, when I was in my cell, I saw the Lord Jesus clothed in a white garment. One hand [was] raised in the gesture of blessing, the other was touching the garment at the breast. From beneath the garment, slightly drawn aside at the breast, there were emanating two large rays, one red, the other pale.... After a while, Jesus said to me, "Paint an image according to the pattern you see, with the signature: Jesus I trust in You. I desire that this image be venerated, first in your chapel, and then throughout the world." (47).

Jesus gave several messages relating to the image. Regarding the spiritual significance of the red and the white rays which are related to baptism and the Eucharist:

The two rays denote Blood and Water. The pale ray stands for the Water which makes souls righteous. The red ray stands for the Blood which is the life of souls.... These two rays issued forth from the depths of My tender mercy when My agonized Heart was opened by a lance on the Cross. These rays shield souls from the wrath of my Father. Happy is the one who will dwell in their shelter, for the just hand of God shall not lay hold of them. I desire that the first Sunday after Easter be the Feast of Mercy. (299)

"My gaze from this image is like My gaze from the cross." (326)

On the need to bless and honor the Image on the Sunday after Easter, the day associated with Jesus' appearance in the Upper Room and the presentation of His wounds to St. Thomas:

"My image already is in your soul. I desire that there be a Feast of Mercy. I want this image, which you will paint with a brush, to be solemnly blessed on the first Sunday after Easter; that Sunday is to be the Feast of Mercy." (49)

"I am King of Mercy. I desire that this image be displayed in public on the first Sunday after Easter. That Sunday is the Feast of Mercy. Through the Word Incarnate I make known the bottomless depth of My mercy." (88)

Promises associated with the image:

"I promise that the soul that will venerate this image will not perish. I also promise victory over its enemies already here on earth, especially at the hour of death. I Myself will defend it as My own glory." (48)

"By means of this Image I shall be granting many graces to souls; so let every soul have access to it." (570)

"I am offering people a vessel with which they are to keep coming for graces to the fountain of mercy. That vessel is this image with the signature: 'Jesus, I trust in you.'" (327)

The Feast of the Divine Mercy

In 1931, Jesus asked that the first Sunday after Easter be proclaimed Mercy Sunday. Fifty-nine years later, on April 30, 2000, Pope John Paul officially declared that every first Sunday after Easter would be celebrated as Mercy Sunday by the Church. The request for Mercy Sunday was made for two central reasons: (1) the redemptive Death and Resurrection of Jesus, which are remembered on this Sunday, are inescapably tied to the Mercy of God; (2) this Sunday is to serve as a special channel of God's mercy and His forgiveness of sin.

"The first Sunday after Easter; that Sunday is to be the Feast of Mercy." (49)

"Ask of my faithful servant that, on this day, he should tell the whole world of My great mercy; that whoever approaches the Fount of Life on this day will be granted complete remission of sins and punishment. Mankind will not have peace until it turns with trust to My mercy.

Oh, how much I am hurt by a soul's distrust! Such a soul professes that I am Holy and Just, but does not believe that I am Mercy and does not trust in My Goodness. Even the devils glorify My Justice but do not believe in my goodness. My heart rejoices in this title of Mercy." (300)

"Your assignment and duty here on earth is to beg for mercy for the whole world. No soul will be justified until it turns with confidence to My mercy, and this is why the first Sunday after Easter is to be the Feast of Mercy. On that day, priests are to tell everyone about My great and unfathomable mercy. (570)

"My daughter, tell the whole world about My inconceivable mercy. I desire that the Feast of Mercy be a refuge and shelter for all souls, and especially for poor sinners. On that day the very depths of My tender mercy are open. I pour out a whole ocean of graces upon those souls who approach the fount of My mercy.

The soul that will go to Confession and receive Holy Communion shall obtain complete forgiveness of sins and punishment. On that day all the divine floodgates through which grace flow are opened. Let no soul fear to draw near to Me, even though its sins be as scarlet. My mercy is so great that no mind, be it of man or angel, will be able to fathom it throughout all eternity. Everything that exists has come forth from the very depths of My most tender mercy. Every soul in its relation to Me will contemplate My love and mercy throughout eternity. The feast of Mercy emerged from My very depths of tenderness. It is My desire that it be solemnly celebrated on the first Sunday after Easter. Mankind will not have peace until it turns to the Fount of Mercy." (699)

There are certain conditions associated with receiving the benefits of this great Promise:

"The soul that will go to Confession and receive Holy Communion — on that day — shall obtain complete forgiveness of sins and punishment." (699)

The Chaplet of the Divine Mercy

This chaplet is a series of prayers, like the Rosary, personally dictated by Jesus and again associated with various graces and promises. The prayers can be said on a Rosary with one specific prayer for the large bead and another shorter prayer for the small beads. The chaplet is to be recited every day and, in the nine days between Good Friday and Mercy Sunday, it is to be applied to a Novena of intentions. The chaplet focuses on reparation for outrages against God by offering up the merits of Jesus and the invocation of God's mercy. In an age like the present, characterized by blasphemy and the systematic, comprehensive and all but universal violation of divine law, the chaplet of Divine Mercy is a powerful antidote and weapon.

"This prayer will serve to appease My wrath. You will recite it for nine days, on the beads of the rosary, in the following manner: First of all, you will say one OUR FATHER and HAIL MARY and the I BELIEVE IN GOD. Then on the OUR FATHER beads you will say the following words: Eternal Father, I offer You the Body and Blood, Soul and Divinity of Your dearly beloved Son, Our Lord Jesus Christ, in atonement for our sins and those of the whole world." On the HAIL MARY beads you will say the following words: "For the sake of His sorrowful Passion have mercy on us and on the whole world." In conclusion, three times you will recite these words: "Holy God, Holy Mighty One, Holy Immortal One, have mercy on us and on the whole world." (476)

The Nine-Day Novena

The chaplet is to be said for a specific intention on each of the nine days between Good Friday and the Sunday after Easter:

"I desire that during these nine days you bring souls to the fount of My mercy, that they may draw therefrom strength and refreshment and whatever graces they need in the hardships of life and, especially, at the hour of death. On each day you will bring to My Heart a different group of souls, and you will immerse them in this ocean of My mercy and I will bring all these souls into the house of My Father. You will do this in this life and in the next. I will deny nothing to any soul whom you will beg My Father, on the strength of My bitter Passion, for graces for these souls." (1209)

First Day: "Today, bring to Me all mankind, especially all sinners, and immerse them in the ocean of My mercy. In this way you will console Me in the bitter grief into which the loss of souls plunges Me." (1210)

Second Day: "Today bring to Me the souls of priests and religious, and immerse them in My unfathomable mercy. It was they who gave Me the strength to endure My bitter Passion. Through them, as through channels, My mercy flows out upon mankind." (1212)

Third Day: "Today bring Me all devout and faithful souls, and immerse them in the ocean of My mercy. These souls brought Me consolation on the Way of the cross. They were that drop of consolation in the midst of an ocean of bitterness." (1214)

Fourth Day: "Today bring to Me the pagans and those who do not yet know me. I was thinking also of them during My bitter Passion, and their future zeal comforted My heart. Immerse them in the ocean of My mercy." (1216)

Fifth Day: "Today bring to Me the souls of heretics and schismatics, and immerse them in the ocean of My mercy. During My bitter Passion they tore at My Body and Heart; that is, My Church. As thy return to unity with the Church, My wounds heal, and in this way they alleviate My Passion." (1218)

Sixth Day: "Today bring to Me the meek and humble souls and the souls of little children and immerse them in My mercy. These souls most closely resemble My Heart. They strengthened Me during My bitter agony. I saw them as earthly Angels, who would keep vigil at My altars. I pour out upon them whole torrents of grace. Only the humble soul is able to receive My grace. I favor humble souls with My confidence." (1220)

Seventh Day: "Today bring to Me the souls who especially venerate and glorify My mercy, and immerse them in My mercy. These souls sorrowed deeply into My Spirit. They are living images of My Compassionate Heart. These souls will shine with a special brightness in the next life. Not one of them will go into the fire of hell. I shall particularly defend each one of them at the hour of death." (1224)

"I myself will defend as My own glory, during their lifetime, and especially at the hour of their death, those souls who will venerate My fathomless mercy." (1225)

Eighth Day: "Today bring to Me the souls who are in the prism of Purgatory, and immerse them in the abyss of My mercy. Let the torrents of My Blood cool down their scorching flames. All these souls are greatly loved by Me. They are making retribution to My justice. It is in your power to bring them relief. Draw all the indulgences from the treasury of My Church and offer them on their behalf. Oh, if you only knew the torments they suffer, you would continually offer for them the alms of the spirit and pay off their debt to My justice." (1226)

Ninth Day: "Today bring to Me souls who have become lukewarm, and immerse them in the abyss of My mercy. These souls wound My Heart most painfully. My soul suffered the most dreadful loathing in the Garden of Olives because of lukewarm souls. They were the reason I cried out: 'Father, take this cup away from Me, if it be your will.' For them, the last hope of salvation is to flee to My mercy." (1228)

Promises

"Say unceasingly the chaplet that I have taught you. Whoever will recite it will receive great mercy at the hour of death. Priests will recommend it to sinners as their last hope of salvation. Even if there were a sinner most hardened, if he were to recite this chaplet only once, he would receive grace from My infinite mercy. I desire that the whole world know My infinite mercy. I desire to grant unimaginable graces to those souls who trust in My mercy." (687)

"At the hour of their death, I defend as My own glory every soul that will say this chaplet; or when others say it for a dying person, the indulgence is the same. When this chaplet is said by the bedside of a dying person, God's anger is placated, unfathomable mercy envelopes the soul." (811)

"The souls that say this chaplet will be embraced by My mercy during their lifetime and especially at the hour of their death." (754)

"My daughter, encourage souls to say the chaplet which I have given to you. It pleases Me to grant everything they ask of Me by saying the chaplet. When hardened sinners say it, I will fill their souls with peace, and the hour of their death will be a happy one. Write this for the benefit of distressed souls: when a soul sees and realizes the gravity of its sins, when the whole abyss of the misery into which it immersed itself is displayed before its eyes, let it not despair, but with trust let it throw itself into the arms of My mercy, as a child into the arms of its beloved mother. These souls have a right of priority to My compassionate Heart, they have first access to My mercy. Tell them that no soul that has called upon My mercy has been disappointed or brought to shame. I delight particularly in a soul which has placed its trust in My goodness. Write that when they say this chaplet in the presence of the dying, I will stand between My Father and the dying person, not as the just judge but as the merciful Savior." (1541)

The Hour of Mercy

The scriptural accounts lead us to conclude that Jesus died at three o'clock in the afternoon. Like most of the other events associated with the Passion and commemorated in numerous devotions and spiritual practices, the hour of the death of Jesus has also taken on great significance. Nowhere is this more apparent than in the Divine Mercy revelation. Jesus tells us what we should do at this hour and again attaches great promises to those who practice this devotion:

"I remind you, My daughter, that as often as you hear the clock strike the third hour, immerse yourself completely in My mercy; adoring and glorifying it invoke its omnipotence for the whole world, and particularly for poor sinners for at that moment mercy was opened wide for every soul. In this hour you can obtain everything for yourself and for others for the asking; it was the hour of grace for the whole world — mercy triumphed over justice. My daughter, try your best to make the Stations of the Cross in this hour, provided that your duties permit it; and if you are not able to make the Stations of the Cross, then at least step into the chapel for a moment and adore, in the Blessed Sacrament, My Heart, which is full of mercy; and should you be unable to step into the chapel, immerse yourself in prayer there where you happen to be, if only for a very brief instant. I claim veneration for My mercy from every creature, but above all from you, since it is to you that I have given the most profound understanding of this mystery." (1572)

"At three o'clock, implore My mercy, especially for sinners; and, if only for a brief moment, immerse yourself in My Passion, particularly in My abandonment at the moment of agony. This is the hour, I will refuse nothing to the soul that makes a request of Me in virtue of My Passion." (1320)

The Spreading of Devotion to the Divine Mercy

In His messages, Jesus emphasizes both the importance of spreading the Divine Mercy devotion and practicing mercy in our daily lives:

"Souls who spread the honor of My mercy I shield through their entire lives as a tender mother her infant, and at the hour of death I will not be a Judge for them, but the Merciful Savior. At that last hour, a soul has nothing with which to defend itself except My mercy. Happy is the soul that during its lifetime immersed itself in the Fountain of Mercy, because justice will have no hold on it." (1075)

"My daughter, if I demand through you that people revere My mercy, you should be the first to distinguish yourself by this confidence in My mercy. I demand from you deeds of mercy, which are to arise out of love for Me. You are to show mercy to your neighbors always and everywhere. You must not shrink from this or try to excuse or absolve yourself from it. I am giving you three ways of exercising mercy toward your neighbor: the first — by deed, the second — by word, the third — by prayer. In these three degrees is contained the fullness of mercy, and it is an unquestionable proof of love for Me. By this means a soul glorifies and pays reverence to My mercy. Yes, the first Sunday after Easter is the Feast of Mercy, but there must also be acts of mercy, and I demand the worship of My mercy through the solemn celebration of the Feast and through the veneration of the image which is painted. By means of this image It is to be a reminder of the demands of My mercy, because even the strongest faith is of no avail without works." (742)

Viewed as a whole, the messages that constitute the Divine Mercy revelation presents us with a program of action and a stunning vision of joy and hope in the midst of darkness and sin. In a nutshell, it does the following:

1. As with all the other accredited visions and messages, it brings us back to the Jesus of the Gospels, making the events and teachings recorded there come alive here and now in all their majesty and urgency. Concurrently it highlights the immediate significance of the Gospel accounts for all of history and for our everyday lives. Far from diverting us from Scripture, the visions and messages draw us deeper into Scripture and closer to Jesus.

2. We are all aware of the severity of the challenges facing us and some of us try in limited ways to apply the teachings of Jesus to contemporary situations. The Divine Mercy revelation in its simplicity and power gives us a divinely directed solution to the problems that both we and the world face. The truth of this message becomes most apparent in its fruits. Only those who practice the Divine Mercy devotion can begin to comprehend its truth and significance.

In addition to the themes outlined above, some of the other messages of Jesus to St. Faustina are of especial interest, first, because they come to us from Jesus and, second, because they give us an insight into many great mysteries:

"Who God is in His Essence, no one will fathom, neither the mind of Angels nor man. Get to know God by contemplating His attributes." (30)

"I desire that priests proclaim this great mercy of Mine towards the souls of sinners. Let the sinner not be afraid to approach Me. The flames of mercy are burning Me — clamoring to be spent; I want to pour them out upon these souls." (50)

"Proclaim that mercy is the greatest attribute of God. All the works of My hands are crowned with mercy." (301)

"I desire that you make an offering of yourself for sinners and especially for those souls who have lost hope in God's mercy." (308)

"As often as you want to make Me happy, speak to the world about My great and unfathomable mercy." (164)

"My daughter, all your miseries have been consumed in the flame of My love, like a little twig thrown into a roaring fire. By humbling yourself in this way, you draw upon yourself and upon other souls an entire sea of My mercy." (174)

"I desire that you know more profoundly the love that burns in My Heart for souls, and you will understand this when you meditate upon souls; I desire their salvation. When you say this prayer, with a contrite heart and with faith on behalf of some sinner, I will give him the grace of conversion. This is the prayer: 'O Blood and Water, which gushed forth from the Heart of Jesus as a fount of Mercy for us, I trust in you.'" (186, 187)

"Do not be surprised that you are sometimes unjustly accused. I myself first drank this cup of undeserved suffering for love of you." (289)

"Act like a beggar who does not back away when he gets more alms [than he asked for], but offer thanks the more fervently. You too should not back away and say that you are not worthy of receiving greater graces when I give them to you. I know you are unworthy, but rejoice all the more and take as many treasures from My Heart as you can carry, for then you will please Me more. And I will tell you one more thing: Take these graces not only for yourself, but also for others; that is in My infinite mercy. Oh how I love those souls who have complete confidence in Me. I will do everything for them." (294)

"The prayer of a humble and loving soul disarms the anger of My Father and draws down an ocean of blessings." (320)

"Pure love gives the soul strength at the very moment of dying. When I was dying on the cross, I was not thinking about Myself, but about poor sinners, and I prayed for them to My Father. I want your last moment to be completely similar to Mine on the cross. There is but one price at which souls are bought, and that is suffering united to My suffering on the cross. Pure love understands these words; carnal love will never understand them." (324)

"There is more merit to one hour of meditation on My sorrowful Passion than there is to a whole year of flagellation that draws blood; the contemplation of My painful wounds is of great profit to you, and it brings Me great joy." (369)

"My heart is sorrowful, because even chosen souls do not understand the greatness of My mercy. Their relationship [with me] is, in certain ways, imbued with mistrust. Oh, how much that wounds My Heart! Remember My Passion, and if you do not believe My words, at least believe My wounds." (379)

"Who will proclaim My great mercy? I shall protect them Myself at the hour of death, as My own glory. And even if the sins of soul are as dark as night, when the sinner turns to My mercy, he gives Me the greatest praise and is the glory of My passion. When a soul praises My goodness, Satan trembles before it and flees to the very bottom of hell." (378)

"I am more deeply wounded by the small imperfections of chosen souls than by the sins of those living in the world. These little imperfections are not all. I will reveal to you a secret of My Heart: what I suffer from chosen souls. Ingratitude in return for so many graces is My Heart's constant food, on the part of [such] a chosen soul. Their love is lukewarm, and My heart cannot bear it; these souls force Me to reject them. Others distrust My goodness and have no desire to experience that sweet intimacy in their own hearts, but go in search of Me, often the distance, and do not find Me. This distrust of My goodness hurts Me very much. If My death has not convinced you of My love, what will? Often a soul wounds Me mortally, and then no one can comfort Me. They use My graces to offend Me. These are souls who despise My graces as well as all the proofs of My love. They do not wish to hear My call, but proceed into the abyss of hell. The loss of these souls plunges Me into deadly sorrow. God though I am, I cannot help such a soul because it scorns Me; having a free will, it can spurn Me or love Me.

You, who are the dispenser of My mercy, tell all the world about My goodness, and thus you will comfort My heart." (580)

"When you reflect upon what I tell you in the depths of your heart, you profit more than if you had read many books. Oh, if souls would only want to listen to My voice when I am speaking in the depths of their hearts, they would reach the peak of holiness in a short time." (584)

"My daughter, know that you give Me greater glory by a single act of obedience than by long prayers and mortifications." (894)

"Souls perish in spite of My bitter Passion. I am giving them the last hope of salvation; that is, the Feast of Mercy. If they will not adore My mercy, they will perish for all eternity. Secretary of My mercy, write, tell souls about this great mercy of Mine, because the awful day, the day of My justice, is near." (965)

"Let the greatest sinners place their trust in My mercy. They have the right before others to trust in the abyss of My mercy. My daughter, write about My mercy towards tormented souls. Souls that make an appeal to My mercy delight Me. To such souls I grant even more graces than they ask. I cannot punish even the greatest sinner if he makes an appeal to My compassion, but on the contrary, I justify him in My unfathomable and inscrutable mercy. Write: before I come as a just Judge, I first open wide the door of My mercy. He who refuses to pass through the door of My mercy must pass through the door of My justice." (1146)

"From all My wounds, like from streams, mercy flows for souls, but the wound in My Heart is the fountain of unfathomable mercy. From this fountain spring all graces for souls. The flames of compassion burn Me. I desire greatly to pour them out upon souls. Speak to the whole world about My mercy." (1190)

"The loss of each soul plunges Me into mortal sadness. You always console Me when you pray for sinners. The prayer most pleasing to Me is prayer for the conversion of sinners. Know, My daughter, that this prayer is always heard and answered." (1397)

"Come to Me, all of you. Be not afraid of your Savior, O sinful soul. I make the first move to come to you, for I know that by yourself you are unable to lift yourself to me. Child, do not run away from your Father; be willing to talk with your God of mercy who wants to speak words of pardon and lavish his graces on you. How dear your soul is to Me! I have inscribed your name upon My hand; you are engraved as a deep wound in My Heart. I am your strength, I will help you in the struggle. My child, do not fear the God of mercy. My holiness does not prevent Me from being merciful. Behold, for you I have established a throne of mercy on earth — the tabernacle — and from this throne I desire to enter into your heart. I am not surrounded by a retinue or guards. You can come to me at any moment, at any time; I want to speak to you and desire to grant you graces. My mercy is greater than your sins and those of the entire world. Who can measure the extent of my goodness? For you I descended from heaven to earth; for you I allowed myself to be nailed to the cross; for you I let my Sacred Heart be pierced with a lance; thus opening wide the source of mercy for you. Come, then, with trust to draw graces from this fountain. I never reject a contrite heart. Your misery has disappeared in the depths of My mercy. Do not argue with Me about your wretchedness. You will give me pleasure if you hand over to me all your troubles and griefs. I shall heap upon you the treasures of My grace. Child, speak no more of your misery; it is already forgotten. Listen, my child, to what I desire to tell you. Come close to My wounds and draw from the Fountain of Life and you will not weary on your journey. Look at the splendors of My mercy and do not fear the enemies of your salvation. Glorify My mercy." (1485)

"There is no way to heaven except the way of the cross. I followed it first. You must learn that it is the shortest and surest way. It is because you are not of this world that the world hates you. First it persecuted Me. Persecution is a sign that you are following in My footsteps faithfully....

"Know, too, that the darkness about which you complain I first endured in the Garden of olives when My Soul was crushed in mortal anguish. I am giving you a share in those sufferings because of My special love for you and in view of the high degree of holiness I am intending for you in heaven. A suffering soul is closest to My Heart. My child, make the resolution never to rely on people. Entrust yourself completely to My will saying, "Not as I want, but according to your will, O God, let it be done unto me." These words, spoken from the depths of one's heart, can raise a soul to the summit of sanctity in a short time. Such a soul fills heaven with the fragrance of her virtue. But understand that the strength by which you bear sufferings comes from frequent Communions. So approach this fountain of mercy often, to draw with the vessel of trust whatever you need." (1487)

"I am pleased with your efforts, O soul aspiring for perfection, but why do I see you so often sad and depressed? Tell Me, My child, what is the meaning of this sadness, and what is its cause? You see, My child, what you are of yourself. The cause of your falls is that you rely too much upon yourself and too little on Me. But let this not sadden you so much. You are dealing with the God of mercy, which your misery cannot exhaust. Remember, I did not allot only a certain number of pardons. My child, know that the greatest obstacles to holiness are discouragement and an exaggerated anxiety. These will deprive you of the ability to practice virtue. All temptations united together ought not disturb your interior peace, not even momentarily. Sensitiveness and discouragement are fruits of self-love. You should not become discouraged, but strive to make My love reign in place of your self-love. Have confidence, My child. Do not lose heart in coming for pardon, for I am always ready to forgive you. As often as you beg for it, you glorify My mercy. My child, life on earth is a struggle indeed; a great struggle for My kingdom. But fear not, because you are not alone. I am always supporting you, so lean on Me as you struggle, fearing nothing. Take the vessel of trust and draw from the fountain of life — for yourself, but also for other souls, especially such as are distrustful of my goodness." (1488)

"A single act of pure love pleases Me more than a thousand imperfect prayers. One of your sighs of love atones for many offenses with which the godless overwhelm Me. The smallest act of virtue has unlimited value in My eyes because of your great love for Me. In a soul that lives on My love alone, I reign as in heaven. I watch over it day and night. In it I find My happiness; My ear is attentive to each request of its heart; often I anticipate its requests." (1489)

"Let souls who are striving for perfection particularly adore My mercy, because the abundance of graces which I grant them flows from My mercy. I desire that these souls distinguish themselves by boundless trust in My mercy. I myself will attend to the sanctification of such souls. I will provide them with everything they will need to attain sanctity. The graces of My mercy are drawn by means of one vessel only, and that is — trust. The more a soul trusts, the more it will receive. Souls that trust boundlessly are a great comfort to Me, because I pour all the treasures of My graces into them. I rejoice that they ask for much. On the other hand, I am sad when souls ask for very little, when they narrow their hearts." (1578)

"Write: I am Thrice Holy, and I detest the smallest sin. I cannot love a soul which is stained with sin; but when it repents, there is no limit to My generosity toward it. My mercy embraces and justifies it. With My mercy, I pursue sinners along all their paths, and My Heart rejoices when they return to Me. I forget the bitterness with which they fed My Heart and rejoice at their return. Tell sinners that no one shall escape My Hand; if they run away from My Merciful Heart, they will fall into My Just Hands. Tell sinners that I am always waiting for them, that I listen intently to the beating of their heart. . . . When will it beat for Me? Write, that I am speaking to them through their remorse of conscience, through their failures and sufferings, through thunderstorms, through the voice of the church. And if they bring all My graces to naught, I begin to be angry with them, leaving them alone and giving them what they want." (1728)

"My daughter, let three virtues adorn you in a particular way: humility, purity of intention and love. Do nothing beyond what I demand of you, and accept everything that My hand gives you. Strive for a life of recollection so that you can hear My voice, which is so soft that only recollected souls can hear it." (1779)

"Daughter, when you go to confession, to this fountain of My mercy, the Blood and Water which came forth from My Heart always flows down upon your soul and ennobles it. Every time you go to confession, immerse yourself entirely in My mercy, with great trust, so that I may pour the bounty of My grace upon your soul. When you approach the confessional, know this, that I Myself am waiting there for you. I am only hidden by the priest, but I myself act in your soul. Here the misery of the soul meets the God of mercy. Tell souls that from this fount of mercy souls draw graces solely with the vessel of trust. If their trust is great, there is no limit to My generosity. The torrents of grace inundate humble souls. The proud remain always in poverty and misery, because My grace turns away from them to humble souls." (1602)

Chapter 7

Other Accredited
Visions and Messages

As noted in the earlier chronology, numerous saints and other holy men and women have reported both visions of Jesus and messages from Him. Here we will focus on messages received by some of the most prominent visionaries of the twentieth century (with the exception of Sr. Mary of St. Peter, who lived in the nineteenth century) who have received ecclesiastical approval. Excerpts from these messages are transcribed here. The visionaries cited are:

1. *Sr. Consolata Betrone* (1903–1946). A Capuchin nun from Turin, Italy, who was instructed in the practice of ceaseless love and received the famous prayer, "Jesus, Mary, save souls."

2. *Sr. Mary of the Trinity* (1901–1942), a Swiss nun who grew up as a Protestant and then joined the Poor Clares in Jerusalem. She did not see Jesus but received inner messages from Him. She died young — within four years of joining the order. At the request of her spiritual director, she wrote down the locutions she received.

3. *Sr. Conchita* (Concepción Cabrera de Armida) of Mexico (1862–1937). Sr. Conchita was a widow with eight children who went on to become the founder of two religious orders. She transcribed over sixty volumes of messages she received in visions of Jesus over a period of forty years. Although she had no formal theological training, the messages concerned some of the deepest theological mysteries. Her writings were introduced with a foreword by Miguel Darío Miranda, the Cardinal-Archbishop of Mexico City, who gave them his full approval.

4. *Sr. Josefa Menéndez* (1890–1923), a Spanish nun who belonged to the Society of the Sacred Heart of Jesus and was stationed in France. Sr. Josefa underwent great physical and spiritual suffering. The messages she transcribed received

almost immediate acceptance both within her order and from ecclesiastical authorities, including the future Pope Pius XII.

5. *Sr. Mary of St. Peter* (1816–1848). Sr. Mary joined the Carmelites in Tours, France, in 1839. She had numerous mystical encounters with Jesus and was entrusted with the task of spreading devotion to the Holy Face and the Holy Name of Jesus in reparation for blasphemy and sacrilege. She was given various prayers and promises by Jesus.

As we noted earlier the accredited private revelations of Jesus constitute a window into the Heart of God. Along with the two great revelations of the Sacred Heart and the Divine Mercy, we have been given several other moving and forceful messages from Jesus, some of which are quoted below. Most of the citations here are excerpted from two invaluable books, *Words of Love*, compiled by Bartholomew Gottemoller (Rockford, Ill.: Tan, 1985), and *The Golden Arrow*, edited by Dorothy Scallan (Rockford, Ill.: Tan, 1990). The name of the visionary is followed by the messages received from Jesus.

Sr. Consolata Betrone

"Think no longer about yourself, about your perfection, on how to attain to sanctity, or about your defects, your present and future troubles. No. I will see to your sanctification, to your sanctity. You must henceforth think only of Me and of souls; of Me to love Me, and of souls to save them!"[1]

"Consolata, it often happens that good and pious souls, and very frequently also souls who are consecrated to Me, wound My heart to Its very depths by some diffident phrase such as: 'Who knows whether I will be saved?'

"Open the Gospel and read My promises. I promised to My sheep: 'I will give them life everlasting; and they shall not perish forever, and no man shall pluck them out of My Hand.' Do you understand, Consolata? No one can take a soul from Me! Now read on: 'That which My Father hath given Me, is greater than all; and no one can snatch them out of the Hand of My Father.' Do you understand, Consolata? No one can snatch a soul from Me....In all eternity they will not perish...because I give them eternal life. For whom have I spoken these words? For all the sheep, for all souls! Why then insult, 'Who knows whether I will be saved?' I have given assurances in the gospel that no one can pluck a soul from Me and that I will give that soul eternal life, and so the soul cannot perish. Believe Me, Consolata, into Hell go only those who really wish to go there; for though no one can snatch a soul from Me, the soul may, through the free will granted her, flee from Me, may betray Me, deny Me, and so go to Satan of her own volition.

"Oh, if instead of wounding My Heart with such distrust, you would give a little thought to the Heaven which awaits you! I did not create you for Hell but for heaven, not as a companion for the devil but to enjoy Me in everlasting love! You see, Consolata, to Hell go only those who wish to go there....How foolish is your fear of being damned! After having shed My Blood in order to save your soul, after having surrounded your soul with graces upon graces all through your entire existence, would I permit Satan, My worst enemy, to rob Me of that soul at the last moment of her life, just when I am about to gather in the fruit of the Redemption and when therefore that soul is on the point of loving Me forever? Would I do that, when in the Holy Gospel I have promised to give the soul eternal life and that no one can snatch her from My Hands? Consolata, how is it possible to believe such a monstrosity? You see, final impenitence is found only in a soul who purposely wishes to go to Hell and therefore obstinately refuses My mercy, for I never refuse to pardon anyone. I offer the gift of My immense compassion to all, for My Blood was shed for all! No, it is not the multiplicity of sins which condemns a soul, for I forgive everything if she repents, but it is the obstinacy of not wishing to be pardoned, of wishing to be damned! Dismas on the cross had only one single act of faith in Me, but many, many sins; he was pardoned in an instant, however, and on the very day of his repentance he entered into My kingdom and is a saint! Behold the triumph of My Mercy and of faith in Me!

"No, Consolata, My father who has given Me the souls is greater and more powerful than all the demons. No one can snatch souls from the Hand of My Father.

"O Consolata, have confidence in Me! Trust Me always! You must have a blind confidence that I will fulfill all the great promises which I have made you, for I am kind, immensely kind and merciful, and 'I desire not the death of the wicked, but that the wicked turn from his way and live.' "[2]

"You see, I long to have My creatures serve Me out of love. Therefore, if a soul avoids some fault for fear of My chastisements, that is not what I am longing for them My creatures. I desire to be loved; I crave the love of My creatures! When they will come to love Me, they will no longer offend Me. When two people really love each other, they never offend each other. That is precisely the way it ought to be between the Creator and His creatures."[3]

"Now do you understand how much My parental Heart is wounded by every severe judgment, reprimand, or condemnation, even though based on truth, and how much comfort, on the other hand, is afforded Me by every act of compassion, indulgence and mercy? You must never judge anyone; never say a harsh word against anyone; instead console My Heart, distract Me from My sorrow; with eager charity make Me see only the good side of a guilty soul. I will believe you, and then I will hear your prayer in her favor and will grant it. If you only knew how I suffer when I must dispense justice! You see My Heart needs to be comforted; It wishes to dispense mercy, not justice!"[4]

"If you should happen to commit some fault, do not grieve over it, but come and place it quickly within My heart; then strengthen your determination to strive for the opposite virtue, but with great calmness. In that manner your every fault will become a step in advance."[5]

"Now, what do you need in order to give Me this continual act of love? You need the twofold silence of thought and word toward everyone, and to see and treat Me in everyone. I will think through you, but you must be intent solely on loving

Me, and loving Me always! That should be your one and only thought from the time of your rising in the morning until you fall asleep at night."[6]

"You see, Consolata, My Heart is won more readily through your wretchedness than through your virtues! Who came away from the temple justified? The publican. For to Me the sight of a humble and contrite soul is irresistible.... That is the way I am."[7]

"I prefer one of your acts of love to all your prayers! 'Jesus, Mary, I love You! Save souls!' This comprises all: the souls in Purgatory and those in the Church Militant, the innocent and the sinful souls, the dying, the godless, etc."[8]

Sr. Mary of the Trinity

"Your value does not lie in your personal capabilities, however brilliant they may be, but in your capacity to receive your Creator and allow Him to live and shine through you."[9]

"It is the sun that gives the earth its beauty and animates it. It is My grace that gives souls their beauty and that animates them. My Omnipotence is limited only by your liberty. It is with coal that I make diamonds. What would I not do with a soul, however black she might be, who would give herself to Me."[10]

"All souls could rapidly attain to the plenitude of their sanctity if they allowed Me to act, without resisting. Oh, the unacknowledged reserves of selfishness which paralyze the omnipotence of the Holy Spirit within you!"[11]

"Yes, I can transform all ugliness into beauty — all poverty into spiritual wealth — all sin into a source of grace — all rancor into forgiveness — into sweetness all bitterness — into joy all sadness — all suffering into Redemption... when you give them to Me and let Me act...."[12]

"A true mother will not consider her child ugly, no matter how much it may be so; to her it is always lovely and so it will always remain in her innermost heart. That is precisely the way My Heart feels toward souls: though they be ugly, soiled, filthy, My love considers them always beautiful. I suffer when their ugliness is confirmed to Me; on the other hand, I rejoice when, in conformity with My parental sentiments, someone dissuades Me about their ugliness and tells Me that it is not true and that they are still beautiful. The souls are Mine; for them I have given all My Blood!

"I cherish each soul with a tenderness of which your human love has no conception. Do you not understand that? They must be loved for my sake. Strive to make it known to all whom I put in your path."[13]

"You must do all that you can, and it is only after that, that you can count infallibly on My help."[14]

"To those who ask with love, that is to say, with unlimited confidence, I cannot prevent Myself from granting even more, far more than what is asked."[15]

"To love Me is to have confidence in Me, not to doubt Me; it is to rely on Me. Wherein lies the limit of My power over you? In your confidence."[16]

"Now you must live by Faith; you must believe that I am there under the humble species, believe without proof. You must believe without proof that I use your sacrifices, you prayers, all your sufferings for the salvation of souls."[17]

"Faith is also a form of obedience: the submission of the mind."[18]

"I wish every soul to understand that I am awaiting her. That beyond this life a boundless love awaits her, and that she must hasten . . . must purify herself to meet Love, and let that be her one object."[19]

"It is not sins that injure your purity, it is your pride, which, so often, does not wish to acknowledge them."[20]

"I love you! Is that not enough to fill every one of your moments with the fullness of joy? I love you and desire that you should know it. Oh, if you knew how much I love you, My little child!"[21]

"Time that is filled with joy, with joy directed toward God, is not lost time."[22]

"This is the only reality. I love you and take care of you."[23]

"I bought you at the price of My blood, the Blood of God. That I might not condemn you, I allowed Myself to be condemned in your place."[24]

"As parents are happy in showing their love to their children, so it is My joy to make My love felt, to reveal it; I do it in a reserved manner, perceptible to those who are attentive to My Presence and who seek it; because I am Spirit, and in order that a soul should really find Me, she must have sought and discovered Me. Then she associates Me with her life and perceives that she had been seeking Me too far away."[25]

"Do you understand that after having loved you so much in My earthly life, I cannot stop loving you — My gifts are without regret — do you understand how ready I am to help you, to give you My grace? You can ask everything of Me; come to Me!"[26]

"I wish each soul to understand that she has her special place in My Heart which awaits her; that her love is necessary to Me; and her cooperation necessary — that I need to see her happy and perfect — because I have loved her even to dying on the Cross for her — yes, each soul."[27]

"I love you because you have always loved Me. You did not know it was I whom you loved in cherishing your family and those whom I placed in your path; you did not know it was I whom you loved in them and whom you wished never to grieve."[28]

"My little daughter, all that you do to others is really done to Me."[29]

"My little daughter, beware of avarice. It unconsciously introduces itself into a soul. It shuts the soul out from My Kingdom. Avarice is the cause of lying — of all crimes, of all denials, of all treason. The attachment to passing goods which one desires to possess and to hold, hates My Spirit and wishes to destroy it. Avarice is the work of death."[30]

"You would not be able to bear the sight of Me; that is why I hide Myself in countenances within reach of you: in the faces that surround you, the faces of duty, of pain, and of pleasure — I am always hidden in the Cross."[31]

"Thus do I change the circumstances in your lives to make them work together for the greater good of your soul — that is a mere game for divine power! And that same power can do nothing in your soul, without your acquiescence."[32]

"Do you know that there is...more happiness in making reparation than in doing additional good works? The soul that makes reparation gives Me two joys: she reestablishes order — and above all: she erases from My heart the pain caused by the unfaithful soul, because by making reparation she arouses repentance — and nothing consoles Me so much as a repentant soul. She becomes My beloved...."[33]

"The more I forgive you, the more you desire to do penance and make reparation. This desire must not be extinguished but enkindled in souls. It is the grace which flows immediately from My pardon."[34]

"No, there is not a single superfluous suffering in your life. Your heart must be rent that My grace may penetrate it; otherwise you remain as a closed garden within you own feelings, your own thoughts, your horizon. Your horizon must be rent, so that you may catch a glimpse of the destiny to which you are called. Your destiny is so great that according to nature, you could not of yourselves imagine it. Your heart must be rent that My grace may penetrate and transform it."[35]

"When a trial befalls you, seek the cause within yourselves: What wrong have you done? What good are you neglecting to do? Be conscious of your responsibilities and the way in which you fulfill them. You must first understand, and then make amends. Then you will see that when the trial is no longer necessary, it will cease."[36]

"Trials should produce a definite result in your souls; if you see that the trial ceases, lay hold of the virtue that it came to teach you, and practice it. Thus if you do your share of penance in your life, I shall not have to send you the sickness which takes the place of neglected mortifications. In the same way, the more simple you are, the more you will avoid great temptations, which are used to destroy in you that which is an obstacle between you and Me."[37]

"These horrors of the war are a small thing compared with the loss of souls. One must thank God if, by them, souls accept their salvation."[38]

Sr. Conchita of Mexico

The Lord told me: "The world is buried in sensuality; no longer is sacrifice loved and no longer is its sweetness known. I wish the Cross to reign. Today it is presented to the world with my Heart, so that it may bring souls to make sacrifices. No true love is without sacrifice. It is only in my crucified Heart that the ineffable sweetness of my Heart can be tasted. Seen from the outside, the Cross is bitter and harsh, but as soon as tasted, penetrating and savoring it, there is no greater pleasure. Therein is the repose of the soul inebriated by love, therein its delights, its life."[39]

The Lord told me: "Do not complain about your sufferings before strangers. Do not let them see how you are in pain: that would lessen your merit. Suffer in silence. Let me work in you and walk the earth silently and obscurely crucified."[40]

The Lord told me: "My Father existed from all eternity. He produced from the depth of himself, of his own substance, of his very essence, his Word. From all eternity too, from the beginning, already there was the Word-God and the Father who is God, the two Persons constituting but one same divine substance. But never, at any moment, were these divine Persons, the Father and the Son, alone or only two. In this same eternity, but inspired by the Father and the Son, the Holy Spirit existed, reflection, substance, essence of the Father and the Son, and equally Person. The Holy Trinity is a divine reflection in the bosom of the same divinity, the reflection of Love in the bosom of Love itself. The Holy Spirit is the reflection of Light itself, and likewise, of all the perfection. This communication of the same substance, of the same essence, of the same life and of the same perfection which form and are in reality one and the same substance, essence, life and perfection, constitute the eternal felicity of one and the same God and the endless complacencies of the august Trinity."[41]

"I wish that above all there be honored the interior sufferings of my Heart, sufferings undergone from my incarnation to the Cross and which are mystically prolonged in my Eucharist. These sufferings are still unsuspected by the world. Nonetheless, I declare to you that from the first moment of my incarnation, the Cross already planted in my heart overburdened me, and the thorns penetrated it. The blow struck by the lance might have been some solace causing to gush from my side a volcano of love and suffering, but I did not consent to that until after my death. I only received ingratitude. That is why my Heart, overflowing with tenderness, will ever feel the thorns of the Cross. In heaven, as God, I cannot suffer. To find this Cross which above did not exist, I descended into this world and became man. As God-Man, I could suffer infinitely to pay the price of the salvation of so many souls. During my life, I never desired anything but the Cross, and ever the Cross, wanting to show the world that which is the sole wealth and happiness on earth, the currency which will buy an eternal happiness."[42]

"When I pronounced these words, 'Do this in memory of me,' I was not addressing myself only to priests. Of course, they alone have the power to change the substance of bread into my holy body and the substance of wine into my blood.

But the power to unite in one single oblation all oblations belongs to all Christians. It belongs to all Christians, members of one single body, to become one with the Victim on the altar by faith and works, offering me as host in propitiation to my eternal Father."[43]

Sr. Josefa Menéndez

"Do you think that anything happens without My permission? I dispose all things for the good of each and every soul."[44]

"A soul who truly surrenders herself to Me gives Me so much joy that in spite of her miseries and imperfections she becomes a very heaven of delight to Me and I take pleasure in abiding in her."[45]

"I can refuse nothing to one who relies entirely on Me. Souls are too little conscious of how much I want to help them and how much I am glorified by their trust."[46]

"Let them give themselves up to thoughts of confidence, not fear, for I am a God of pity, ever ready to receive them into My Heart."[47]

"Nothing, indeed, is wanting to My heavenly beatitude, which is infinite, but I yearn for souls.... I thirst for them, and want to save them."[48]

"Ah, if souls only understood how ardently I desire to communicate Myself to them! But how few do understand...and how deeply this wounds My Heart."[49]

"A soul will profit even after the greatest sins, if she humbles herself."[50]

"Never go to rest at night with the slightest shadow obscuring your soul. This I recommend to you with great insistence. When you commit a fault, repair it at once. I wish your soul to be as pure as crystal. Do not let your falls, however many, trouble you. It is trouble and worry that keep a soul from God."[51]

"Those whose generosity is not equal to these daily endeavors and sacrifices will see their lives go by full only of promise which never comes to fruition. But in this, distinguish: to souls who habitually promise and yet do no violence to themselves nor prove their abnegation and love in any way, I say: 'Beware lest all this straw and stubble which you have gathered into your barns take fire or be scattered in an instant by the wind!' But there are others, and it is of them I now speak, who begin their day with a very good will and desire to prove their love. They pledge themselves to self-denial or generosity in this or that circumstance.... But when the time comes they are prevented by self-love, temperament, health, ... from carrying out what a few hours before they quite sincerely purposed to do. Nevertheless they speedily acknowledge their weakness and, filled with shame, beg for pardon, humble themselves, and renew their promise.... Ah! Let them know that these souls please Me as much as if they had nothing with which to reproach themselves."[52]

"I do not say that by the fact of My choice, a soul is freed from her faults and wretchedness. That soul may and will fall often again, but if she humbles herself, if she recognizes her nothingness, if she tries to repair her faults by little acts of generosity and love, if she confides and surrenders herself once more to My heart...she gives Me more glory and can do more good to other souls than if she had never fallen. Miseries and weaknesses are of no consequence; what I do ask of them is love."[53]

"Love gives Itself as food to Its own and this food is the substance which gives them their life and sustains them. Love humbles Itself before Its own...and in so doing raises them to the highest dignity. Love surrenders Itself in totality, It gives in profusion and without reserve. With enthusiasm, with vehemence It is sacrificed, It is immolated, It is given for those It loves....The Holy Eucharist is love to the extreme of folly."[54]

"A soul will profit even after the greatest sins, if she humbles herself. It is pride that provokes My Father's wrath, and it is loathed by Him with infinite hatred."[55]

"The less there is of you, the more I shall be your life, and you will be My heaven of rest...on earth My heaven is in souls."[56]

"They have not understood My Heart. For it is their very destitution and failings that incline My goodness towards them. And when, acknowledging their helplessness and weakness, they humble themselves and have recourse to Me trustfully, then indeed they give Me more glory than before their fault."[57]

"I am not attracted by your merits but by My love for souls."[58]

"My Heart is not so much wounded by sin, as torn with grief that they will not take refuge with Me after it."[59]

"As soon as a soul throws itself at My feet and implores My forgiveness, Josefa, I forget all her sins."[60]

"As soon as your soul is touched by grace, and before the struggle has even begun, hasten to My Heart; beg of Me to let a drop of My Blood fall on your soul. Ah! hasten to My heart...and be without fear for the past; all has been swallowed up in the abyss of My mercy, and My love is preparing new graces for you. The memory of your lapses will be an incentive to humility and a source of merit, and you cannot give Me a greater proof of affection than to count on My full pardon and to believe that your sins will never be as great as My mercy, which is infinite."[61]

"I pursue sinners as justice pursues criminals. But justice seeks them in order to punish, I, in order to forgive."[62]

"Nothing, indeed, is wanting to My heavenly beatitude, which is infinite, but I yearn for souls....I thirst for them, and want to save them."[63]

"I will make it known that My work rests on nothingness and misery—such is the first link in the chain of love that I have prepared for souls from all eternity. I will use you to show that I love misery, littleness and absolute nothingness."[64]

"I withdrew into the Garden of Gethsemane, that is to say into solitude. God is to be sought within, away from distraction and noise. To find Him the soul must enforce silence on all the disturbances by which nature often fights against grace; on interior arguments prompted by self-love or sensuality. These constantly tend to stifle the inspirations of grace and keep her from finding God within."[65]

"I do not ask you to free yourself, for I know it is not always in your power, but what I do ask of you is to keep up the struggle against your passions."[66]

Sr. Mary of St. Peter

Shortly afterwards our Lord invited me to apply myself particularly to honoring His divine Heart and also the Heart of His holy Mother, promising me that He would favor me in the future with graces even more extraordinary than those which He had in the past conferred upon me.

I did what our Lord assigned to me, and honoring the Heart of Jesus and the Heart of Mary, I applied myself with great devotion to these two hearts. However, before granting me further graces our Lord prepared my soul now by plunging it into great interior sufferings. I began to experience during prayer a loving and a burning attraction to the Three Persons of the Most Blessed Trinity. Feeling myself constrained repeatedly to renew my vows, I henceforth dedicated the three powers of my soul to the Three adorable Persons in God, Who now operated great marvels in my soul, but in a manner which I am unable to explain. I was plunged in an abyss of suffering born as it were of my immense desire to glorify God, but recognizing my extreme misery, I felt annihilated and incapable of anything good.

Finally, our Lord having purified my soul according to His designs, in spite of my unworthiness, communicated Himself to me on August 26, 1843, speaking to me for the first time about His great Work of the Reparation for blasphemy, destined to redound to the glory of the holy Name of God.[67]

At the beginning of prayer I make an examination of conscience after which I humble myself at the feet of our Lord for my infidelities as I beg Him mercifully to purify my soul. After that I treat the Saviour with much simplicity, as a child would treat its father. The following is one method of prayer which our Lord one day gave me, although I cannot say whether He did this by speaking His interior words to me or merely by giving me an illumination:

> Empty your soul by recollection,
> Purify it by an act of contrition,
> Then fill it with God.[68]

I obeyed and begged our Lord to forgive me my faults. At that particular time, however, my soul was extremely perturbed and it was difficult for me to pray at all. My imagination was like a runaway horse that I could not control. Nevertheless I implored the Saviour to restore my soul to a state of prayerful meditation since the prioress had ordered me to ask for this grace.

Our Lord at once had the goodness to hear my prayers addressed to him through obedience for I believe it was on the following morning, as I awoke, that I heard an interior voice saying:

"Return to the house of your Father, which is none other than My Heart."

These words produced a great peace in my soul. As soon as I entered the choir for mental prayer, I united myself to our Lord in the Blessed Sacrament, and immediately I heard Him say to me:

"Apply yourself diligently to honor My Sacred Heart and also the Heart of My Mother. Never separate these two hearts. It is My desire that you pray to these two hearts for yourself and for sinners. I in turn will forget your past faults and furthermore I will grant you even more graces than before because you are now more completely united to Me through your Vows."

As there arose within me a doubt as to whether it was really our Lord Who had spoken to me, I then heard Him say:

"It is I, Jesus, present in the Blessed Sacrament Who speaks to you. I have various ways of communication with souls. Are you not able to perceive how calm and how united your soul is to Me at present, whereas only recently it was a prey to many distractions? Begin to do as I tell you and you will soon experience many beneficial results."

After that our Lord made me understand that I should not become attached to a devotion which gratifies the sense merely, and He gave me the light to see that people often follow after interior sweetness, thinking that they are following after Him."[69]

On August 26, 1843 (the day after the Feast of St. Louis, the crusader against blasphemy), there was a terrible storm during which I felt the justice of angry God as I had never before felt in my life. Kneeling, so that my forehead touched the ground, I ceaselessly offered our Saviour, Jesus Christ, to His Eternal Father, for the expiation of my sins and for the needs of holy Church.

Since one of the nuns in our convent experienced on the day the same emotion as I did, when the hour for evening prayer arrived, I placed myself in spirit at the foot of the cross, and approaching our Lord familiarly, I spoke to Him about the incident of the storm. After that I asked Him to tell me the reason why I felt so strongly on that day the roused anger of His Eternal Father.

Although recently I had experienced much aridity in prayer, now as soon as I had addressed our Saviour, He at once relaxed His manner towards me and said:

"My daughter, I have heard your sighs and your groans, and I have also witnessed your ardent desire to glorify Me, which desire does not spring from yourself, for it is I Who have given it birth in your soul."

Then gathering the powers of my soul, our Lord opened His Heart to me and said:

"My Name is everywhere blasphemed! There are even children who blaspheme!"

He then made me see that this frightful sin wounds His divine Heart more grievously than all other sins, showing me how by blasphemy the sinner curses Him to His Face, attacks Him publicly, nullifies his redemption, and pronounces his own judgment and condemnation.

Our Lord then made me visualize the act of blasphemy as a poisoned arrow continually wounding His divine Heart. After that He revealed to me that He wanted to give me a "Golden Arrow" which would have the power of wounding Him delightfully, and which would also heal those other wounds inflicted by the malice of sinners.

The following is the formula of the "Golden Arrow" which is an Act of Praise that our Lord Himself dictated to me, notwithstanding my unworthiness, for the reparation of blasphemy against His Holy Name:

THE GOLDEN ARROW

May the most holy, most sacred, most adorable, most incomprehensible and unutterable Name of God be always praised, blessed, loved, adored and glorified in heaven, on earth and in the hells, by all the creatures of God and by the Sacred Heart of our Lord Jesus Christ in the Most Holy Sacrament of the Altar. Amen.

Since I felt somewhat astonished at the words which our Lord used which He said to me, "in the hells," He made me understand that His Justice was also glorified there. I furthermore beg that notice be taken of this that our Lord did not say to me "in hell," but He said, "in the hells," which can be understood to include also purgatory, where He is loved and glorified by His suffering souls. Then too, the word "hell" applies not only to the abode of the reprobate, for faith teaches us that our Lord Himself after His death descended into hell, which was the place where the souls of the just awaited Him. Besides, does not Holy Church pray her Divine Spouse to deliver the souls of her children from the gates of hell? . . .

After our Lord finished dictating this prayer which He called the "Golden Arrow" He added a warning: "Be careful to utilize this grace because I shall demand an account of it from you," and at that moment I believe I saw streaming from the Sacred Heart of Jesus, delightfully wounded by this "Golden Arrow," torrents of graces for the conversion of sinners. . . .

Ever since the revelation on the "Golden Arrow" I have felt my soul completely changed, and wholly occupied in glorifying the Most Holy Name of God. In addition to the "Golden Arrow": our Lord also inspired me to compose a little exercise of Reparation in the form of twenty-four Acts of Adoration to atone for the blasphemies uttered to reveal to me that this exercise of Reparation which I performed was agreeable to Him, and that He desired this devotion to be spread everywhere. The Saviour then made me share His own ardent longing to see the

Name of His eternal Father glorified. He further made me understand that just as the Angels sing, Sanctus, Sanctus, Sanctus, without ceasing, so must I apply myself to glorifying His Holy Name. By doing this, He assured me that I would fulfill the command which he had given me a short while ago when He told me to honor His Sacred Heart and also the heart of His holy Mother, for these two hearts were continually being wounded by blasphemy.[70]

Our Lord inspired me at this time to compose certain prayers of reparation in the form of a chaplet, or a small rosary. This chaplet is made up of thirty-three small beads, on which is recited thirty-three times the prayer, "Arise, O Lord, and let Your enemies be scattered, and let those that hate You flee before Your Face," and also six large beads on which are recited the ejaculation: "My Jesus, mercy," followed by the doxology: Glory be the Father, etc.

One day after Holy Mass our Lord appeared to me presenting me with a similar chaplet which I saw was made of precious stones strung on a fine gold chain. Deeming myself quite unworthy of possessing such a treasure, I begged the Blessed Virgin to keep this beautiful rosary for me by placing it in her Immaculate Heart, and I also begged our Lord to attach indulgences to the recitation of this chaplet.[71]

Immediately after receiving Holy Communion on the Feast of our holy father, St. John of the Cross, our Lord seized possession of the powers of my soul and made me hear the following words:

> "Until now I have shown you only in part the plans of My Heart but today I want to reveal them to you in all their fullness."

He then continued:

> "The whole earth is covered with crimes and the violation of the first three of the Ten Commandments of God has aroused the anger of My Father. The crimes that fill up the cup of wickedness are blasphemies against God's Holy Name and the profanation of Sundays. These sins have reached to the very throne of Almighty God, and they have provoked Hs wrath which is about to strike everywhere unless His Justice be appeased. Never before have these crimes reached such a peak."

After that our Lord said:

> "I desire, and this most urgently, that there be formed to honor the Name of My Father an Association, properly approved and well organized. Your superiors have good reasons to take only such steps in this devotion which are well founded, for otherwise My designs would not be fulfilled."[72]

My soul is terrified at what our Lord has just made me hear during prayer this morning, charging me with the duty of transmitting His message to my superiors without any fear of being deceived. He said He was incensed with anger against our nation, and that He has sworn in His wrath to avenge Himself if Reparation to the honor of His Divine Father were not made for all the blasphemies of which the people are guilty, making me hear that He could no longer remain among men who, like vipers, were tearing at the entrails of His mercy. He said that as for the contempt shown to Himself, He would still endure it patiently, but that He was roused to anger by the outrages committed against His Eternal Father. He then declared that His Mercy was on the verge of giving way to His Justice, and that His wrath would overflow with a fury such as had never yet been heard of before.

Greatly frightened, I pleaded, "My Lord, permit me to ask You if You would grant our nation pardon if this Atonement for which You ask were made to God?"

Our Lord answered me:

> "Yes, I will grant it pardon once more, but mark my word, once! And since this crime of blasphemy extends over the whole nation, and since it is public, I demand that Reparation be extended to all the cities and that it be public. Woe to those cities that will not make this Reparation!"[73]

Finally, our Lord told me that He desired each member of the Association to wear a special cross, and that on one side of this cross should be engraved the words, "Blessed be the Name of God," and on the reverse side should be the words, "Begone, Satan!" To all those wearing this holy cross our Lord promised a special resourcefulness to conquer the demon of blasphemy, adding that every time one hears a curse, he should repeat the two short inscriptions written on each side of the cross, and he will thus overcome the evil one and render glory to God.

At the end our Lord warned me, saying that the demon would do everything in his power to crush this Work which springs from the Sacred Heart. I then felt that I would willingly shed the last drop of my blood for such a holy association.[74]

"I therefore demand, and most urgently, that this Work be established," our Lord said, making me understand that His Sacred Heart desires through this means to bestow mercy on mankind.

I also hear this Divine Jesus from the depths of the tabernacle addressing us with these words:

> "Oh, you, who are my friends, and my faithful children, look and see if there be any sorrow like mine. Everywhere My enemies despise and insult both my Eternal Father and My Church, the cherished Spouse of My Heart. Will no one rise up to console Me by defending the glory of My Father, and the honor of My Spouse, which has been so cruelly attacked? I can no longer remain in the midst of a people that will continue to be so heedless and so ungrateful. Look at the torrents of tears that stream from My eyes! Can I find no one to wipe away these tears by making reparation to My Father, and imploring forgiveness for the guilty?"[75]

During holy Mass our Lord showed me the enormity of the crime of blasphemy, saying to me:

> "You cannot comprehend the malice and abomination of this sin. If My Justice were not restrained by My Mercy, indeed, it would instantly crush the guilty. In fact, all creatures, even those that are inanimate, would avenge

this outrage against their Creator's majesty, but I have an eternity in which to punish the guilty."[76]

"My child, have courage and confidence! Moreover, engrave these two words, courage and confidence, in your heart. Oh, if you only knew the profit which accrues to your soul from suffering these pains, you would thank me for having given them to you. I come to pay you a visit merely, but not to remain with you in a way which would gratify your senses. You shall, instead, drink the chalice, but be consoled, for although you will not see Me, I will not be far from you. In fact, it will be I, Myself, who will hold the chalice to your lips while you drink it, and after this trial is past, I will again allow you to taste My consolations. You have deserved these sufferings through your many infidelities; however, it is not in vengeance but rather through charity that I give you these trials."[77]

Immediately after that our Lord carried me in spirit to the road leading up to Calvary, and there He vividly showed me the pious deed of charity which St. Veronica performed towards Him when with her veil she wiped His Most Holy Face covered with spittle, dust, sweat, and blood. Then this Divine Saviour told me that in our present age the wicked, by their blasphemies, renew all those outrages that disfigured His Holy Face on that occasion. I was enlightened to see that all the blasphemies which wicked men hurl against the Divinity, Whom they cannot reach, fall back like the spittle of the mob upon the Holy Face of our Lord, Who offered Himself a victim for sinners.

Our Lord then instructed me saying that I must imitate the courage of St. Veronica, who bravely broke through the mob of His enemies to reach Him, and that He now presented her to me as my protectress and as my model.

Following this, our Lord told me that by practicing Reparation for blasphemy, we render Him the same service as did the pious Veronica and that just as He looked with kindly eyes upon this holy woman during His passion, so would He regard with affection all those who make reparation. I could see from our Lord's attitude that He had a very tender love for St. Veronica.[78]

Drawing me strongly to the contemplation of His adorable Face, our Divine Saviour made me see through a ray of light issuing from His august Countenance that the Holy Face which He presented to mankind for their adoration, was indeed the mirror of those unutterable Divine Perfections comprised and contained in the Most Holy Name of God.

It is impossible for me to express in words all that I understood through this intellectual vision, unless it be by those words of the Apostle St. Paul: "The Head of Christ is God." Coming upon this text recently, I was deeply impressed by it because I recognized in these words the truth of that which was revealed too me in my vision.

I then understood by this illumination that as the Sacred Heart of Jesus is the exterior object offered for our adoration to represent his boundless love in the most Holy Sacrament of the Altar, so in a parallel manner, in the Work of Reparation, the adorable Face of our Lord is the exterior object offered for the adoration of the members. I saw that by thus honoring and venerating this Sacred Countenance covered anew with outrages, we could atone for blasphemers who attack the Divinity of which this Holy Face is the figure, the mirror and the expression.[79]

"By My Holy Face you will work wonders!" He made known to me that He desired to see his Holy Face offered as the exterior object of adoration to all His children who would be associated in the Work of Reparation for Blasphemy. Inviting me to make known His Holy Face from this standpoint, our Lord then declared that the gift of His adorable Countenance which He presented to me on that day was, next to the sacraments, the greatest gift He could bestow on me.

He showed me how He had prepared me for its reception by tilling the ground of my soul with severe interior trials which I had recently endured, making me understand, however, that He never tempted His children beyond their strength.[80]

The devotion to the Holy Face requested in these messages reached its culmination in the formation of an Archconfraternity of the Holy Face. Several promises were attached to this devotion. In addition to those outlined above, Sr. Mary also received the following promises:

1. "In proportion to your care in repairing the injuries My Face receives from blasphemers, will I take care of yours, which has been disfigured by sin."

2. "I will impress My Divine Likeness to souls who honor My Holy Face."

3. "The sight of My Face is so pleasing to the Father, that nothing that you ask in virtue of My Holy Face will be refused you."

4. "Those who on earth contemplate the wounds of My Face will also contemplate It shining with glory in Heaven."

In the twentieth century, Mother Maria Pierina (1890–1945) of the Daughters of the Immaculate Conception received messages on devotion to the Holy Face from both Jesus and Mary. The messages from Jesus echo those received by Sr. Mary of St. Peter:

1. "I have given My Heart as the sensible proof of my great love for men, and I give My Face as the sensible object of my grief for the sins of mankind."

2. "I desire that My Face, which shows My soul's deepest anguish, My Heart's sorrow and love, be more honoured."

3. "Whoever contemplates Me, consoles Me."

4. "Contemplate My Face and you will enter into My Heart's abysses of sorrow."

5. "Every time that anyone gazes at My Face, I will pour My Love into hearts."

6. "And by means of the Holy Face, the salvation of many souls will be obtained."

7. "Offer My Holy Face without ceasing to the Eternal Father. With this offering, you will obtain salvation and sanctification of many souls. When henceforth you offer it through My priests, they will perform miracles."

8. "I desire that My Holy Face be honoured in a special way on Tuesdays."

9. "I desire that My Face be honoured by a special Feast on Quinquagesima Tuesday [Tuesday on the fifth week before Easter Sunday], a Feast preceded by a Novena, in which all the faithful will make reparation to me, thus uniting and participating in My grief."[81]

In her messages, the Blessed Virgin offered a scapular of the Holy Face, which is now circulated as a medal. The following promises are associated with this medal:

"This scapular is a weapon of defense, a shield of strength, a pledge of love and mercy which Jesus wishes to give to the world in these times of sensuality and hatred of God and of the Church. Diabolic snares are being laid to tear the faith from men's hearts, and evil spreads, true apostles are few, a Divine remedy is necessary, and the remedy is the Holy Face of Jesus. All those who wear a scapular like this, and will make, if possible, a visit to the Blessed Sacrament every Tuesday, in reparation for the outrages that the Holy Face of my Son Jesus received during His Passion, and which He receives each day in the Eucharistic Sacrifice, will be fortified in the Faith, made able to defend it and to overcome all difficulties within and without, and in the end will have a happy death under the loving gaze of my Divine Son."

Devotions Centered on the Incarnation

The Incarnation of God in Christ has also been made tangible and accessible to the everyday experience of humanity through a variety of events and devotions centered on the life of Jesus. The chief devotions directly related to the Incarnation are:

- The Eucharist
- The Childhood of Jesus
- The Passion of Jesus (this includes the Stations of the Cross as well as devotions centering on the physical body of Jesus, in particular the Holy Face, the Sacred Heart, the Five Wounds, and the Shoulder Wound)

The central characteristics of these devotions are the following:

- They began through a supernatural event experienced by one or more of the faithful.
- Verification of the veracity of the devotion comes primarily through miracles and answered prayer followed by ecclesiastical approval.

The Eucharist is treated in more detail in the next section. The Passion of Jesus is a central theme of the private revelations treated here. In addition, such devotions as the Stations of the Cross and veneration of the Holy Face and the Wounds of Jesus have been a source of grace for millions of devout Christians.

The devotion to the Childhood of Jesus has rapidly become one of the most significant themes in the life of popular worship. The most important subset of this devotion is the devotion to the Infant of Prague.

The Infant of Prague is a statue of the Infant Jesus clothed in royal splendor that was brought to a religious order in Prague in the Czech Republic in the seventeenth century. Among the promises made by the Infant are the following: "The more you honor me the more I will bless you." The devotion to the Infant is particularly associated with prayers for the family and good health.

The Stigmatists

We have said that the Passion was the fundamental theme of the messages of Jesus in His visions. As if to underline the importance of this theme, the climactic moments of the Passion have literally been incarnated in the lives of over three hundred privileged individuals in the course of Christian history (over sixty of them have been canonized or beatified). That is to say, the wounds of Christ, called the Sacred Stigmata, have mysteriously appeared on their bodies — on their hands, legs, sides, or heads — in all their painful reality. In most of the prominent cases, the wounds were verified by medical authorities, although their origin was inexplicable on a natural level. In calling them privileged individuals we are not suggesting that they had glamorous lives. On the contrary, the wounds were extremely painful, and those who bore them were often publicly humiliated. What is most impressive about this phenomenon is that all of the stigmatists willingly, even enthusiastically, offered up their suffering to their Lord.

On the following page is a brief overview of the best-known stigmatists taken from the best-selling book *They Bore the Wounds of Christ: The Mystery of the Sacred Stigmata* by Michael Freze (Huntington, Ind.: Our Sunday Visitor, 1989) with the kind permission of the author.

Several of the famous visionaries of this century who have reported apparitions of the Virgin Mary have also received the stigmata. These include: Maria Esperanza of Venezuela; Mirna Nazour of Damascus, Syria; Gladys Quiroga De Motta of San Nicolás, Argentina; Barbara Reuss of Marienfried, Germany; Sr. Agnes Sasagawa of Akita, Japan; and Christina Gallagher of Ireland.

Blessed Padre Pio of Pietrelcina, Italy (1887–1968), is by far the most famous stigmatist of this century and perhaps the most extraordinary stigmatist of all. He bore the Five Sacred Wounds for fifty-eight years from 1910 — the longest period of any stigmatist. When he celebrated Mass, blood would begin to gush from his hand wounds. The stigmata disappeared a few days before his death.

Stigmatist	Date	Description of Wound/History?
St. Francis of Assisi	1182–1226	Received the wounds of Christ on September 14, 1224. The wounds remained on him until his death.
St. Clare of Montefalco	d. 1308	In addition to bearing the stigmata, an imprint of the wounds was found on her heart after her death.
St. Catherine of Siena	1347–1380	Received the stigmata in 1375. At her request to the Lord, the wounds later disappeared but reappeared at her death.
St. Lydwine of Holland	1380–1433	Received the stigmata in 1407 and carried it for the rest of her life.
St. Rita of Cascia	1381–1457	A wound from the crown of thorns on forehead. Received 1441.
Bl. Osanna of Mantua	1449–1505	After she requested the Lord to share in His Passion, she received first the wounds of the crown of thorns and then the five wounds.
St. Teresa of Avila	1515–1582	Recipient of transverberation, a stigma on the heart.
St. Catherine Dei Ricci	1522–1590	In 1542 she received the wounds on both feet, her hands, her side and the crown of thorns.
St. Rose of Lima	1586–1617	Received the Five Wounds.
St. Margaret Mary Alacoque	1647–1690	Received the stigmata invisibly.
St. Veronica of Giuliani	1660–1727	Received the wound of Christ's heart in 1697.
St. Mary Frances of the Five Wounds	1734–1791	Received the stigmata on hands, feet and side.
Anne Catherine Emmerich	1774–1824	Stigmata appeared in 1812 after she asked for a share in the Passion. Her wounds were medically examined but no natural cause for them could be found.
Louise Lateau	1850–1883	The Five Wounds and later the wounds from the Crown of Thorns. Her wounds were examined by medical authorities.
St. Gemma Galgani	1878–1903	Received the stigmata, which remained invisible at her request.
Sr. Josefa Menéndez	1890–1923	Received the stigmata and underwent severe sufferings.
St. Faustina Kowalska	1905–1938	Invisible stigmata.
Berthe Petit	1870–1943	Invisible stigmata.
Alexandrina da Costa	1904–1955	Received the stigmata.
Theresa Neumann	1898–1962	Bore the stigmata for thirty-six years. She carried all the wounds of the Passion: hand and foot wounds, wound to the heart, shoulder wound, thirty scourge marks and nine head wounds.
Marthe Robin	1902–1981	In 1930 she received the Five Wounds and the Crown of Thorns wounds.

PART THREE

CORPUS CHRISTI

Chapter 8

The Bible Code

In recent years, much prominence has been given to claims that the Hebrew text of the Bible conceals codes foretelling future events and individuals. These messages were reportedly detected when specific combinations of letters and words in the surface text were subjected to statistical analysis using sophisticated computers. Whether or not there is merit to such claims — and they have, of course, been challenged and dismissed — there is a far more important Bible Code that seems to have been hidden from the modern age although it had been cracked in the Apostolic Age.

This Code pertains to the explosive emergence and maturation of key common themes and concepts across both Testaments. Thus we read in the Old Testament about Abel's sacrifice of a first-born lamb; Melchizedek's offering of bread and wine; Abraham obeying God and offering his son in sacrifice (only to be stopped by an angel); the sons of Israel being protected by the sacrifice of a lamb as the Angel of Death passed over Egypt; the manna that fed the Israelites in the desert; the Holy of Holies constructed by the Israelites; the annual sacrifice of the Passover celebrated by Israel; Malachi's prophecy of a future perfect sacrifice to be performed by the pagans from the rising of the sun to its setting. In the New Testament, we read about the miracles of the loaves which are followed by Jesus' command to eat His Flesh; the Passover meal at which Jesus tells the Apostles that they must remember Him by offering up His Body and Blood under the appearance of bread and wine; the sacrifice of Christ the "Paschal Lamb" on Calvary; the two disciples traveling to Emmaus who discover Jesus in the "breaking of bread"; the Apostles continuing the tradition of "breaking the bread"; the continuing intercession of Christ in Heaven shown in the Epistles to the Hebrews and the Romans; and the mysterious Lamb that was slain in the Book of Revelation.

When something is encrypted, when a code is constructed, those most qualified to help us read between the lines or, better yet, read the lines as they were meant to be read, are precisely those who lived and taught the encoded message, those for whom the code was a familiar language — namely, the contemporaries of the Apostles and the generations that came immediately after them. Two instances of such decoding will illustrate this. St. Irenaeus of Lyons (c. 130–c. 200) writes,

> [St. Paul] is speaking of the anatomy of a real man, consisting of flesh, nerves and bones, which is nourished by his chalice, the chalice of his blood, and gains growth from the bread which is his body.

St. Cyprian (d. 258):

> Just as we say "Our Father," because he is the Father of those who know and believe in him, so we call Christ "our bread," because he is the bread of those who are feasted on his body. We ask for this bread every day in order not to be separated from the body of Christ by some serious sin, which would prevent us from communion in the daily Eucharist, the bread of salvation, and from the heavenly bread. He himself has proclaimed: "I am the living bread who has come down from heaven. Whoever eats this bread will live for ever. The bread that I shall give is my flesh for the life of the world" (John 6:51). When he says that anyone who eats his bread lives for ever, he clearly declares that this pertains only to those who eat his body and who have the right to share in the eucharistic communion.

Today, two thousand years after Christ, most of us are so familiar with His command to eat His Body and drink His Blood that we do not realize how extraordinary it was not just to His hearers but in the context of religious history as a whole. Never in recorded history had any leader of a religion made such a demand. No prophet of Israel, no Hindu, Buddhist, Taoist, or Confucian sage had ever asked his followers to consume him. But this is exactly what Jesus commanded, adding that only those who followed this command would receive eternal life. He was Life and to receive this Life, to share in the divine Life, one would have to eat His Flesh. His hearers knew what He was saying and that is why even many of His disciples left Him. "Hard saying" though it was, the first Christians felt compelled to take Jesus at His word. Second-century writers like Tertullian and Minucius Felix noted that cannibalism was one of the primary charges made against Christians. So important was this command of Christ that it is specifically recorded in every Gospel and repeated by the greatest of the missionaries, St. Paul, who said that He personally "received" it "from the Lord." It is this great revelation that the Bible Code speaks about. Before considering the revelation in more detail we will first consider the biblical texts that constitute the Bible Code.

In the course of time Cain brought an offering to the Lord from the fruit of the soil, while Abel, for his part, brought one of the best firstlings of his flock. The Lord looked with favor on Abel and his offering, but on Cain and his offering he did not. (Gen. 4:3–5)

The Eighth-Century Eucharistic Miracle of Lanciano, Italy

(Courtesy of Dr. Bryan Thatcher of the Eucharistic Apostles of Divine Mercy, Florida, and the Franciscan priests of the Santuario del Miracolo Eucaristico in Lanciano, Italy.)

The Eucharistic Miracle of Siena, Italy - 1730

(Courtesy of Dr. Bryan Thatcher of the Eucharistic Apostles of Divine Mercy, Florida.)

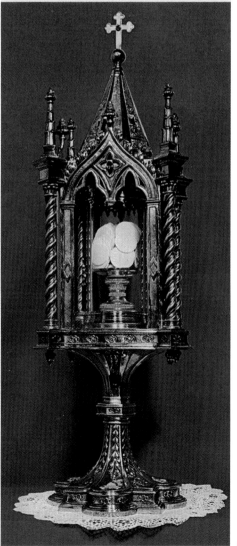

The Eucharistic Miracle of Orvieto, Italy

(Courtesy of Dr. Bryan Thatcher of the Eucharistic Apostles of Divine Mercy, Florida.)

The Thirteenth-Century Eucharistic Miracle of Santarem, Portugal

(Courtesy of Dr. Bryan Thatcher of the Eucharistic Apostles of Divine Mercy, Florida.)

The Eucharistic Miracle of Daroca, Spain - 1239

(Courtesy of Dr. Bryan Thatcher of the Eucharistic Apostles of Divine Mercy, Florida.)

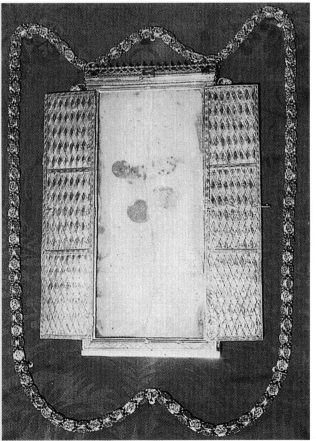

The Infant Jesus of Prague

(Courtesy of The National Shrine of the Infant Jesus of Prague Shrine, in Prague, Oklahoma.)

The Face of Jesus as seen
on Veronica's veil

*(Courtesy of the Discalced Carmelite
sisters of Dallas, Texas.)*

The Divine Mercy - artist unknown

*(Courtesy of Dr. Bryan Thatcher
of the Eucharistic Apostles of Divine
Mercy, Florida.)*

The Appearance of the Sacred Heart of Jesus in 1675
to St. Margaret Mary. Painting by Filippo Costaggini, 1887.

*(Courtesy of Msgr. George W. Rost, Rector, The Basilica of the Sacred
Heart of Jesus, Hanover, Pennsylvania.)*

The Holy Face of Jesus (retouched from the Holy Shroud)

(Courtesy of the Sylvestrine-Benedictine Monks of the Monastery of the Holy Face of Jesus, Clifton, New Jersey.)

The Eucharistic Miracle of Cascia, Italy - 1330

(Courtesy of Dr. Bryan Thatcher of the Eucharistic Apostles of Divine Mercy, Florida.)

The Theme of Sacrifice through the Bible
Sketch—Copyright © by Brian P. Hanlon 2000 (Used with permission.)

From top right: 1. The breaking of the bread at Emmaus (Luke 24:13-31);
2. Noah's holocaust of thanksgiving (Genesis 8:20-21); 3. The sacred bread (Leviticus 24:5-9);
4. The Passover ritual (Exodus 12); 5. The patience of Job (Job);
6. Abraham offers up Isaac (Genesis 22:2; 9-13); 7. The sacrifice of Abel (Genesis 4:4)

Middle background: The Last Supper (Matthew 17:22-23); *upper middle:* The Crucifixion;
lower middle: The Pietá

Then Noah built an altar to the Lord, and choosing from every clean animal and every clean bird, he offered holocausts on the altar. When the Lord smelled the sweet odor, he said to himself: "Never again will I doom the earth because of man." (Gen. 8:20–21)

Melchizedek, king of Salem, brought out bread and wine, and being a priest of God Most High, he blessed Abram with these words: "Blessed be Abram by God Most High, the creator of heaven and earth; and blessed be God Most High, who delivered your foes into your hand." Then Abram gave him a tenth of everything. (Gen. 14:18–20)

Then God said: "Take your son Isaac, your only one, whom you love, and go to the land of Moriah. There you shall offer him up as a holocaust on a height that I will point out to you...." Abraham built an altar there and arranged the wood on it. Next he tied up his son Isaac, and put him on top of the wood on the altar. Then he reached out and took a knife to slaughter his son. But the Lord's messenger called to him from heaven, ..."Do not lay your hand on the boy," said the messenger. "Do not do the least thing to him. I know now how devoted you are to God, since you did not withhold from me your own beloved son." As Abraham looked about, he spied a ram caught by its horns in the thicket. So he went and took the ram and offered it up as a holocaust in place of his son. (Gen. 22:2, 9–13)

The Lord said to Moses and Aaron in the land of Egypt, "The lamb must be a year-old male and without blemish....It shall be slaughtered during the evening twilight. They shall take some of its blood and apply it to the two doorposts and the lintel of every house in which they partake of the lamb. That same night they shall eat its roasted flesh with unleavened bread and bitter herbs....It is the Passover of the Lord. For on this same night I will go through Egypt, striking down every first-born of the land....But the blood will mark the houses on where you are. Seeing the blood, I will pass over you; thus, when I strike the land of Egypt, no destructive blow will come upon you. This day shall be a memorial feast for you, which all your generations shall celebrate with pilgrimage to the Lord, as a perpetual institution....You may not take its flesh outside the house. You shall not break any of its bones." (Exod. 12:1, 5–8, 11–14, 46)

In the morning a dew lay all about the camp, and when the dew evaporated, there on the surface of the desert were fine flakes like hoarfrost on the ground. On seeing it, the Israelites asked one another, "What is this?" for they did not know what it was. But Moses told them, "This is the bread which the Lord has given you to eat...." The Israelites called this food manna. It was like coriander seed, but white, and it tasted like wafers made with honey. (Exod. 16:13–15, 31)

Then, having sent certain young men of the Israelites to offer holocausts and sacrifice young bulls as peace offerings to the Lord, Moses took half of the blood and put it in large bowls; the other half he splashed on the altar. Taking the book of the covenant, he read it aloud to the people, who answered, "All that the Lord has said, we will heed and do." Then he took the blood and sprinkled it on the people, saying, 'This is the blood of the covenant which the Lord has made with you in accordance with all these words of his." (Exod. 24:5-8)

"They shall make sanctuary for me, that I may dwell in their midst. This Dwelling and all its furnishings you shall make exactly according to the pattern that I will now show you. You shall make an ark of acacia wood...." (Exod. 25:8-10)

Then the cloud covered the meeting tent, and the glory of the Lord filled the Dwelling. Moses could not enter the meeting tent, because the cloud settled down upon it and the glory of the Lord filled the Dwelling. (Exod. 40:34-35)

"You shall take fine flour and bake it into twelve cakes, using two tenths of an ephah of flour for each cake. These you shall place in two piles, six in each pile, on the pure gold table before the Lord. On each pile put some pure frankincense, which shall serve as an oblation to the Lord, a token offering for the bread. Regularly on each Sabbath day this bread shall be set out afresh before the Lord, offered on the part of the Israelites by an everlasting agreement. It shall belong to Aaron and his sons, who must eat it in a sacred place, since, as something most sacred among the various oblations to the Lord it is his by perpetual light." (Lev. 24:5-9)

The Philistines, having captured the ark of God, transferred it from Ebenezer to Ashdod.... Now the Lord dealt severely with the people of Ashdod. He ravaged and afflicted the city and its vicinity with hemorrhoids; he brought upon the city a great and deadly plague of mice that swarmed in their ships and overran their fields.... The ark of God was next sent to Ekron; but as it entered that city, the people there cried out, "Why have they brought the ark of the God of Israel here to kill us and our kindred?" (1 Sam. 5:1, 6, 10)

The descendants of Jeconiah did not join in the celebration with the inhabitants of Beth-shemesh when they greeted the ark of the Lord, and seventy of them were struck down. (1 Sam. 6:19)

"Give me five loaves, or whatever you can find." But the priest replied to David, "I have no ordinary bread on hand, only holy bread; if the men have abstained from women, you may eat some of that." David answered the priest: "We have indeed been segregated from women as on previous occasions. Whenever I go on a journey, all the young men are consecrated — even for a secular journey...." So the priest gave him holy bread. (1 Sam. 21:4-7)

When they came to the threshing floor of Nodan, Uzzah reached out his hand to the ark of God and steadied it, for the oxen were making it tip. But the Lord was angry with Uzzah; God struck him on that spot, and he died there before God. (2 Sam. 6:6-7)

The ark of the Lord remained in the house of Obededom the Gittite for three months, and the Lord blessed Obededom and all that belonged to him. (2 Sam. 6:11)

That night the Lord spoke to Nathan and said: "Go, tell my servant David, 'Thus says the Lord: Should you build me a house to dwell in? I have not dwelt in a house from the day on which I led the Israelites out of Egypt to the present, but I have been going about in a tent under cloth. In all my wanderings everywhere among the Israelites, did I ever utter a word to any one of the judges whom I charged to tend my people Israel, to ask: Why have you not built me a house of cedar?'" (2 Sam. 7:4–7)

When Solomon awoke from his dream, he went to Jerusalem, stood before the ark of the covenant of the Lord, offered holocausts and peace offerings, and gave a banquet for all his servants. (1 Kings 3:15)

The priest brought the ark of the covenant of the Lord to its place beneath the wings of the cherubim in the sanctuary, the holy of holies of the temple.... When the priests left the holy place, the cloud filled the temple of the Lord so that the priests could no longer minister because of the cloud, since the Lord's glory had filled the temple of the Lord. Then Solomon said, "The Lord intends to dwell in the dark cloud; I have truly built you a princely house, a dwelling where you may abide forever.... Can it indeed be that God dwells among men on earth? If the heavens and the highest heavens cannot contain you, how much less this temple which I have built! Look kindly on the prayer and petition of your servant, O Lord...." The king and all Israel with him offered sacrifices before the Lord. (1 Kings 8:6, 10–13, 27–28, 62)

After Solomon finished building the temple of the Lord... the Lord appeared to him a second time, as he had appeared to him in Gibeon. The Lord said to him: "I have heard the prayer of petition which you offered in my presence. I have consecrated this temple which you have built. I confer my name upon it forever, and my eyes and my heart shall be there always." (1 Kings 9:1–3)

He was pierced for our offenses, crushed for our sins. Upon him was the chastisement that makes us whole, by his stripes we were healed.... Like a lamb led to the slaughter or a sheep before the shearers, he was silent and opened not his mouth. (Isa. 53:5, 7)

The days are coming, says the Lord, when I will make a new covenant with the house of Israel and the house of Judah. It will not be like the covenant I made with their fathers the day I took them by the hand to lead them forth from the land of Egypt; for they broke my covenant and I had to show myself their master. (Jer. 34:31–32)

His sons used to take turns giving feasts.... And when each feast had run its course, Job would send for them and sanctify them, rising early and offering holocausts for every one of them. For Job said, "It may be that my sons have sinned and blasphemed God in their hearts." This Job did habitually. (Job 1:4–5)

The Lord said to Eliphaz the Temanite,... "Now, therefore, take seven bullocks and seven rams, and go to my servant Job, and offer up a holocaust for yourselves;

and let my servant Job pray for you; for his prayer I will accept, not to punish you severely." (Job 42:7–8)

From the rising of the sun, even to its setting, my name is great among the nations; And everywhere they bring sacrifice to my name, and a pure offering; for great is my name among the nations, says the Lord of hosts. (Mal. 1:11)

"Give us today our daily bread." (Matt. 6:11)

As they were gathering in Galilee, Jesus said to them, "The Son of Man is to be handed over to men, and they will kill him, and he will be raised on the third day." And they were overwhelmed with grief. (Matt. 17:22–23)

The disciples then did as Jesus had ordered, and prepared the Passover.... While they were eating, Jesus took the bread, said the blessing, broke it, and giving it to his disciples said, "Take and eat; this is my body." Then he took a cup, gave thanks, and gave it to them, saying, "Drink from it, all of you, for this is my blood of the covenant, which will be shed on behalf of many for the forgiveness of sins." (Matt. 26:17, 26–28)

He advanced a little and fell prostrate in prayer saying, "My Father, if it is possible, let this cup pass from me; yet, not as I will, but as you will." (Matt. 26:39)

While they were eating, he took bread, said the blessing, broke it, and gave it to them, and said, "Take it, this is my body." Then he took a cup, gave thanks, and gave it to them, and they all drank from it. He said to them, "This is my blood of the covenant, which will be shed for many." (Mark 14:22–24)

He said to them, "I have eagerly desired to eat this Passover with you before I suffer, for I tell you, I shall not eat it [again] until there is fulfillment in the kingdom of God." Then he took a cup, gave thanks and said, "Take this and share it among yourselves; for I tell you [that] from this time on I shall not drink of the fruit of the vine until the kingdom of God comes." Then he took the bread, said the blessing, broke it, and gave it to them, saying, "This is my body, which will be given for you; do this in memory of me." And likewise the cup after they had eaten, saying, "This cup is the new covenant in my blood, which will be shed for you." (Luke 22:15–20)

And it happened that, while he was with them at table, he took bread, said the blessing, broke it, and gave it to them. With that their eyes were opened and they recognized him, but he vanished from their sight. (Luke 24:30–31)

In the beginning was the Word, and the Word was with God, and the Word was God.... And the Word became flesh and made his dwelling among us. (John 1:1, 14)

As he watched Jesus walk by, he said, "Behold, the Lamb of God." (John 1:36)

For God so loved the world that he gave his only Son, so that everyone who believes in him might not perish but might have eternal life. For God did not send his Son into the world to condemn the world, but that the world might be saved through him. (John 3:16–17)

The Jewish feast of Passover was near.... Jesus answered and said to them, "...I am the bread of life. Your ancestors ate the manna in the desert, but they died; this is the bread that comes down from heaven so that one may eat it and not die. I am the living bread that came down from heaven; whoever eats this bread will live forever; and the bread that I will give is my flesh for the life of the world." The Jews quarreled among themselves, saying: "How can this man give us [his] flesh to eat?" Jesus said to them, "Amen, amen, I say to you, unless you eat the flesh of the Son of Man and drink his blood, you do not have life within you. Whoever eats my flesh and drinks my blood has eternal life, and I will raise him on the last day. For my flesh is true food, and my blood is true drink. Whoever eats my flesh and drinks my blood remains in me and I in him. Just as the living Father sent me and I have life of the Father, so also the one who feeds on me will have life because of me. This is the bread that came down from heaven. Unlike your ancestors who ate and still died, whoever eats this bread will live forever." (John 6:4, 43, 48–58)

Jesus then said to the Twelve, "Do you also want to leave?" Simon Peter answered him, "Master, to whom shall we go? You have the words of eternal life." (John 6:67–68)

"I come so that they might have life and have it more abundantly." (John 10:10)

"I am the way and the truth and the life. No one comes to the Father except through me." (John 14:6)

They devoted themselves to the teaching of the apostles and to the communal life, to the breaking of the bread and to the prayers. (Acts 2:42)

This was the scripture passage he was reading: "Like a sheep he was led to the slaughter, and as a lamb before its shearer is silent, so he opened not his mouth...." Then the eunuch said to Philip in reply, "I beg you, about whom is the prophet saying this? About himself, or about someone else?" Then Philip opened his mouth and, beginning with this scripture passage, he proclaimed Jesus to him. (Acts 8:32, 34–35)

It is Christ Jesus who died, rather, was raised, who also is at the right hand of God, who indeed intercedes for us. (Rom. 8:34)

Clear out the old yeast, so that you may become a fresh batch of dough, inasmuch as you are unleavened. For our paschal lamb, Christ, has been sacrificed. Therefore let us celebrate the feast.... (1 Cor. 5:7)

The cup of blessing that we bless, is it not a participation in the blood of Christ? The bread that we break, is it not a participation in the body of Christ? (1 Cor. 10:16)

For I received from the Lord what I also handed on to you, that the Lord Jesus, on the night he was handed over, took bread, and after he had given thanks, broke it and said, "This is my body that is for you. Do this in remembrance of me." In the same way also the cup, after supper, saying, "This cup is the new covenant in my blood. Do this, as often as you drink it, in remembrance of me." For as often as you eat this bread and drink the cup, you proclaim the death of the Lord until he comes. Therefore whoever eats the bread or drinks the cup of the Lord unworthily will have to answer for the body and blood of the Lord. A person should examine himself, and so eat the bread and drink the cup. For anyone who eats and drinks without discerning the body, eats and drinks judgment on himself. That is why many among you are ill and infirm, and a considerable number are dying. (1 Cor. 11:23–30)

Therefore, he is always able to save those who approach God through him, since he lives forever to make intercession for them. (Heb. 7:25)

We have such a high priest, who has taken his seat at the right hand of the throne of the Majesty in heaven, a minister of the sanctuary and of the true tabernacle that the Lord, not man, set up. Now every high priest is appointed to offer gifts and sacrifices; thus the necessity for this one also to have something to offer. (Heb. 8:1–3)

When he speaks of a "new" covenant, he declares the first one obsolete. (Heb. 8:13)

Now [even] the first covenant had regulations for worship and an earthly sanctuary. For a tabernacle was constructed, the outer one, in which were the lampstand, the table, and the bread of offering; this is called the Holy Place. Behind the second veil was the tabernacle called the Holy of Holies, in which were the gold altar of incense and the ark of the covenant entirely covered with gold. In it were the gold jar containing the manna, the staff of Aaron that had sprouted, and the tablets of the covenant. (Heb. 9:1–4)

According to the law almost everything is purified by blood, and without the shedding of blood there is no forgiveness. Therefore, it was necessary for the copies of the heavenly things to be purified by these rites, but the heavenly things themselves by better sacrifices than these. For Christ did not enter into a sanctuary made by hands, a copy of the true one, but heaven itself, that he might now appear before God on our behalf. (Heb. 9:22–24)

Through these, he has bestowed on us the precious and very great promises, so that through them you may come to share in the divine nature. (2 Pet. 1:4)

Every spirit that acknowledges Jesus Christ come in the flesh belongs to God, and every spirit that does not acknowledge Jesus does not belong to God. (1 John 4:2–3)

Then I saw standing in the midst of the throne and the four living creatures and the elders, a Lamb that seemed to have been slain. (Rev. 5:6)

Then God's temple in heaven was opened, and the ark of his covenant could be seen in the temple. There were flashes of lightning, rumblings, and peals of thunder, an earthquake, and a violent hailstorm. (Rev. 11:19)

Then the angel said to me, "Write this: Blessed are those who have been called to the wedding feast of the Lamb." (Rev. 19:9)

Certain common and consistent themes are obvious in the scriptural passages cited above:

1. Sacrifice
2. The Passover
3. The Lamb
4. The Covenant
5. The Holy of Holies
6. Bread from Heaven
7. The Breaking of Bread
8. The Body and Blood of Christ
9. The Continuing Heavenly Intercession of Christ
10. The Wedding Feast

But how are we to understand the true import of these themes and their application in the scheme of things? St. Paul, one of the earliest New Testament witnesses, says two things that are of interest here. Somehow "the bread that we break" is "a participation in the body of Christ" (1 Cor. 10:16). Moreover, "anyone who eats and drinks without discerning the body, eats and drinks judgment on himself. That is why many among you are ill and infirm, and a considerable number are dying" (1 Cor. 11:30). These passages indicate that "the breaking of the bread," which had become a fundamental part of Christian life (Acts 2:42), was not simply a symbolic meal or a memorial service. It had tangible effects and unworthy participation was an invitation to sickness, even to death. And this was a teaching that St. Paul "received from the Lord."

There is also an obvious pattern of parallels. Melchizedek, King of Salem (Jerusalem), offers a sacrifice of bread and wine at the commencement of the Old Covenant. Likewise Jesus Christ, King of Jerusalem, Who is "declared by God high priest according to the order of Melchizedek" (Heb. 5:10), offers a sacrifice of bread and wine to introduce a New and Everlasting Covenant. Among the multitude of other parallels, those shown in the table on p. 22 above are particularly significant here.

This overview does not by any means demonstrate or explain the meaning and significance of these biblical accounts. One of the great follies of our time is the idea that a mere reading of a scriptural passage is enough to either understand what it denotes or prove a doctrine. This idea is demonstrably false because (1) every one of these passages can be considered and interpreted in terms of multiple, mutually incompatible perspectives and frameworks and (2) fundamental

Christian doctrines did not as a matter of historical fact simply emerge overnight from a devout or learned reading of Scripture. The most fundamental of Christian doctrines — who was Jesus? — was comprehensively clarified and explained only in the seventh century. It was the Sixth Council of Constantinople (680–81 A.D.) that answered one final question: did Jesus have one will or two? The answer to this question is not obvious from reading Scripture, but the Council, in the face of opposition, came to the conclusion on theological grounds that Jesus had both a divine and a human will. If it took nearly seven centuries, under the guidance of the Holy Spirit, to reach this conclusion, we must be wary of any "fast food" approach to biblical exegesis.

How then are we to crack the Bible Code or at least understand the true sense of biblical texts? Historically speaking, the answer is as plain as day. What we call Christian doctrine, indeed what we call Christianity, is the interpretation and explanation of both individual scriptural passages and of Scripture as a whole laid down in three forums: the writings of the Fathers, the decrees of the great Councils, and the texts of the ancient liturgies. To know what the first Christians believed we have simply to examine what they preached and practiced. Once we get a good idea of the content of their beliefs, we are faced with a choice. Either their understanding of Christian doctrine was true to the teaching of Christ or it was not. If it was not true to His teaching, we probably have no chance of ever deciphering what He really intended to teach. Why should the exegesis of someone who lives two thousand years after Christ be considered more reliable or accurate than the exegesis of someone who lived within a generation of Christ's Apostles? The choice comes down to this: either we rely on the hard facts currently available, namely, the texts of the Fathers, Councils, and liturgies or we retreat to the speculation of skeptics and scholars. But no matter how profound or plausible, speculation as such cannot support a single doctrine. Thus a Christianity without Fathers, Councils, and liturgies is a Christianity without doctrine. And, as noted above, if we wish to crack the Bible Code, we have to rely on those for whom the Code was a language: the contemporaries and disciples of the Apostles and the liturgies and letters they have bestowed on posterity.

As we will see in the next chapter, the Eucharist played a central role in the ancient liturgies and Councils and the writings of the Fathers. Eucharistic doctrine and worship was both implicitly and explicitly proclaimed in all three forums. A full-blooded, fully fleshed-out Christianity inevitably centered on the Flesh and Blood of Christ. The Eucharistic story of Scripture may be summarized as follows:

From the first days of the human race, God had implanted in the human race a desire to make sacrifices to Him in praise and thanksgiving but also for expiation, atonement, and propitiation for sin. The blood of innocence was offered as propitiation for guilt to appease God's wrath. The Old Testament shows us the sacrifices that pleased God: the sacrifices of Abel and Noah, of Melchizedek and Abraham, of Moses, David, Solomon, and Job. Embedded in this theme of sacrifice there were other themes: the idea of the sacrifice of one's first-born son, the notion that the blood of the sacrificed victim would be used to seal a covenant with God and that this blood offered protection from death, the requirement of offering a male lamb without blemish and of consuming its flesh to complete the celebration, the comparison of the Messiah Who atones by His Death for the sin of His People with a lamb led to its slaughter, the prediction that a "pure" sacrifice would one day be offered without ceasing in every corner of the world. In parallel with the theme of sacrifice there was a persistent awareness that God wanted to dwell with His People in a tangible manner: thus the Ark of the Covenant became the vehicle of the divine Presence. While the Holy of Holies offered protection to the People of God, It would not tolerate defilement and ultimately the sins of the Israelites led to the loss of the Ark.

The themes traced out by the Old Testament were fulfilled and consummated in the New. Jesus is identified as the Messiah, the Lamb of God, Whose sacrifice on the cross will save His People from their sins. While the Sacrifice on Calvary was a once-for-all event (Hebrews), the Lamb Who was sacrificed continues in Heaven (Hebrews) to apply the effects of the Sacrifice to those who need it. Calvary does not guarantee Heaven: it only makes it possible. The continual application of the graces won at Calvary through the heavenly Manna aids us on the journey to the Promised Land through the desert of trial and temptation. After preparing the minds of His disciples with the miracles of the multiplication of loaves and the transformation of water into wine, Jesus instructs them to continually celebrate His salvific death through a new and enduring event: the transformation of bread into His Body and wine into His Blood. He is the Paschal Lamb and to complete the Paschal celebration we must eat His Flesh. Without eating His Flesh we cannot receive His Life. The shedding of blood was so important in the Old Testament sacrifices because blood was symbolic of the life of the animal, and its life had to be offered to achieve atonement. In the New Testament sacrifice, the Blood of the Paschal Lamb had to be offered to seal the New Covenant and His Flesh and Blood had to be consumed to receive His Life. The breaking of bread became the central act of worship of the Apostles because it was expressly commanded by Christ and because, as St. Paul said, it was a mystical participation in the Body and Blood of Christ and a proclamation of His death. The disciples at Emmaus ceased to see their Lord in His glorified Body at the breaking of bread because He was now present to them under the appearance of bread.

With this overview, we will consider a few common questions about the Eucharistic teachings of the New Testament:

1. Was Jesus using symbolic language at the Last Supper when He spoke of the bread and wine as His Body and Blood?

2. Was Jesus using symbolic language in John 6 when He spoke of the need to eat His Flesh to receive eternal life?

3. Are there any other indications in Scripture that doctrines of the Eucharist and the Mass are warranted?

Each of these issues and many others relating to the biblical and historical background of the Eucharist and the Mass are comprehensively and incisively treated in *Not by Bread Alone,* a recent study by Robert Sungenis. Here our intent is simply to provide an introduction to a few of the scriptural passages relevant to Eucharistic doctrine.

The Last Supper

The so-called Institution Narratives, the passages in Matthew, Mark, and Luke and in St. Paul's Epistle to the Corinthians, in which Jesus institutes the Eucharist at the "Last Supper," are central to Eucharistic doctrine and practice. Jesus' words, "This is my body. . . . This is my blood," lie at the core of every Eucharistic liturgy. Like the Word that brought all things into being (John 1:3), these Words are words of creation and transformation that actually bring about what they pronounce. Biblical scholars hold that the Institution formulas used in the various narratives were actually in use in the liturgies of the early Church. About these texts, we can say the following. When Jesus said, "Take and eat; this is my body," He meant His statement to be taken either symbolically or literally. A study of the earliest liturgies and the early Fathers will show that the first Christians certainly understood Him literally. That Jesus intended to be taken literally seems certain in view of the following:

1. The Synoptic Gospels and St. Paul testify unanimously to the same basic format of institution.

2. This was a grave, even tragic, occasion and it seems unlikely that Jesus would have allowed any scope for misunderstanding Him. Certainly, He made no attempt to explain His words in terms of symbolism or a parable.

3. He tied His Words of Institution to the Covenant. Significantly, the only time that Jesus uses the word "covenant" is on this momentous occasion. The covenants of Israel were sealed with the blood of the sacrificial victim. Here Jesus was speaking of a New Covenant and the Blood that would seal it was to be His Own (and this Blood is miraculously provided, an idea nowhere found in the Old Testament). We are also commanded to continue the covenantal offering of His Body and Blood ("Do this") through which the new covenant is renewed and re-presented. And whereas the Paschal Meal of the Old Covenant was eaten in memory of Yahweh, the New Paschal Meal is centered on Jesus ("Do this in remembrance of me."). Moreover, the New Covenant could not be in any sense inferior to the Old. Central to the Old Covenant was the localized Presence of Yahweh with His People in the Holy of Holies. Likewise, the New Covenant is built around the permanent physical Presence of Jesus with His People in His Body and Blood — contrast "I am with you always, until the end of the age" (Matt. 28:20) with "I will be with you" (Exod. 3:12).

4. The meaning of the Crucifixion — the final triumph of the Savior — is given in these narratives: His Blood is shed "on behalf of many for the forgiveness of sins."

5. When the Institution narratives are read in conjunction with John 6 — see below — there is no further room for doubt about whether or not the Words of Institution are to be taken literally, as they always have been.

In the narrative in Luke, Jesus says, "Do this in memory of me." The "this" that we are supposed to do is the offering of His Body. The word used here for "in memory" is *anamnesis,* one out of nine possible words in Greek with the same meaning. This particular word is used because it is associated with sacrifice and as used here, writes Robert Sungenis, "*anamnesis* does not refer merely to remembering a past event or a past sacrifice; rather it refers to remembrance brought about by the act of sacrifice."[1] The Anglican Eric Mascall gives a similar interpretation of *anamnesis:*

> If *anamnesis* means not a psychological act of remembering but a genuine recalling into the present of an act which is past as an event of history but is eternalised in the heavenly places, the act when recalled will be recalled before God and man alike, and for the matter of that before the angels and the devils as well. It is not a recalling before this or that spectator; it is simply a *recalling,* a re-presentation, a sacramental instantiation, of the tremendous act and event itself.[2]

Similarly the Reformed theologian J. Leenhardt writes that

> remembrance [*anamnesis*] was not for him [St. Paul] mental recollection, an evocative thought. Remembrance was for him the restoration of a past situation which has for the moment disappeared. To remember is to make present and actual.... What happens [in the Lord's Supper] is what took place during the ministry; it is what is going to happen on the Cross; it is the same gift under different forms, it is the same sacrifice which accomplishes the same service, which realizes the same ministry.[3]

John 6

We will begin by saying that there are clearly instances in this chapter where Jesus intends to speak symbolically. Just as clearly there are instances here where He is speaking literally. Thus, when He says, "whoever believes in me will never thirst," He is speaking symbolically, and when He says, "whoever eats my flesh and drinks my blood has eternal life," He is speaking literally.

How do we know when He is speaking symbolically and when He is speaking literally? For one thing, we know that in every instance in the New Testament when Jesus' teaching provoked the Jews to anger it was for proclaiming a literal truth. His parables and metaphorical language simply as stated did not rouse their wrath. (It might be said that His teaching about rebuilding the temple in three days is an exception, but "temple" was often used to refer to the body in the New Testament and Jesus was here referring to His Body.) When Jesus said, "Before Abraham was I AM," there was no question that He meant His statement literally — and hence the Jews sought to kill Him.

In John 6, Jesus is teaching two great truths, the first about Who He was and the second about the Eucharist. First, He says that He is the Bread of Life Who has come from Heaven and that anyone who believes in Him will not hunger or thirst and will have eternal life. This claim angers the Jews who know Him as the son of Joseph. Second, He says that the bread that He gives is His Flesh "for the life of the world" and that only those who eat His Flesh and drink His Blood will have life. This second teaching was too much for even many of His disciples who now left Him ("This saying is hard; who can accept it?"). The Apostles, however, accepted this mysterious teaching, although they could not comprehend it, because they had already accepted Him as "the Holy One of God."

We know that Jesus' command that we eat His Flesh and drink His Blood is to be taken literally for the following reasons:

1. There is not a single instance of a symbolic command to eat the Flesh and drink the Blood of Christ or God in either Testament.

2. If Jesus intended to speak symbolically, He could simply have said this was the case to the scandalized Jews. Instead He proceeded to elaborate on this command, thus further enraging them and running the risk even of losing His Apostles. In other instances, when He was using symbolic language, He explained the true meaning of what He said to His disciples.

3. In 6:63 Jesus says, "It is the spirit that gives life, while the flesh is of no avail. The words I have spoken to you are spirit and life." It is obvious here that the flesh He is referring to is not His Flesh — if He did the prior teaching that the Word became flesh for our salvation would be meaningless. The "flesh" referred to here is the carnal way in which unbelievers look at spiritual things, including the carnal refusal to accept Christ's command to eat His Flesh and drink His Blood.

4. The Greek word for "eat" in the verses where Christ asks us to eat His Flesh is translated "chew" or "gnaw" and is quite obviously physical in meaning; a symbolic interpretation would be a stretch.

5. Liberal Protestant exegetes like Rudolf Bultmann admitted that John 6:54–58 is to be taken literally: "It is a matter of real eating and not simply of some sort of spiritual participation."[4] (Bultmann's way around this "hard saying" was to regard it as a later addition.) In addition to Bultmann, Robert Sungenis draws our attention to such other prominent Protestant exegetes as Alastair Heron and C. K. Barrett, who argued for a Eucharistic interpretation of John 6.[5]

6. St. Paul and the authors of the other Gospels also took Christ's teaching quite literally because they record His command to eat His Body and drink His Blood without giving any indication that this command is to be taken symbolically.

7. The first Christians were accused of being cannibals precisely because their beliefs and practices called for them to eat the Flesh and drink the Blood

of the Lord. The literal interpretation of John 6 is found also in the texts of the ancient Fathers, Councils, and liturgies.

8. If Jesus intended John 6:53 to be interpreted symbolically, it might be said that "eating flesh" is an unlikely candidate for symbolism. If in this verse He actually meant us to receive Him into our hearts or to enter into a personal relationship, other metaphors would have been more appropriate. The Cambridge philosopher Elizabeth Anscombe writes, "For why would anyone want to eat someone's flesh or drink his blood? 'I will drink your blood' might be a vow made against an enemy. Indeed in Old Testament language eating a man's flesh and drinking his blood is an idea expressive of just such deadly enmity."[6]

9. We might add here that a denial of the reality of Christ's flesh in the Eucharist is implicitly a denial of Christ coming in the flesh from God since both truths were taught forcefully in the same discourse. Hence the author of the Gospel in which this discourse appears writes in his first epistle, "Every spirit that acknowledges Jesus Christ come in the flesh belongs to God, and every spirit that does not acknowledge Jesus does not belong to God" (1 John 4:2–3.)

In a profound commentary on John 6, Edward Holloway writes,

There are other grounds too, on which any meaning less than realist must be rejected for the words of Christ.... It is possible perhaps for Western man to consider the words of Christ as a beautiful parable, illustrative of the divine action, even more perfectly fulfilled in the Incarnation, of God the Life-giver upon the nature of man. It is totally impossible for the semitic mind, and if the words of Jesus Christ were a parable of any sort, expressed as they were, left unrepentantly literal as they were, they could only be blasphemous and unclean, the very epitome of gaucherie, in no way flattering to the divine wisdom of him for whom Christianity claims Godhead enfleshed. Because the Jew was forbidden either to eat meat with the blood, or to drink of blood by itself, such was for him an abomination, and to this day the devout Jew tries to observe the precept and to obtain meat that is "kosher." This most ancient precept, repeated several times in the Old Law, goes back for the Hebrew tradition as far as the days of Noah; it signified that God alone was Lord of life and death, "for the life is in the blood, and I have given you it that with it you may make atonement upon the altar for your souls...," but also with significance it seems that the principle of the life belongs to the sovereignty of God, and for man to assume it was a form of blasphemy. Looked at across the ages as a prophecy in type of the expiation of Christ upon the Cross, it has also a unique significance, as the author of the epistle to the Hebrews is not slow to appreciate. But there it was, and because of this strict precept, the violation of which under the law of Leviticus at least carried sentence of both excommunication and death, such a figure of speech, no matter how sacred its reference, could not be beautiful or meaningful for the Jew at all. Why then did Christ use it at all? Because he meant it, and it was no figure. Quite different will be the case when indeed "the Life is in the blood" and the Life which is in the blood is the Divinity itself, the principle of the beginning, of the development, and of the fulfillment of men.[7]

Other Scriptural Witnesses

Although many volumes (for instance, Eugene LaVerdiere's *The Eucharist in the New Testament and the Early Church*) have been written about various episodes and passages in the New Testament that are Eucharistic in origin and import, we will consider two areas that are rarely considered for their Eucharistic message. The first is the Lord's Prayer and the second is the Book of Revelation.

The Relation of the Lord's Prayer to the Lord's Supper

It has been plausibly argued that the Lord's Prayer is actually a Eucharistic prayer. Here we will compare the Lord's Prayer to the four Eucharistic Prayers used most commonly in the Latin liturgy (the first and the second prayers being the most ancient).

Like every Eucharistic Prayer, the Lord's Prayer is addressed to the "Father in Heaven." "The first Eucharistic Prayer begins, "We come to you, Father."

We then say, "Hallowed be your name." The counterpart is the opening of the Second Eucharistic Prayer, "Lord you are holy indeed, the fountain of all holiness."

Then "Your kingdom come." Here Eucharistic Prayer I turns to the Kingdom of God on earth and in Purgatory and Heaven: "We offer them for your holy catholic Church...for all who hold and teach the catholic faith that comes to us from the apostles." "Remember, Lord, those who have died and have gone before us marked with the sign of faith." "Lord, remember all of us gathered here before you....In union with the whole Church we honor Mary...the apostles and martyrs." It is remarkable too that in the accounts of the Lord's Supper in the Synoptic Gospels Jesus says that He will not again eat of the Passover or drink of the fruit of the vine "until the kingdom of God comes." With His death on the Cross, the kingdom of God has come—and hence Jesus in the person of His priest can eat of the Passover and drink of the fruit of the vine.

The next verse goes to the heart of the Sacrifice of the Mass: "Your will be done, on earth as in heaven." How is the Father's will being done in Heaven? In Heaven, Christ appears "before God on our behalf" and "lives forever to make intercession" for us "at the right hand of God." How is this will done on earth? "From age to age you gather a people to yourself, so that from east to west a perfect offering may be made to the glory of your name" (Eucharistic Prayer III) and "We come to you...through Jesus Christ your Son. Through him we ask you to accept and bless these gifts we offer you in sacrifice" (Eucharistic Prayer I). The Mass is the earthly incarnation of the Heavenly intercession of Christ: it is offered "through him, with him, in him" to the Father.

"Give us today our daily bread" is just as significant because the expression "our daily bread" is unique in the New Testament and there is good reason to believe that it refers specifically to the "Eucharistic bread." The word used for "daily bread" is the Greek word *epiousios,* a word that is not found in any other work of Greek literature. It appears only in the texts for the Lord's Prayer in Matthew and Luke and the Didache. According to Eugene La Verdiere there is no real English translation of this word, and "daily" is simply an approximation. He notes that the first Christians had to create a new word in order to fully describe the new reality and new experience that is the Eucharist, the Bread of Life received in the "breaking of the bread." The most accurate translation he can think of for the text "our daily bread" is "our Eucharistic bread." The "our" in the text refers to the fact that the Lord's Supper was a special event experienced and shared in common by the first Christians.

> The key element in the Greek expression for "our daily bread," *ho artos hemon ho epiousios* is the adjective *epiousios,* usually translated into English as "daily." ... The word *epiousios* was nowhere to be found in ancient Greek literature. ... In the New Testament, the term appears exclusively in the two traditional texts of the Lord's Prayer. ... Why then did the early Christians use such an undefinable and untranslatable word? ... Coining a new word presupposes a new reality, a new experience, or at least a new way of viewing something. Meals in which the risen Lord appeared and was present to the disciples were a new reality with a totally new experience, which could not have been foreseen. Such a new reality called for a new word, hence *epiousios.* ... *Epiousios* is a proper adjective for Eucharist. To know what it means, one must know what it means to celebrate Eucharist.[8]

All of the Eucharistic Prayers, of course, center on "our daily bread": "he took bread in his sacred hands. ... He broke the bread, gave it to his disciples" (Eucharist Prayer I); "On the night he was betrayed, he took bread and gave you thanks and praise. He broke the bread" (Eucharistic Prayer III).

"And forgive us our debts, as we forgive our debtors." All the Eucharistic prayers implore God's mercy and forgiveness: "Though we are sinners, we trust in your mercy and love. Do not consider what we truly deserve, but grant us your forgiveness" (Eucharistic Prayer I).

"And do not subject us to the final test": "Grant us your peace in this life, save us from final damnation" (Eucharistic Prayer I).

"But deliver us from the evil one." The Eucharistic prayers proclaim the Eucharist as the source of strength against evil: "As we receive from this altar the sacred body and blood of your Son, let us be filled with every grace and blessing" (Eucharistic Prayer I). "Grant that we, who are nourished by his body and blood, may be filled with his Holy Spirit, and become one body, one spirit in Christ."

The Book of Revelation

In his recent masterpiece on the Mass, *The Lamb's Supper,* the biblical scholar Scott Hahn argues that the Book of Revelation is a descriptive account of the

Mass (although it can be legitimately interpreted at other levels as well). This liturgical view of Revelation has been held by Church Fathers from the second to the sixth centuries and various Protestant scholars. In Revelation we see Heaven coming down to earth in the Mass, a vision that is continued in the great Eastern liturgies. Among the many parallels that Hahn sees between the Mass and the worship shown in the Book of Revelation, the following are especially relevant:[9]

The Mass	*Book of Revelation*
Sunday worship	1:10
A high priest	1:13
An altar	8:3–4; 11:1; 14:18
Priest (*presbyteroi*)	4:4; 11:15; 14:18
Vestments	1:13; 4:4; 6:11; 7:9; 15:6; 19:13–14
Consecrated celibacy	14:4
Lamp stands, or Menorah	1:12; 2:5
Penitence	ch. 2 and 3
Incense	5:8; 8:3–5
The book or scroll	5:1
The Eucharistic Host	2:17
Chalices	15:7; ch. 16; 21:9
The Sign of the Cross (the *tau*)	7:3; 14:1; 22:44
The Gloria	15:3–4
The Alleluia	19:1, 3, 4, 6
Lift up your hearts	11:12
The "Holy, Holy, Holy"	4:8
The Amen	19:4; 22:21
The "Lamb of God"	5:6 and throughout
The prominence of the Virgin Mary	12:1–6; 13–17
Intercession of angels and saints	5:8; 6:9–10; 8:3–4
Devotion to St. Michael, Archangel	12:7
Antiphonal chant	5:8–11; 5:9–14; 7:10–12; 18:1–8
Reading from Scripture	ch. 2–3; 5; 8:2–11
The priesthood of the faithful	1:6; 20:6
Catholicity, or universality	7:9
Silent contemplation	8:1
The marriage supper of the Lamb	19:9, 17

Once for All

One other question is often asked about the Mass and the Eucharist: Does the continual celebration of the Mass contradict the verses in Hebrews that speak of Jesus' Sacrifice being a once-for-all event? This question is treated in some detail in the chapter "How the Paschal Supper, Calvary, and the Heavenly Intercession Become Present Here and Now in the Holy Mass," but here we can say four things.

1. The command to continually celebrate the Lord's Supper came from the Lord Himself.

2. The Epistles to the Hebrews and to the Romans show Jesus continuing to make intercession for us before the Father. This means that His redemptive

death on the cross and the application of the effects of His death through His intercession in Heaven are two separate actions, the second being one that is carried on until the end of time. "Hebrews 8:1–2," writes Sungenis,

> specifies that "we do have such a high priest who sat down at the right hand of the throne of the Majesty in heaven, and who serves in the sanctuary, the true tabernacle." Christ does more than merely take His seat at the right hand of God; He continually serves as a priest in the Most Holy Place and does the things that priests do, namely, "to offer gifts and sacrifices for sins" (Heb. 5:1). In the same way, Hebrews 7:24 says that Christ has a "permanent priesthood," for His priesthood did not stop when His life on earth was over.... Moreover, we must add that Romans 8:34 states that Christ "is at the right hand of God and is also interceding for us." If his work is completely finished, then there is no reason for Him to continue interceding on our behalf, unless one is willing to say that Christ does such things as a mere figurehead without meaning.[10]

Additionally, notes Sungenis, over half the verses in Hebrews warn of Christians losing their salvation. Although Christ's death is definitive and never-to-be-repeated, it does not ensure salvation for everyone, not even for Christians. The graces won on the Cross have to be applied to every soul particularly through our "participation in the blood of Christ?...[and] in the body of Christ."

3. Christ's death on the Cross and His continual intercession before the Father have to be understood in relation to the doctrine of the Holy Trinity. The Eucharistic celebration reenacts in time the eternal presentation of God the Son to God the Father. If Christ was just a holy man who died on behalf of his people, his sacrifice could not become present to us today. But His eternal self-offering to the Father can be continually mirrored in time precisely because He is the Incarnate Son of God.

4. The famous theologian Max Thurian explained that "once for all" in the Epistle to the Hebrews is not to be interpreted in a past or static sense: "The expression signifies rather the absolute, definitive and perpetual character of the sacrifice of Christ; it does not imply a unique instant with no repercussion (except for repetition) under the diverse modes which recall and actualise it.... [It is equivalent to] for eternity."[11]

Protestant Exegesis

The Eucharistic interpretations of Scripture given here have also been expounded by Protestant and Anglican exegetes and theologians (and, in fact, in his famous Marburg debate with Ulrich Zwingli, Martin Luther staunchly defended the Real Presence, asserting that "God is more powerful than all our ideas, and we must submit to his Word. Prove that Christ's body is not where the Scripture says it is when Christ says 'this is my body....' It is God who commands, 'take, eat, this is my body.'")

In his book *Corpus Christi*, Eric Mascall declared that "it is the words with which our Lord accompanied the distribution of the elements that indicate the change that they have undergone. At the moment of reception they are no longer ordinary bread and wine, but have become the Body and Blood of Christ."[12]

The Swedish Lutheran theologian Gustaf Aulen says in *Eucharist and Sacrifice:* "The real presence of the sacrifice is inseparably connected with the presence of the living Lord. The real presence and the sacrifice belong together. This sacrifice is present because the living Lord is present. But the living Lord cannot be present without actualising the sacrifice."[13]

The Eucharist, a joint document of the Lutheran-Roman Catholic Joint Commission that was published by the Lutheran World Federation in 1980, reached the following conclusion:

> In the sacrament of the Lord's Supper, Jesus Christ, true God and true man, is present wholly and entirely in his body and blood, under the signs of bread and wine. Through the centuries Christians have attempted various formulations to describe this presence. Our confessional documents have in common affirmed that Jesus Christ is "really," "truly" and "substantially" present in this sacrament. This manner of presence "we can scarcely express in words," but we affirm this presence because we believe in the power of God and the promise of Jesus Christ. "This is my body.... This is my blood...." Our traditions have spoken of this presence as "sacramental," "supernatural" and "spiritual." These terms have different connotations in the two traditions, but they have in common a rejection of a spatial or natural mode of presence and a rejection of an understanding of the sacrament as only commemorative or figurative.[14]

Similarly, the Anglican-Roman Catholic International Commission in its September 7, 1971, report concluded that "Communion with Christ in the Eucharist presupposes his true presence, effectually signified by the bread and wine which, in this mystery, become his body and blood.... The elements are not mere signs; Christ's body and blood become really present and are really given."[15]

Chapter 9

Heaven Here and Now: The Teaching of the Fathers, Councils, and Ancient Liturgies on the Bread That Becomes the Word Made Flesh

The Eucharistic teaching of Scripture was unanimously consolidated, magnified, and celebrated in the exegesis of the Eastern and Western Fathers of the Church, the decrees of the great Ecumenical Councils, and the fundamental forms of worship adopted by all the Christian communities of the ancient world. This Eucharistic interpretation, understanding, and explanation of the words of Scripture was so universal and so ancient that any rejection of Eucharistic doctrine has to be regarded as both novel and unscriptural. It is a question here of drawing the line because any reading of Scripture that rejects a scriptural interpretation consistently held as central by Christians from ancient times is ipso facto suspect. Many modern exegetes have rejected interpretations of Scripture that teach the doctrines of the Trinity and Christ's divinity. If all interpretations are equal, then these exegetes and their views have the same standing as the Fathers and the Councils. But if either the concept of "Christianity" or a belief in the guidance of the Holy Spirit in the reading of Scripture is to have any intelligible content, we must anchor them in a body of exegesis and teaching that is ancient, universal, and consistent. We cannot say the doctrine of Christ's divinity is definitive while simultaneously holding that there are no definitive doctrines. Hence the scriptural interpretations of the Fathers, the Councils, and the liturgies, when universal and consistent, must be regarded as both authoritative and definitive in determining what Scripture actually teaches on central issues.

In the present context, we will consider what we have heard from these sources on the profusion of scriptural passages on the Lord's Supper, the Breaking of Bread, the Flesh that gives eternal life, and the Sacrifice offered from the rising of the sun to its setting. The following sequence is adopted: first the exegesis of the Fathers, second the teaching of the Councils, then the structure of the liturgies. In the next chapter, we will offer a defense of the traditional doctrine.

It is important to note here that the doctrine of the Eucharist is not a belief that first surfaced with the definition of the dogma of Transubstantiation by the Fourth Lateran Council in 1215 A.D. Polemicists have often charged that the doctrine of the Real Presence of Christ in the Eucharist was invented by the medieval Church in this Council. The most cursory survey of the teachings of the Fathers, starting with St. Ignatius of Antioch (d. 107), the texts of the earliest liturgies, and even the Acts of the Council of Ephesus (431) will show that this was not the case. "The Eucharist," writes the Protestant historian J. N. D. Kelly, "was also, of course, the great act of worship of Christians, their sacrifice. The writers and liturgies of the [pre-Nicene] period are unanimous in recognizing it as such."[1] All these ancient authorities held that during the celebration of the Lord's Supper the reality that was bread and wine becomes an entirely different Reality, namely, the Body and Blood of the Risen Lord, all the while leaving in place the physical properties of bread and wine. There was no doubt in the Christian mind that this Transformation took place. The only question was how the Transformation should be conceptually described.

Over a period of several centuries the language of Transubstantiation was deployed to provide such a description. But whether or not the Transformation took place was never at issue. Moreover the Transformation Itself remained as much a mystery after the definition of the dogma as It was before. A similar instance where the fundamental truth of a doctrine was grasped many centuries before a philosophical description was formulated concerns the dogmas of Christology. The early Christians believed that Jesus Christ was fully God and fully man. But it was only at the Councils of Nicaea, Constantinople, Ephesus, and Chalcedon that an acceptable description of this truth and its implications, deploying such concepts as *homoousion,* was defined. This was a process that took several centuries, finally ending with the Third Council of Constantinople in 680. The final definition helped clarify earlier imprecisions, but the belief it embodied remained the same before and after the fuller description. Once defined as a description of the truth always held by the faithful, the language of Transubstantiation was accepted by virtually all Christians of the time, including the Eastern Orthodox.

The Fathers

The first great expositors of Scripture, the earliest "witnesses" after the Apostles, were the saintly thinkers of the early Christian world later christened "the

Fathers." In citing the Fathers, we will focus on their teachings on both the Transformation of the bread and wine and on the nature of the ritual involved, i.e., on the Holy Eucharist and the Sacrifice of the Mass.

Now it has been said that at least a few of the Fathers have implied that the change in the bread and wine was symbolic while others have stated that the bread and wine continue to co-exist with the Body and Blood after the consecration. These objections are not nearly as weighty as they seem.

The two Fathers most often cited as using symbolist language are Clement of Alexandria and Tertullian. Clement (150–215) wrote that "Scripture called wine the mystic *sumbolon* of the sacred blood" and Tertullian (160–225) interprets "This is my body" as "This is the *figura* of my body." But in neither case is a heterodox reading justified because "symbol" and "figure" meant something very different in the ancient Church than they do today. The Lutheran historian Adolf Von Harnack notes, "What we nowadays understand by 'symbol' is a thing which is not that which it represents; at that time 'symbol' denoted a thing which in some kind of way really is what it signifies."[2] Tertullian, when speaking of the Word taking flesh in Mary's womb, says He took *caro figuratus* — evidently he was not denying here that Christ took actual flesh by saying He only took a figure of flesh. As Aidan Nichols has shown, Tertullian understands "represent" to mean "making present" — *re*-presenting — what is now invisible.[3]

In his reflection on these issues, Eric Mascall remarks,

> It is perhaps well to remember how extremely realistic and unmetaphorical the doctrine of the early fathers on the Eucharistic presence is. "The Eucharist," writes Ignatius, "is the flesh of our Saviour Jesus Christ, which flesh suffered for our sins and which God the Father raised up...." In the face of expressions like these it is obviously impossible to interpret such words as *antitypon, figura, symbolon,* and the like, when used of the elements, as indicating belief in a merely metaphorical presence.... In the earlier period, the question which is in effect being asked is, "How can bread and wine be the body and blood of Christ?" and the answer is, "By the fact that they are the *figures* or *symbols* of the body and blood"; where "figures" and "symbols" mean outward signs of invisibly present realities.[4]

The single most important fact to keep in mind here is the fact that virtually every Father used strongly realistic language in affirming the presence of the actual Flesh and Blood of Jesus at the communion table.

Concerning the second objection (relating to the co-existence theory), it must be admitted that at least some of the Fathers — a distinct minority — left room for the view that bread and wine continue to subsist in their reality alongside the Body and Blood of Christ. The main impetus for this view was an attempt to understand the mystery of Christ actually taking human flesh and continuing to retain His human nature over eternity. These thinkers rashly tried to use the idea of the co-existence of bread and wine with the Body and Blood as an argument from analogy for the doctrine of human and divine natures subsisting in the one Person of Christ. *It must be noted here that none of these thinkers denied the truth that Christ actually becomes present during consecration.* The only confusion was over what happens to the bread and wine: do they also remain after consecration or are they transformed in their entirety? Although presented with good intentions, this co-existence theory gave rise to insurmountable conceptual problems and was rejected by the vast majority of Fathers. (It is one thing to say that Jesus has both human and divine natures for in both instances it is *His* nature, distinct natures of *one* Person, we are talking about; but we cannot make any sense of the view that one and the same object is simultaneously bread *and* the Flesh of Jesus.) In the formulation accepted in 1215, the original insight of the Transformation was preserved while the improbable speculation about the co-existence of bread and wine with Flesh and Blood was dropped.

We present now the witness of the Fathers, first on the Real Presence and second on the Eucharistic Sacrifice.

The Fathers on the Real Presence of Christ in the Eucharist

St. Ignatius of Antioch (c. 35– c. 107)

There is no pleasure for me in any meats that perish, or in the delights of this life; I am fain for the bread of God, even the flesh of Jesus Christ, who is the seed of David; and for my drink I crave that blood which is love imperishable.[5]

Make certain that, therefore, that you all observe one common Eucharist.[6]

For there is but one body of our Lord Jesus Christ, and but one cup of union with his blood, and one single altar of sacrifice.[7]

St. Justin Martyr (c. 100– c. 165)

No one may share in the Eucharist except those who believe in the truth of our teachings and have been washed in the bath which confers forgiveness of sins and rebirth and who live according to Christ's commands, for we do not receive this food as ordinary bread and as ordinary drink; but just as Jesus Christ our Savior became flesh through the word of God, and assumed flesh and blood for our salvation, so too we are taught that the food over which the prayer of thanksgiving, the word received from Christ, has been said, the food which nourishes our flesh and blood by assimilation, is the flesh and blood of this Jesus who became flesh.[8]

St. Irenaeus of Lyons (c. 130– c. 200)

We offer to him what belongs to him, as we appropriately recall our fellowship and union and confess the resurrection of flesh and spirit. For as the earthly bread, once it has received the invocation of God upon it, it is no longer ordinary bread, but the Eucharist, and is made up of two elements, heavenly and earthly, so too our bodies, once they have received the Eucharist, are no longer corruptible, but contain within themselves the hope of resurrection.[9]

If the flesh is not saved, then the Lord did not redeem us with his blood, the chalice of the Eucharist is not a share in his blood, and the bread which we break is not a share in his body. For the blood cannot exist apart from veins and flesh and the rest of the human substance which the Word of God truly became in order to redeem us with his blood, as his own apostle states: "In him we have redemption, the forgiveness of sins." (Eph. 1:7)

Since we are his members, and are nourished by his creation, and since he also gives us his creation, by making his sun rise and rain fall according to his own good pleasure, he declared that the chalice of his creation is his own blood, from which he augments our own blood, and he affirmed that the bread of his creation is his own body, from which he gives growth to our bodies.

So when the mixed chalice and the baked loaf receive the word of God, and when the eucharistic elements become the body and blood of Christ, which bring growth and sustenance to our bodily frame, how can it be maintained that our flesh is incapable of receiving God's gift of eternal life? For our flesh feeds on the Lord's body and blood, and is his member.

So St. Paul writes in his letter to the Ephesians: "We are members of his body, of his flesh and his bones" (Eph. 5:30). He is not speaking about some spiritual and invisible man, "for a spirit has not flesh and bones as you see that I have" (Luke 24:39); on the contrary, he is speaking of the anatomy of a real man, consisting of flesh, nerves and bones, which is nourished by his chalice, the chalice of his blood, and gains growth from the bread which is his body.[10]

Clement of Alexandria (c. 150–c. 215)

Now, the blood of the Lord is twofold: one is corporeal, redeeming us from corruption (1 Pet. 1:18); the other is spiritual, and it is with that we are anointed. To drink the blood of Jesus is to participate in his incorruption (cf. John 6:55). Yet, the Spirit is the strength of the Word in the same way that blood is of the body. Similarly, wine is mixed with water and the Spirit is joined to man; the first, the mixture, provides feasting that faith may be increased; the other, the Spirit, leads us on to corruption. The union of both, that is, of the potion and the Word, is called the Eucharist, a gift worthy of praise and surpassingly fair; those who partake of it are sanctified in body and soul for it is the will of the Father that man, a composite made by God, be united to the Spirit and to the Word. In fact, the Spirit is closely joined to the soul depending upon him, and the flesh of the Word, because it was for it that "the Word was made flesh" (John 1:14).[11]

Origen (c. 185–c. 254)

You who are wont to take part in the divine mysteries know how carefully and reverently you guard the body of the Lord when you receive it, lest the least crumb of it should fall to the ground, lest any thing should be lost of the hallowed gift. For you regard, and rightly regard, yourselves as culpable if any part should fall to the ground through your carelessness.[12]

That which is "sanctified through the word of God and prayer" (1 Tim. 4:5) does not of its own accord sanctify the recipient; for if this were so it would sanctify him who eats the bread of the Lord unworthily and no one through this food would become "ill or weak" or "sleep" (1 Cor. 11:30). Thus even in respect of the bread of the Lord the advantage to the receiver depends on his partaking of the bread with a pure mind and a clear conscience.[13]

Tertullian (c. 160 – c. 225)

The flesh feeds on the body and blood of Christ that the soul may also feast on God.[14]

Marcion [a heretic] fails to appreciate that bread was prefigured as the body of Christ in Jeremiah, through whom already Christ said: "They were hatching their plots against me, saying, 'Let us give him a taste of wood with his bread'" (Jer. 11:19), that is, the cross pertaining to his body. So, he who clarifies the past showed just what "bread" he intended by calling his body "bread." In the same way, when he established the covenant sealed with his blood in speaking of the cup, he likewise demonstrates his body's reality. For only a living body of flesh has blood....In order that you may discern also the ancient figure of blood in wine, listen to Isaiah: "Who is this that comes from Edom, in crimsoned garments from Bozrah, he that is glorious in his apparel, marching in the greatness of his strength? Why is thy apparel red, and thy garments like his that treads in the wine press?" (Isaiah 63:1–2)....Thus, he who once signified his blood by wine now has consecrated his blood into wine.[15]

St. Cyprian (d. 258)

No one is more a priest of the Most High God than our Lord Jesus Christ: he sacrificed to God the Father, offering nothing other than what Melchisedech had offered, namely, bread and wine, his body and blood.[16]

In the Lord's prayer we go to ask: "Give us this day our daily bread." These words can have both a spiritual and a literal meaning. Both senses can be understood, through God's goodness, as fostering our salvation. Christ is truly the bread of life (John 6:35). This bread is ours, and not for everyone. Just as we say "Our Father," because he is the Father of those who know and believe in him, so we call Christ "our bread," because he is the bread of those who are feasted on his body. We ask for this bread every day in order not to be separated from the body of Christ by some serious sin, which would prevent us from communion in the daily Eucharist, the bread of salvation, and from the heavenly bread. He himself has proclaimed: "I am the living bread who has come down from heaven. Whoever eats this bread will live for ever. The bread that I shall give is my flesh for the life of the world" (John 6:51). When he says that anyone who eats his bread lives for ever, he clearly declares that this pertains only to those who eat his body and who have the right to share in the eucharistic communion. On the other hand, it is necessary to fear and to pray lest by keeping away from the body of Christ one may not become separated and remain far from salvation. For we must heed the warning which he himself gave: "If you do not eat the flesh of the Son of man and drink his blood, you shall not have life in you" (John 6:53). For this reason we ask to be given every day our bread, that is, Christ. Thus, abiding and living in Christ, we are not cut off from his sanctification and from his body.[17]

St. Athanasius (c. 296–373)

St. Athanasius was the moving force behind the Council of Nicaea, the first great Council of the Church, and his testimony to the Real Presence of Christ in the Eucharist shows how fundamental this doctrine was to Christianity even before the Councils.

You shall see the levites bring loaves and a chalice of wine, and place them on the table. As long as the invocation and prayers have not begun, there is only bread and wine. But after the great and wonderful prayers have been pronounced, then the bread becomes the body of our Lord Jesus Christ, and the wine becomes his blood. Let us come to the celebration of the mysteries. As long as the prayers and invocations have not taken place, this bread and wine are simply (bread and wine). But after the great prayers and invocations have been pronounced, the Word descends into the bread and wine, and the body of the Word is.[18]

St. Ephraem (c. 306–c. 373)

In your sacraments we welcome you every day and receive you into our bodies. Make us worthy to experience within us the resurrection for which we hope. By the grace of baptism we conceal within our bodies the treasure of your divine life. This treasure increases as we eat at the table of your sacraments. Let us rejoice in your grace.[19]

St. Cyril of Jerusalem (c. 313–387)

The Blessed Paul's teaching (cf. 1 Cor. 11:23–25) itself gives you ample and full assurance about the divine mysteries into which your admission has made you one body and blood with Christ.... Since, then, Christ himself clearly described the bread to us in the words, "This is my body," who will dare henceforward to dispute it? And since he has emphatically said, "This is my blood," who will waver in the slightest and say it is not his blood?

So let us partake with the fullest confidence that it is the body and blood of Christ. For his body has been bestowed on you under the figure of bread, and his blood under the figure of wine, so that by partaking of Christ's body and blood you may become one body and blood with him. This is how we become bearers of Christ, since his body and blood spreads throughout our limbs; this is how, in the blessed Peter's words, "we become partakers in the divine nature" (2 Pet. 1:4).[20]

Do not, then, regard the bread and wine as nothing but bread and wine, for they are the body and blood of Christ as the master himself has proclaimed. Though your senses suggest otherwise, let faith reassure you.

You have been taught and fully instructed that what seems to be bread is not bread, though it appears to be such to the sense of taste, but the body of Christ; that what seems to be wine is not wine, though the taste would have it so, but the blood of Christ; that David was speaking of this long ago when he said, "Bread strengthens the heart of man that he may make his face glad with oil" (Ps. 103:15). So strengthen your heart by partaking of that spiritual bread, and gladden the face of your soul.[21]

St. Basil the Great (c. 330–379)

To communicate every day, to be a sharer in the holy body and blood of Christ is, indeed, a good and beneficial practice, for He says plainly: "He who eats my flesh and drinks my blood, has eternal life" (John 6:55).[22]

St. Gregory of Nyssa (c. 330–395)

But since human nature is twofold, a composite of soul and body, those who are being saved must grasp Him who leads the way towards life by means of both. Now the soul, being blended with Him by faith, received from it the beginnings of its salvation. For the union with Life involves a sharing of life. But the body comes into association and blending with its Savior in a different way.... But it is not possible for anything to enter the body, unless it is mingled with the vital organs by way of food and drink. Therefore the body must receive the life-giving power in the way that its nature permits....

It is admitted that the subsistence of the body comes from nourishment, and that this nourishment is food and drink, and that in food bread is included, and in drink water sweetened with wine.... We believe that now also the bread which is sanctified by the word of God is changed into the body of God the Word.... Not by the process of being eaten does it go on to become the body of the Word, but it is changed immediately into the body through the word, even as the Word has said: "This is my body."[23]

And this He bestows by power of the eucharistic prayer (*eulogia*), transforming the nature of the visible elements into that immortal thing.[24]

St. Augustine (354–430)

I remember my promise. For last night I promised you who have been baptized a sermon in which I would explain the Sacrament of the Lord's table, which you now behold and which you became partakers of last night. You should understand what you have received, what you will receive, indeed what you should receive daily. That bread that you see on the altar and that has been sanctified by the word of God is the Body of Christ. That chalice—rather, that which the chalice contains— has been sanctified by the word of God and is the Blood of Christ. Through these things the Lord Christ wished to entrust to us his Body and his Blood, which he shed for us unto the remission of sins. If you receive them well, you are that which you receive. The Apostle says, "One bread and we, the many, are one body."[25]

He took earth from earth, because flesh is from the earth, and he took Flesh of the flesh of Mary. He walked on earth in that same Flesh, and gave that same Flesh to us to be eaten for our salvation. Moreover no one eats that Flesh unless he has first adored it... and we sin by not adoring. Who is the Bread of heaven except Christ? But in order that man might eat the bread of angels, the Lord of the angels became a man. If this had not happened, we would not have his Flesh: if we did not have his Flesh, we would not eat the Bread of the altar.[26]

The Fathers on the Sacrifice of the Mass

St. Ignatius of Antioch

Let me be no more than a libation [cf. Phil. 2:17] for God while an altar of sacrifice is still at hand.[27]

St. Justin Martyr

Concerning the sacrifices once offered by you Jews, God, as I have already said, has spoken through Malachi the prophet, who was one of the Twelve [minor prophets]: "I have no pleasure in you," says the Lord, "and I do not accept your sacrifices from your hands, because from the rising of the sun to its setting my Name has been glorified among the Gentiles. And in every place incense and a pure sacrifice are offered to my Name, because my Name is great among the Gentiles, says the Lord, while you have profaned it." Already, then, did he prophesy about those sacrifices that are offered to him in every place by us Gentiles, speaking, that is, about the Bread of the Eucharist and the cup of the Eucharist. And he added that his Name is glorified by us and profaned by you.[28]

St. Irenaeus of Lyons

Therefore the offering which the Lord taught to be offered throughout the whole world is considered by God a pure sacrifice and is acceptable to him.[29]

Mystagogic Catechesis (attributed to St. Cyril of Jerusalem)

Then, after the spiritual sacrifice our unbloody worship has been accomplished over that sacrifice of propitiation, we beg God for the common peace of the Church.[30]

St. John Chrysostom

When you see the Lord immolated and lying upon the altar, and the priest bent over that sacrifice praying, and all the people empurpled by that precious Blood, can you think that you are still among men and on earth? Or are you not lifted up to heaven? Is not every carnal affection deposed? Do you not with pure mind and clean heart contemplate the things of heaven?[31]

St. Augustine

Was not Christ immolated in himself once and for all? Nevertheless is he not immolated for the people in the Sacrament not only at the Paschal solemnities but every day, so that anyone who replies to a questioner that he is immolated does not lie? For if the Sacrament did not bear a certain similarity to those things for which they are sacraments, they would not be sacraments at all. Therefore as the Sacrament of the Body of the Lord is in a certain way the Body of the Lord and the Sacrament of the Blood of Christ is the Blood of Christ, so the Sacrament of the Faith is the Faith. Believing is nothing else than having faith. And so when it is replied that the little child believes, even though he does not yet have an experience of the Faith, the response is given because he has the Sacrament of the Faith and has converted himself to God because of the sacrament of conversion.[32]

The Councils

For most Christians, whether Catholic, Orthodox or Protestant, the first seven Ecumenical Councils of the Church have an authoritative place in the formation of Christian doctrine. The proclamations of these Councils — on the Trinity, the Incarnation, and various other issues — are regarded as binding interpretations of the revelation of God found in Holy Scripture. There is no sense in contrasting the complexity of the Councils with the simplicity of Scripture. The Councils were called precisely because there were controversies over how Scripture was to be interpreted. The job of the Councils was to determine and define the accurate and authentic interpretation of Scripture. Thus one cannot set Scripture against Council for a Council simply is a way of reading Scripture, a way accepted as authoritative through most of Christian history.

Council of Nicaea (325)

It has come to the knowledge of the holy and great Synod that, in some districts and cities, the deacons administer the Eucharist to the presbyters, whereas neither canon nor custom permits that they who have no right to offer should give the Body of Christ to them that do offer. And this also has been made known, that certain deacons now touch the Eucharist even before the bishops. Let all such practices be utterly done away with, and let the deacons remain within their own bounds, knowing that they are the ministers of the bishop and the inferiors of the presbyters. Let them receive the Eucharist according to their order, after the presbyters, and let either the bishop or the presbyter administer to them.[33]

Council of Ephesus (431)

Proclaiming the death, according to the flesh, of the only begotten Son of God, that is Jesus Christ, confessing his resurrection from the dead, and his ascension into heaven, we offer the Unbloody Sacrifice in the churches, and so go on to the mystical thanksgivings, and are sanctified, having received his Holy Flesh and the Precious Blood of Christ the Saviour of us all. And not as common flesh do we receive it; God forbid: nor as of a man sanctified and associated with the Word according to the unity of worth, or as having a divine indwelling, *but as truly the Life-giving and very flesh of the Word himself.* For he is the Life according to his nature as God, and when he became united to his Flesh, he made it also to be Life-giving, as also he said to us: Verily, verily, I say unto you, Except ye eat the flesh of the Son of Man and drink his Blood. For we must not think that it is flesh of a man like us (for how can the flesh of man be life-giving by its own nature?)

but as having become truly the very own of him who for us both became and was called Son of Man.

The Second Council of Nicaea (787)

Never did the Lord or the apostles or the Fathers call the bloodless sacrifice which is offered by the priest an image but the body itself and the blood itself.[34]

The Fourth Lateran Council (1215)

In this Church Jesus Christ is both priest and sacrifice. In the Sacrament of the Altar, under the species of bread and wine, his Body and Blood are truly contained, the bread having been transubstantiated into his Body and wine into his Blood by divine power.

The Orthodox Confession (1640)

This statement was approved by the Eastern Orthodox Patriarchs of Constantinople, Alexandria, Antioch, and Jerusalem, all the Eastern Sees, in 1643.

Christ is now in heaven only and not on earth after that manner of the flesh wherein He bore it and lived in it when He was on earth; but after the sacramental manner, whereby He is present in the Holy Eucharist, the same Son of God, God and Man, is also on earth by way of TRANSUBSTANTIATION [*kata metousiosis*]. For the SUBSTANCE of the bread is changed into the SUBSTANCE of His holy body, and the SUBSTANCE of the wine into the SUBSTANCE of His precious blood.

Where it is fitting to WORSHIP and ADORE the Holy Eucharist even as our Savior Jesus Himself.

The priest must know that at the moment when he consecrates the gifts the SUBSTANCE itself of the bread and the SUBSTANCE of the wine are changed into the SUBSTANCE of the real body and blood of Christ through the operation of the Holy Ghost, whom the priest invokes at that time, consecrating this mystery by praying and saying, "Send down Thy Holy Ghost on us and on these gifts set before Thee, and make this bread the precious body of Thy Christ and that which is in this cup the precious blood of Thy Christ, changing them by Thy Holy Ghost."

For immediately after these words the TRANSUBSTANTIATION [*metousiosis*] takes place, and that bread is changed into the real body of Christ, and the wine into His real blood. ONLY THE SPECIES WHICH ARE SEEN REMAIN, and this by the ordinance of God, first, that we may not see the body of Christ, but may believe that it is there....

The honor which it is fitting to give to these awful mysteries is of such a kind as that which is given to Christ Himself.... This mystery is also OFFERED AS A SACRIFICE on behalf of all orthodox Christians, both the living AND THOSE WHO SLEEP in hope of a resurrection to eternal life; and the SACRIFICE shall never fail until the last Judgment.

The fruits of this mystery are these: first, the commemoration of the sinless passion and death of Christ...secondly...this mystery is a PROPITIATION AND ATONEMENT WITH GOD FOR OUR SINS BOTH OF THE LIVING AND OF THE DEAD...thirdly...that each Christian who shall frequent this SACRIFICE and partake of this mystery may be delivered by means of it from the temptation and danger of the devil.

The Liturgies

As we believe so do we pray. Nothing embodies the content of our faith better than the content of the worship it inspires. To discover what Christians in ancient times believed we must consider then their prayers and liturgies. At the center of their world of worship, starting with St. Paul, lies the celebration of the Eucharist. This celebration entailed three assumptions:

1. The bread and wine are transformed into Christ's Body and Blood.

2. The Eucharistic liturgy is also a Sacrifice mystically united with Calvary.

3. The raison d'être for this celebration is the command of Christ.

The Eastern centers of Christendom were Jerusalem, Alexandria, Antioch, and Byzantium/Constantinople. The major liturgical families of the East were composed in these centers, with at least two of them linked in popular belief to the age of the Apostles:

- The liturgies of Jerusalem and Antioch originating from the liturgy of St. James;

- the liturgies of Egypt and Ethiopia originating from the liturgy of St. Mark, further developed (in the case of the Coptic Church in Egypt) by St. Cyril of Alexandria, St. Basil, and St. Gregory of Nazianzus;

- the Byzantine liturgies of St. Basil and St. John Chrysostom (both of Antiochian origin).

Other Eastern liturgies appeared in later years: the liturgies of Mesopotamia and Persia — including that of the Chaldean Church — primarily composed by Sts. Addai and Mari; and the Armenian and Maronite liturgies (the first of Byzantine origin and the second of Antiochian). The Byzantine rite was easily the most influential of the Eastern rites because it was the official rite of the Byzantine Empire. The roots of the liturgies used in the Byzantine rite go back to liturgies used in Palestine, Antioch, and Cappadocia. As it spread, the Byzantine rite was celebrated in other liturgical languages, including Russian and Romanian.

Whether or not the liturgies of St. James or St. Mark actually go back to the Apostle and the Evangelist remains a topic of debate among historians. Without question, certain texts were added to these liturgies over the years. But the following general observations are hardly disputable:

- The Eucharistic consecration using the words of Jesus Christ in Scripture lies at the center of the three major liturgical families of the East (as well as of the Latin liturgies of the West).

- The invocation of the Holy Spirit is prominent in all the Eastern liturgies.

- All the liturgies take it for granted that after the consecration the elements of bread and wine are transformed into the Body and Blood of Jesus.

- These liturgies were and are used in every part of the ancient Christian world from Egypt to India, from Rome to Jerusalem.

- Despite the variety of geographical, linguistic, and cultural influences at play in these liturgies, what remains remarkable is their theological unity with respect to the Eucharist.

Distinct from the Eastern liturgies is the Western liturgy with its origin rooted firmly in Rome. Although St. Justin Martyr had described the rites of worship adopted in Rome, the first document with the actual text of a Eucharistic liturgy is Hippolytus's *Apostolic Tradition,* which appeared circa 225 A.D. The liturgical text in Hippolytus's work is now the Second Eucharistic Prayer in the Roman Missal. The First Eucharistic Prayer in the Missal, known as the Roman Canon, is believed to have existed in its fundamental structure at least by the fourth century; references to it are found in St. Ambrose of Milan (339–397). There were also a number of other Latin liturgies, including the sixth-century Gallican liturgy (influenced also by the East) of the Franks and the seventh-century Mozarabic liturgy of Spain. Again, despite diversity of language and expression, there was an underlying focus on the centrality of the Eucharistic consecration in all these liturgies.

To see how central was the doctrine of the Real Presence of Christ in the mind and heart of the Christian world, we must read for ourselves the texts of the major Eucharistic liturgies. To this end, we cite relevant passages from these liturgies.

Liturgy of St. James (Aramaic)

PRIEST: When he, the one without sin, was about to accept for us sinners his voluntary and life-giving death through a cross, on the night he was given up, or rather gave himself up, for the life and salvation of the world [*here the priest takes the bread*], taking bread in his holy, immaculate and unblemished and immortal hands, looking up to heaven and showing it to you, his God and Father, giving thanks, blessing, sanctifying and breaking it, he shared it among his holy and blessed Disciples and Apostles, saying: [*here he replaces the bread*] Take, eat. This is my body which is broken and distributed for you for the forgiveness of sins.

PEOPLE: Amen.

PRIEST: [*taking the cup*] Likewise after supper, taking the cup and mixing wine and water, gazing up to heaven and showing it to you, his God and Father, giving thanks, blessing, sanctifying, filling it with the Holy Spirit, he shared it among his holy and blessed Disciples and Apostles, saying: [*putting down the cup*] Drink from this all of you. This is my blood of the new covenant, which is poured out and distributed for you and for many for the forgiveness of sins.

PEOPLF: Amen.

PRIEST: Do this in memory of me. For as often as you eat this bread and drink this cup, you proclaim the death of the Son of Man, and confess his resurrection, until he comes.

PEOPLE: We believe and confess. Your death, Lord, we proclaim, and your resurrection we confess.

PRIEST: Therefore, we sinners too, remembering his life-giving sufferings and the saving Cross, his death and burial, and resurrection from the dead on the third day, his ascension into heaven and sitting at your right hand, his God and Father, and his second, glorious and fearsome coming, when he comes in glory to judge the living and the dead, when he will render to each according to their works — Spare us, O Lord! [*thrice*] — or rather according to his compassion, offer to you, Master, this dread sacrifice without shedding of blood, asking that you do not act towards us according to our sins, but that, according to your kindness and ineffable love for humankind, setting aside and wiping out the record of the debt against us your suppliants, you would grant us your heavenly and eternal gifts, which eye has not seen, nor ear heard, nor has it entered the human heart the things that you have prepared, O God, for those who love you. And do not reject your people because of me and because of my sins, O Lord who love humankind.... Your same all-holy Spirit, Lord, send down on us and on these gifts here set forth, that having come by his holy, good and glorious presence, he may sanctify this bread and make it the holy body of Christ,

PEOPLE: Amen.

PRIEST: and this Cup the precious blood of Christ,

PEOPLE: Amen.

PRIEST: that they may become for all those who partake of them for forgiveness of sins and everlasting life. For sanctification of souls and bodies. For a fruitful harvest of good works.

Coptic Liturgy of St. Mark

PRIEST: He instituted for us this great mystery of godliness. For being determined to give himself up to death for the life of the world.

PEOPLE: We believe.

PRIEST: He took bread into his holy, spotless, unblemished, blessed and life-giving hands.

PEOPLE: We believe that this is true. Amen.

PRIEST: He looked up towards heaven to you, O God, who are his Father and Master of every one. He gave thanks,

PEOPLE: Amen.

PRIEST: He blessed it,

PEOPLE: Amen.

PRIEST: And he sanctified it.

PEOPLE: Amen. We believe, we confess, and we glorify.

PRIEST: He broke it, gave it to his own holy disciples and saintly apostles saying "Take, eat of it all of you. For this is my body, which shall be broken for you and for many, to be given for the remission of sins. Do this in remembrance of me."

PEOPLE: This is true. Amen.

PRIEST: Likewise also the cup after supper he mixed it of wine and water. He gave thanks,

PEOPLE: Amen.

PRIEST: He blessed it,

PEOPLE: Amen.

PRIEST: And he sanctified it.

PEOPLE: Amen. Again, we believe, we confess, and we glorify.

PRIEST: He tasted, and gave it also to his own holy disciples and saintly apostles saying, "Take, drink of it all of you. For this is my Blood for the new covenant which shall be shed for you and many, to be given for the remission of sins. Do this in remembrance of me."

PEOPLE: This is also true. Amen.

PRIEST: For every time you shall eat of this bread and drink of this cup, you proclaim my death, confess my resurrection, and remember me till I come.

PEOPLE: Amen. Amen. Amen. Your death, O Lord, we proclaim. Your holy resurrection and ascension, we confess. We praise you, we bless you, we thank you, O Lord, and we entreat you, O our God.

PRIEST: Therefore, as we also commemorate his holy passion, his resurrection from the dead, his ascension into heaven, his sitting at your hand, O Father, and his second coming which shall be from the heavens, awesome and full of glory; we offer unto you your oblations from what is yours, for every condition, concerning every condition and in every condition.

DEACON: Worship God in fear and trembling.

PEOPLE: We praise you, we bless you, we serve you, we worship you.

PRIEST: And we ask you, O Lord, our God, we, your sinful and unworthy servants. We worship you by the pleasure of your goodness, that your Holy Spirit descend upon us and upon these gifts set forth, and purify them, change them and manifest them as a sanctification of your saints.

DEACON: Let us attend. Amen.

PRIEST: And this bread he makes into his Holy Body.

PEOPLE: We believe.

PRIEST: Our Lord, God and Saviour Jesus Christ, given for the remission of sins and eternal life to those who shall partake of him.

PEOPLE: Amen.

PRIEST: And this cup also, into the precious blood of his new covenant.

PEOPLE: Again, we believe. Amen.

PRIEST: Our Lord, God and Saviour Jesus Christ, given for the remission of sins and eternal life to those who shall partake of him.

PEOPLE: Lord have mercy. Lord have mercy. Lord have mercy.

Byzantine Liturgy of St. John Chrysostom

PRIEST: Together with these blessed powers, merciful Master, we also proclaim and say: You are holy and most holy, You and Your only begotten Son and Your Holy Spirit. You are holy and most holy, and sublime is Your glory. You so loved Your world that You gave Your only begotten Son so that whoever believes in Him should not perish, but have eternal life. He came and fulfilled the divine plan for us. On the night when He was delivered up, or rather when He gave Himself up for the life of the world, He took bread in His holy, pure, and blameless hands, gave thanks, blessed, sanctified, broke and gave it to His holy disciples and apostles, saying: Take, eat, this is my Body which is broken for you for the forgiveness of sins.

PEOPLE: Amen.

PRIEST: Likewise, after supper, He took the cup, saying: Drink of it all of you; this is my Blood of the new Covenant which is shed for you and for many for the forgiveness of sins.

PEOPLE: Amen.

PRIEST: Remembering, therefore, this command of the Savior, and all that came to pass for our sake, the cross, the tomb, the resurrection on the third day, the ascension into heaven, the enthronement at the right hand of the Father, and the second, glorious coming, We offer to You these gifts from Your own gifts in all and for all.

PEOPLE: We praise You, we bless You, we give thanks to You, and we pray to You, Lord our God.

PRIEST: Once again we offer to You this spiritual worship without the shedding of blood, and we ask, pray, and entreat You: send down Your Holy Spirit upon us and upon these gifts here presented. And make this bread the precious Body of Your Christ. [*The priest blesses the holy Bread.*]

DEACON: Amen.

PRIEST: And that which is in this cup the precious Blood of Your Christ. [*The priest blesses the holy Cup.*]

DEACON: Amen.

PRIEST: Changing them by Your Holy Spirit. [*He blesses them both.*]

DEACON: Amen. Amen. Amen.

PRIEST: So that they may be to those who partake of them for vigilance of soul, forgiveness of sins, communion of Your Holy Spirit, fulfillment of the kingdom of heaven, confidence before You, and not in judgment or condemnation....

[*When the priest-celebrant receives communion, he says:*] The blessed and most Holy Body of our Lord and God and Saviour Jesus Christ is communicated to me, N., priest, for the remission of my sins and life everlasting. I, N., priest, partake of the pure and Holy Blood of our Lord and God and Saviour Jesus Christ, for the remission of my sins and life everlasting.

[*When he gives communion to the deacon, he says:*] N., the holy deacon, is made partaker of the precious, holy and spotless Body of our Lord and God and Saviour Jesus Christ, for the remission of his sins and life everlasting.

The Eucharistic Liturgy in Hippolytus's *Christian Tradition* (ca. 225) now incorporated into the Roman Missal as the Second Eucharistic Prayer

BISHOP: We render thanks to you, O God, through your most beloved child Jesus Christ...who, when he was betrayed to voluntary suffering that he might destroy death, and break the bonds of the devil, and tread down hell, and shine upon the righteous, and fix a term and manifest the resurrection, took bread and gave thanks to you, saying, 'Take, eat; this is my body, which shall be broken for you'; who also [took] the cup saying, 'This is my blood, which is shed for you; when you do this, you make my remembrance.' Remembering therefore his death and resurrection, we offer to you the bread and the cup, giving you thanks because you held us worthy to stand before you and minister to you. And we ask that you would send your Holy Spirit upon the offering of your holy Church; that, gathering her into one, you would grant to all who receive the holy things [to receive] the fullness of the Holy Spirit for the strengthening of faith in truth."[35]

As is evident from this survey of the proclamations and invocations of the entire Christian universe of the first millennium, the teaching that the consecration of bread and wine at the Mass transforms them into vehicles of the divine Life was universally and enthusiastically accepted by the faithful. All those who believed that the Word became Flesh also believed that His Flesh was made present, as He promised, at the communal "breaking of bread." The memory of the Christian message preserved in the liturgies and the content of this message transmitted by the Fathers and Councils both testified to the fundamental truth of the transformation of the Eucharistic elements. As noted earlier, in the same breath that the Councils defined the flesh of Christ as "the flesh of God the Word" (Constantinople III) they also proclaimed that "when he became united to his Flesh, he made it also to be Life-giving, as also he said to us: Verily, verily, I say unto you, Except ye eat the flesh of the Son of Man and drink his Blood. For we must not think that it is flesh of a man like us (for how can the flesh of man be life-giving by its own nature?) but as having become truly the very own of him who for us both became and was called Son of Man" (*Council of Ephesus*).

Chapter 10

The Progressive
Elevation of Matter:
Toward a New Understanding of
the Astounding Claim That God Is
Present in the Holy Eucharist

Imagine a scenario where a well-known anchorman on a major television network announces on the evening news that scientists have now confirmed the ancient doctrine of Transubstantiation, the teaching that bread and wine change into the Flesh and Blood of Jesus Christ during Mass. Given the fact that many people accept the veracity of the network news, it would hardly be a surprise if a majority of viewers accepted the anchorman's pronouncements without further ado. Likewise, in the domain of modern theology: if one of today's daring theologians propounds a radical new theory about the Eucharist, the burden of proof would already be stacked in his (or her) favor in much of the academic community.

The point of these two examples is this: Like it or not, most of us make up our minds or form our beliefs on the basis of "pronouncements" made by scientists, media persons, celebrities, and other authority figures. Trust in authority is not necessarily bad when such trust is warranted — when the authority in question is truly an authority. When it comes to the Eucharist, the options are limited. If we believe that Jesus Christ is the God-man and that He teaches with authority, then we will believe the truths He taught. On the Eucharist, the New Testament texts seem clearly to indicate that He taught His Real Presence in what was once bread and wine. We have good reason to conclude that this is what He intended to teach because this was the interpretation adopted by all the Fathers, East and West, all the ancient liturgies, and all the major Councils. In addition to these teachings, we have the supernatural verification offered by the great Eucharistic miracles of history in which the Host and the consecrated "wine" turned to actual Flesh and Blood, primarily in response to doubt and desecration, and the experiential verification offered by millions of the faithful throughout the world and across history.

What does it mean to say that the bread and wine at Mass change into the Body and Blood of Christ at the moment of consecration? The traditional description of this change is the doctrine of Transubstantiation — the substance of the bread and wine are changed but not its appearances. The purpose of the present chapter is to offer a new paradigm drawn from contemporary experience to describe the mystery of this dramatic change. We are trying not to replace the language of Transubstantiation but to understand its truth in the context of another dimension — that of life at all levels. What takes place at consecration, we might say, is the transformation of lifeless matter into a vehicle of the divine Life and therefore every instance of the genesis of life — from the cellular level to the creation of the conscious self — is a pointer to the unfathomable mystery of this Event. A description is not an explanation, of course, and neither the doctrine of Transubstantiation nor the version of it presented here diminish, in any respect, the depth of the mystery involved.

The emphasis here on the Eucharist as the vehicle of divine Life mirrors the emphasis that Jesus Himself placed both on His identity as divine Life incarnate and the urgency of our receiving this Life: "I am the way and the truth and the *life*. No one comes to the Father except through me" (John 14:6). "Just as the Father has life in himself, so also he gave to his Son the possession of *life* in himself" (John 5:26). "I am the bread of *life*" (John 6:48). "Whoever eats my flesh and drinks my blood has eternal *life*" (6:54). "Just as the living Father sent me and I have *life* because of the Father, so also the one who feeds on me will have *life* because of me" (6:57). "I come so that they might have *life* and have it more abundantly" (John 10:10).

Here we see that (1) Jesus not only has the divine Life but *is* the divine Life incarnate, (2) our eternal life depends on our living with His divine Life, and (3) to receive His divine Life one must eat the flesh and drink the blood of "the bread of life." The focus on the Eucharist as the vehicle of divine Life is important, above all, because the whole point of receiving communion is to receive the divine Life, to be "partakers of the divine nature."

Right from the beginning, the Fathers of the Church recognized that the conversion of bread and wine into the Body and Blood was not just another miracle. Remarkably, the closest analogy they could bring to bear in describing this event was the creation of the Universe from nothing. Both events represented changes of the most fundamental nature. While one described the coming to be of natural reality as a whole, the other was concerned with the transformation of the natural into the supernatural. Paradoxically, the latter transformation did not

THE PROGRESSIVE ELEVATION OF MATTER

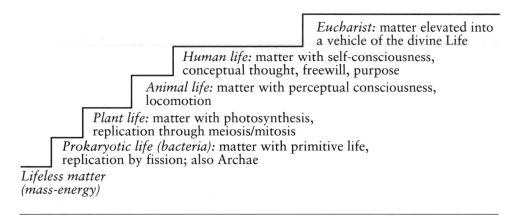

Eucharist: matter elevated into a vehicle of the divine Life

Human life: matter with self-consciousness, conceptual thought, freewill, purpose

Animal life: matter with perceptual consciousness, locomotion

Plant life: matter with photosynthesis, replication through meiosis/mitosis

Prokaryotic life (bacteria): matter with primitive life, replication by fission; also Archae

Lifeless matter (mass-energy)

---

involve any change of appearance. The natural becomes the supernatural while retaining the appearance of the natural (and here there is an analogy — but only an analogy — in terms of identity of appearance between a living being and a nonliving replica).

Metamorphic Creation

For our purposes here, these two ontologically fundamental miracles of nature may be described as "Creatio ex nihilo" and "Metamorphic Creation."

Creatio ex nihilo: creation of physical reality as a whole out of nothing

Metamorphic Creation: transformation of an existing physical reality into a preexisting supernatural reality while retaining the appearances of the physical reality

Two things must be noted about these descriptions. In describing *creatio ex nihilo* as the creation of physical reality, we imply (intentionally) that the creation of nonphysical realities involves distinct creative acts (be these direct or indirect in nature). In using the terms "metamorphic" and "creation" together, we mean something different from what the terms would mean if they were used separately (as is the case with the terms "Chinese philosophy"). We do not imply that there is only a change of form or shape of a thing that remains the same throughout (like the change of a caterpillar into a butterfly); nor do we imply that there is a creation out of nothing. The value of using the terms together is in highlighting the fact that the Event involved is a transformation of something already existing but a transformation so fundamental that its nearest analogy is creation of something out of nothing. "Creation" is used because something that was previously not present is now here, and "metamorphosis" conveys the truth that this new Presence comes through a transformation. The mystery of this transformation lies not just in the fact that one thing changes totally into another but in What it changes into.

Both acts of creation involve God. Both acts take place all the time. *Creatio ex nihilo,* the creation of the universe out of nothing, involves God continuing to hold all things in being at every instant; and Metamorphic Creation takes place at every Mass. Both acts, by their very nature, cannot be scientifically proved or disproved. Both acts are believed on the basis of divine authority, and both acts make sense of a wide variety of phenomena.

Transubstantiation

In talking of the paradigm of Metamorphic Creation — of consecration as the transformation of nonliving matter into a vehicle of the divine Life — we are inevitably led to the traditional teaching of Transubstantiation. The paradigm of Metamorphic Creation can be understood only in the context of the basic insight so powerfully expressed by the concept of Transubstantiation. Recent attempts to describe the Eucharistic Event as Transignification and Transfinalization turn out, in the final analysis, to be reductionistic since they deny the fundamental truth of the actual presence of Christ in the Eucharist. This is not the case with the paradigm of Metamorphic Creation, which is merely one more way of illustrating the truth of Transubstantiation.

Let us assume for a moment that when Jesus said, "This is my body.... This is my blood," He meant His words to be taken literally. That there is a Change in the bread and the wine during the words of consecration uttered by Christ speaking through the person of His priest has always been accepted among Christians. That the Change involves the true indwelling, the actual Presence of God in what was once bread and wine was also widely, even fervently, professed by the faithful. But accepting the fact of this Change is one thing. It is quite another thing to describe what we mean when we talk of such a Change and try to explain how it is possible for this Change to take place. The famous doctrine of Transubstantiation was introduced precisely in order to clarify and magnify the nature of the Change without pretending to make it any less mysterious.

The essence of the doctrine of Transubstantiation is the following: there are objects independent of us in the world; in any and every object in the world, there is a distinction between the object's properties and qualities and the physical substrate, or substance, in which these properties inhere and that endures over a period of time; the qualities and properties of an object (color, size, etc.) are part of the object but cannot exist independently of its physical substrate (the redness of a brick cannot exist independently of the brick); although more "independent" than its properties, the substrate of any and every object ultimately derives from and is constantly dependent for its continued existence on the creative action of God; God, Who has made every object out of nothing and Who keeps it in existence as the specific being that it is with its particular substrate and properties, can change a given object into a wholly different kind of being by changing its physical substrate while allowing it to retain the properties of the original being. As applied to the Eucharist, when the bread and the wine are consecrated at Mass, a change of physical substrate or substance, appropriately called "Transubstantiation," takes place whereby these now become the substance of the Body and Blood of Christ while still retaining the properties or appearances of bread and wine.

The genius of St. Thomas Aquinas was to locate this transformation within the context of the creative activity of God and each object's existence as a finite participation in God's infinite Act of Being. Only an awareness of the mystery of the entire and constant dependence of each object on God both for its existence and its existence with the kind of physical substrate and properties that it has will prepare our minds for the greater mystery of Transubstantiation.

Ultimately, the description of the whole Event in terms of substance and appearances is not the issue. The truth being taught is that the reality that was bread and wine becomes an entirely different Reality, namely, the Body and Blood of the Risen Lord, all the while leaving in place the physical properties of bread and wine. Just as the *same reality* endures through *different appearances* in the metamorphosis of a caterpillar into a butterfly, in the case of the Eucharist the *same appearances* endure through *different realities*.

The idea of a differentiation between a reality and its appearances is more plausible today since it is generally accepted that there are differentiations even at the level of appearances — for instance, between the quantum and the classical realms, between mass and energy, between the virtual environments of cyberspace and the real world, between hardware and software. In taking the creation of life as an analogy of the Change that takes place at Transubstantiation, we might be able to clarify some of the more common misconceptions about this doctrine.

The Paradigm of Life

Both the origin and nature of life remain as much a mystery today as ever before. Life here is understood as any system that processes energy and information and replicates.[1] We have no conclusive proof — accepted with any degree of consensus by the scientific establishment — concerning the origin of cellular life at the most basic level or of the processes of metabolism and replication that are required to sustain and transmit life. The problem applies just as much to prokaryotic (bacteria, algae) as to eukaryotic cells (plants and animals); the discovery that archaeal cells form a distinct class has been followed by discoveries that reduce the likelihood of there being a linear sequence from archae to eukaryotes.[2] The magnitude of the problem becomes even more apparent as we ascend the hierarchy of life from mere biological life through the conscious life of animals to the rational, self-conscious life of the human person.

One can evade the problem by asserting that life originated from some process of chemical self-organization that could take place again given appropriate conditions. This is an evasion because we are ignoring the more fundamental questions: where did these chemicals come from and how did they acquire these characteristics of self-organization? Dr. Werner Arber, winner of a Nobel Prize for his work in molecular genetics, rightly noted that "the most primitive cells may require at least several hundred different specific biological macro-molecules. How such already quite complex structures may have come together, remains a mystery to me. The possibility of the existence of a Creator, of God, represents to me a satisfactory solution to this problem."[3] In his recent book, *What Remains to Be Discovered,* John Maddox, former editor of the journal *Nature,* writes, "We now know when life appeared on Earth's surface, but we do not yet know how it began. . . . Mere arithmetic shows that the chance that such a molecule [the simplest of enzyme molecules] will be assembled from its el-ementary components by random processes is so small as to be virtually zero."[4] Moreover, all forms of life in matter are guided by the genetic code, and the information or meaning-content that constitutes this code is, like all meaning-content, intrinsically immaterial. Exhaustive efforts to map thousands of genes, commendable as they are, in no way answer the question of how, to begin with, such information was inbuilt in matter.

Moving to human life, we are (1) conscious, (2) aware of being conscious, and (3) just as clearly conscious that our consciousness is dramatically different from anything material or physical. Could consciousness and other fundamen-tal features of the human condition such as images, concepts, intentions, and choices — features which we are directly and constantly aware of and aware of as intrinsically immaterial — have arisen from lifeless, purposeless mass-energy given not just a few billion years but an infinite period of time? It seems obvious that we cannot give any credence to the idea that a certain bundle of mass-energy that just happened to exist (without beginning or end) then evolved without any direction or guidance over time into *thought.* We cannot seriously believe that intellect sprang out of mindless mass-energy, consciousness out of lifeless matter, intelligence out of blind force fields. In *Cosmos, Bios, Theos,* Sir John Eccles, a Nobel Prize–winning brain scientist, affirms that "the only certainty we have is that we exist as unique self-conscious beings" and that "the conscious self" is "a divine creation."[5] Another contributor to the volume, Nobelist Sir Nevill Mott, noted, "There is one 'gap' for which there will never be a scientific explana-tion, and that is man's consciousness. No scientist in the future, equipped with a supercomputer of the twenty-first century or beyond, will be able to set it to work and show that he is thinking about it."[6] Once we truly recognize that we are conscious thinking agents, we can never again conceive of our coming to be from anything less than a conscious thinking agent. Only Mind can beget mind; only an infinite Intelligence, an intelligence that has no limitation of any kind, can create beings with any kind of intelligence. I think and therefore know that I cannot as a thinking being have come into existence from nonthinking matter.

The upshot of these reflections is that the existence of any form of life is a profound mystery. But it is a mystery that illuminates a greater mystery yet — the appearance of the divine Life clothed in the medium of matter. Here a con-sideration of the hierarchy of life in the world is relevant (see the diagram on p. 167):

1. Matter

2. Cellular life: incorporates matter

3. Plant life: incorporates matter and cellular life

4. Animal life: incorporates matter, cellular life, some characteristics of plant life and includes perceptual consciousness and communication

5. Human life: incorporates all of the above and includes conceptual thought and communication, freewill, and the consciousness of the self

6. Angelic life: pure conceptual thought and will

7. The divine Life: the infinite Energy, Goodness, Love that created all other forms of life and holds them in being

Other than the divine Life Itself — from which flows all other life — and the angelic life which preceded other created life, the appearance of each one of these kinds of life involved a quantum leap from the previous kind, a leap that is not explicable or comprehensible in terms of physics and chemistry. We know without any shadow of doubt that even given a trillion years a nonliving rock cannot suddenly come to life. Nevertheless, in the case of those forms of life that have a material matrix, each higher form incorporates all of the capabilities of the forms below it.

This drama of the manifestation of progressively higher forms of life in the world, which began with the creation of matter out of nothing and continued with the elevation of matter into various forms of life, reaches its climax with a transformation as dramatic as the initial creation out of nothing: namely, the elevation of matter into a vehicle for the highest form of life, the divine Life that underlies all of creation. This last transformation is what we call Metamorphic Creation.

To understand the idea of Metamorphic Creation, we have only to look at life itself. It is surely significant that matter is involved in every instance of the creation of life in this world. Because we are creatures of flesh and blood, we have to touch, see, and smell life at all its levels to understand it and work with it. This need is met in the supreme instance of the appearance of a new kind of life in the world: it is a creative act whereby matter is transformed into that which contains the preexisting Life of God while continuing to manifest the characteristics of matter. And just as God works through created agents in the creation of new life, so too in the Metamorphic Creation God works through human agents endowed with the required supernatural authority.

If someone were to ask what there is that is different about the Host before and after consecration, the answer, in a word, is the Life that is now present in it. The Eucharist throbs, pulsates, literally explodes with the infinite Energy of the divine Life. But this Energy can be experienced only by the soul because it is literally soul-food. Can we see this Life, it may be asked. The answer is no, for the simple reason that neither human nor divine Life is something you can see. Human life, of course, manifests itself through various actions such as locomotion, speech, and the like. The divine Life, the Life that creates and transforms, manifests itself in the soul.

Even in our everyday experience, the huge amounts of energy latent in what appears to be the most inert units of matter are hidden to view. The equivalence of mass and energy expressed in Albert Einstein's formula $e=mc^2$ tells us that the energy contained in any material object at rest is derived by multiplying its mass m by c^2 the square of the speed of light (186,000 miles per second) — or, as Einstein put it, "The energy that belongs to the mass m is equal to this mass, multiplied by the square of the enormous speed of light — which is to say, a vast amount of energy for every unit of mass." The fact that something is motionless says nothing about whether or not it is actually exploding with energy. Einstein himself noted this paradox: "So long as none of the energy is given off externally, it cannot be observed. It is as though a man who is fabulously rich should never spend or give away a cent; no one could tell how rich he was."[7] The equivalence of mass and energy was confirmed most dramatically (and tragically) by the atom bomb. The relevance, albeit indirect, of the mass-energy equation to the doctrine of the Eucharist is simply this: *the physical characteristics of an object rarely reflect its inherent power.*

If we wonder how the power and glory of the Divine can be hidden in as humble a vessel as the Host, we must first consider the fact that just twenty pounds of plutonium can blow up an entire city with a destructive force of seventy million pounds of TNT. Even more mysterious is the fact that two and a half pounds of gray matter unveiled the precise mechanism that made this conversion of mass to energy possible. The point of these examples is not to prove the presence of the divine Life in a tiny sliver of matter but to broaden the horizons of both the intellect and the imagination. We cannot forget that when God became man, He came as one "without beauty, without majesty . . . no looks to attract our eyes; a thing despised and rejected by men" (Isa. 53:2). It is only to be expected that this humility of appearance would continue as He invites us anew in the mystery of the Eucharist.

In saying that the presence of the divine Life will be apparent only to the soul, we are not suggesting that the resultant experience is simply a matter of feelings or abstractions. St. Thomas Aquinas notes that the sacrament of the Eucharist has the appearance of food and drink because it does for the soul what bread and wine do for the body: it sustains, builds up, restores. Reception of the Eucharist *can* shake us to the very foundations of our being, cleanse us in the most profound sense, strengthen character as we confront choices at every instant and give direction and momentum in our daily voyage to the Divine. We say "can" because the explosion cannot take place without the critical mass or a chain reaction. The Energy that is released is, of course, not physical energy but the Energy that holds all things in being.

To perceive and receive the divine Life our hearts must thirst for It, our minds must have at least a dim recognition of Who is present, and our wills must be at least minimally turned to God and not against Him. The Eucharist has no effect on a soul hardened in deadly sin for the same reason that food given to a corpse does not energize it. "Mortal" sin like a "mortal" wound destroys life. But the divine Life that leaves the soul in mortal sin will return to it if there is repentance, reparation, and recourse to the sacrament of reconciliation. And each instance of the physical reception of the Eucharist, if accompanied by a receptivity of the soul, replenishes and intensifies the divine Life already present in us. On the impact of the Eucharist on the soul, St. Thomas writes, "It invigorates the weak, brings back health to the sick; it increases virtue, makes grace abound, purges away vices, refreshes the soul, renews life in the languid, binds together all the faithful in the union of charity! This Sacrament of Faith also inspires hope and increases charity."[8]

We have spoken of the Eucharist as the vehicle of divine Life because it is the Flesh and Blood of Him in Whom "dwells the whole fullness of the deity *bodily*" (Col. 2:9), namely, the Second Person of the Trinity in His human nature. In the case of human beings, there is no physical separation from the presence of the life of a person and the person itself. Thus I am present wherever my life is present. Likewise, every encounter with the divine Life that is in the Eucharist is simultaneously an encounter with Him Who possesses that Life, the Risen Christ. It is the presence of Christ in us in His divine Life that led the Apostle Paul to write, "Yet I live, no longer I, but Christ lives in me" (Gal. 2:20).

This understanding of the Eucharist as a vehicle of the divine Life is confirmed in Faustina's account of a message she received from Jesus:

> When I steeped myself in prayer, I was transported in spirit to the chapel, where I saw the Lord Jesus, exposed in the monstrance. In place of the monstrance, I saw the glorious face of the Lord, and He said to me, "What you see in reality, these souls see through faith. Oh, how pleasing to Me is their faith! You see, although there appears to be no trace of life in Me, in reality it is present in its fullness in each and every Host. But for Me to be able to act upon a soul, the soul must have faith. O how pleasing to Me is living faith!"[9]

In another extraordinary revelation, Faustina was shown that the effect of the Eucharist on the soul — specifically in the transmission of the divine Life — is directly proportionate to the soul's openness to this Life:

> When I was receiving Holy Communion today, I noticed in the cup a Living Host, which the priest gave to me. When I returned to my place I asked the Lord, "Why was one Host alive, since You are equally alive under each of the species?" The Lord answered me, "That is so. I am the same under each of the species, but not every soul receives Me with the same living faith as you do, My daughter, and therefore I cannot act in their souls as I do in yours."[10]

Applications and Implications

The new paradigm of the Real Presence outlined here might help clarify features of the doctrine of Transubstantiation that have seemed opaque to some critics.

Take the allegation that it is unintelligible to say that appearances can remain the same despite a change of substance. The confusion here can be clarified by a consideration of the appearance and disappearance of life. A physical entity that receives life becomes a different kind of entity from what it was before receiving this life: it is now a living being. Every physical component is now a part of this new being and the being itself is present in its every part. But when it dies, even if there is no change in weight or of components, what was once part of this being becomes mere waste. Once the sparkling eyes close and the heart no longer beats, then the person is no longer present and the body is no longer a body. The parallel to the Eucharist is quite simple. At the creation of the human soul at conception, the particles that were simply bits and pieces of matter become bits and pieces of a person. At consecration, the particles comprising the bread and wine suddenly become particles comprising the Flesh and the Blood of Christ. In the case of human life, when the bits and pieces of matter "give out," the person dies — and what is left of the bits and pieces is no longer a part of a human body. Likewise, when the appearances of bread and wine cease to exist, either through natural corruption or digestion, then the divine Life is no longer present and the remnants of the vehicle of divine Life are now merely instances of matter in motion.[11]

In conclusion, we will briefly address a few misconceptions about the Real Presence

1. Jesus Christ is sacramentally present in the Eucharist in His physical reality but not dimensively and visibly. The appearance of bread and wine was perhaps chosen because it is, on the one hand, unbloody, and, on the other, does not overwhelm us as we surely would be overwhelmed if we saw Christ in all His glory.

2. It is true that God — and this means the Trinity — is present everywhere. But God Incarnate, Christ in His human nature, is today present only in Heaven and in the Eucharist. At consecration, Christ does not come down from Heaven to the Host but the Host rises to Him; the reality that is bread and wine is transformed into a reality that is identical with His Body and Blood.

3. It is the Risen Christ who is present in the Eucharist — and He is present in every particle of the Host, every drop of the Precious Blood.

4. The Eucharist elevates matter to its highest level and it is perhaps a prefiguring of the new heaven and the new earth that is to come.

5. There is no better analogy of complete union than the processes of eating and drinking because what is eaten and drunk become a part of the person who eats and drinks. Thus to receive the Eucharist is to bring the divine Life into one's being in a manner as intimate as the physical act of eating and drinking. The physical reception of the Eucharist is an exact image of the reception of the divine Life in the Eucharist into one's soul.[12]

The View from the Other Side

Four other entries from St. Faustina Kowalska's *Diary* of her encounters with Jesus help us to grasp the importance that God Himself gives to our reception of the Eucharist.

"My daughter, do not omit Holy Communion unless you know well that your fall was serious; apart from this no doubt must stop you from uniting yourself with Me in the mystery of My love. Your minor faults will disappear in My love like a piece of straw thrown into the great furnace. Know that you grieve Me much when you fail to receive Me in Holy Communion."[13]

"I desire to unite myself with human souls; My great delight is to unite Myself with souls. Know, My daughter, that when I come to a human heart in Holy Communion, My hands are full of all kinds of graces which I want to give to the soul. But souls do not even pay attention to Me; they leave Me to Myself and busy themselves with other things. Oh, how sad I am that souls do not recognize Love! They treat Me as a dead object."[14]

"Oh, how painful it is to Me that souls so seldom unite themselves to Me in Holy Communion. I wait for souls, and they are indifferent toward Me. I love them tenderly and sincerely, and they distrust Me. I want to lavish My graces on them, and they do not want to accept them. They treat Me as a dead object, whereas My heart is full of love and mercy. In order that you may know at least some of My pain, imagine the most tender of mothers who has great love for her children, while those children spurn her love. Consider her pain. No one is in a position to console her. This is but a feeble image and likeness of My love."[15]

"My child, that you may answer my call worthily, receive Me daily in Holy Communion. It will give you strength."[16]

Chapter 11

How the Paschal Supper, Calvary, and the Heavenly Intercession Become Present Here and Now in the Holy Mass

From His teachings in the Gospel and that of His entire Church through history, it is clear that the bread and wine at Mass become the Body and Blood of Jesus Christ and that He becomes physically present among us. But why? On one level, He is here to offer us His Life which we receive when we receive Him in communion. But on a more important level, His Presence makes the Mass a true sacrifice, one in which He is both Priest and Victim.

In what sense, it may be asked, is the Mass a sacrifice, since there is no slaughter of animals on the altar, no blazing fires, or eerie incantations. More important, the claim that the Mass is a participation in the Sacrifice of Calvary raises the questions of how exactly it "participates" in Calvary and whether this claim of participation implies a "repetition" of Christ's "once for all death" on Calvary. Let it be said first that the Mass is not a "repeat" of Calvary. But neither is it merely symbolic of Calvary. The Mass makes the sacrifice of Calvary sacramentally present to us with all the graces, glory, and power that flow from that sacrifice. What does it mean to say that not just Jesus Himself but His sacrifice on Calvary become "sacramentally present" to us — and why is this second "presence" necessary?

Calvary and the Mass

The first thing to note is the fundamental difference between the Redemption from Original Sin brought about by Jesus' Death on the Cross and the application of the effects of this Death throughout time for the salvation of souls. The Act of Redemption, whereby the barrier of Original Sin was removed and Heaven once again became possible for humanity, took place only once — on Calvary. But the fruits of the Redemptive Act are manifested soul by soul, act by act, choice by choice. Calvary opens the Gate of Heaven. Prayer, the practice of the beatitudes taught in the Sermon on the Mount, participation in the "signs" instituted as salvific by Jesus (for instance, baptism) and, above all, the Mass, draw us step by step through the celestial Gate. The Fall was a lethal computer virus in the system that prevented the rocket from lifting off. Calvary killed the virus, provided the means to repair most of the damage it caused to the system, and launched the rocket. But now that the rocket is in flight, the question is whether it will stay on course or even "make it," given that its damaged system needs constant attention. Constant upgrades on the basic anti-virus software are required to kill new bugs spawned in parts of the system that were corrupted by the original virus; sometimes new programs have to be written to replace these corrupted parts if there is an imminent crash of the hard drive. Calvary redeemed us "once for all" from Original Sin. Participation in the sacramental presence of Calvary today gives us the sanctifying power and spiritual strength we need at every moment to stay the course. Calvary made salvation possible. The sacramental presence of Calvary in the Mass makes salvation actual.

Intention, Execution, Application: Passover, Passion, Heaven

The second issue concerns the coherence of speaking of the Mass as a participation in Calvary. We say it is a participation because this is what we are taught in Scripture and the understanding of Scripture given us by the Fathers and Councils of the Church. Moreover, the Mass is a participation not just in Calvary but in both the Last Supper and the heavenly intercession that Jesus continues to make on our behalf before the Father. If we look at Scripture, we see three events relating to the Mass that flow from each other. At the Paschal Meal, Jesus announces His intention to lay down His life in atonement for sin — and called on His followers to eat His Flesh and drink His Blood as a memorial of this Event. At Calvary, He executes His intention. And, finally, in Heaven, He continues to intercede for us before the Father (Hebrews, Revelation).

There is an obvious connection between these three great Acts: intention then execution then application. The prophecy of Isaiah speaks of the Servant who is taken as a lamb to its slaughter. The prophetic Book of Revelation shows the Lamb Who now reigns in Heaven — but a Lamb who now and forever is a Lamb that has been slain. Each offering of the Lamb subsumes in its reality and significance all that was done before: Calvary subsumes the Paschal Meal and the Intercession in Heaven subsumes both Calvary and the Paschal

Meal. Each offering gives meaning to the next: the offering made at the Last Supper shows the purpose of the Passion, and the Passion makes possible the intercession in Heaven.

The Mass in turn brings all three offerings before us here and now. It is by no means a repetition or a new offering: it is simply a manifestation in earthly terms of the one continuous Act of Offering in Heaven made by the Son before the Father. Since this Act incorporates both the Passover Promise and the Sacrifice of Calvary, the Mass too is a participation in the Paschal Meal and its incarnation on Calvary. The Son's intercession in Heaven is intended to "apply" the salvific and sanctifying effects of His death for the continued well-being of the human race. The Mass, as the earthly manifestation of this heavenly offering, is a vehicle of these very same effects in a localized setting. This understanding of the Mass is reflected in the New Testament, from the Epistles to the Book of Revelation, and in all the great liturgies. Moreover, the Mass is not an idea conjured up by the Christian community. It is celebrated in obedience to the command of Christ Himself, Who said that His followers were to continue making His Sacrifice present before them ("Do this in memory of me"). The early Church faithfully followed this command, and the "breaking of the bread" was in fact their fundamental religious ritual. The Lord's Supper is a union of heaven and earth for, as St. John Chrysostom said,

> We have our victim in heaven, our priest in heaven, our sacrifice in heaven. ... When you see the Lord sacrificed and lying as an oblation, and the priest standing by the sacrifice and praying, and all things reddened with that precious blood, do you think that you are still among men and standing on earth?[1]

Addressing this very same theme, Eric Mascall writes,

> The purpose of a sign is to represent; and the purpose of that particular kind of sign which is a sacrament is to *re*-present, to make present, to effect, that which is represented.... In the sacramental order the Mass contains and communicates the whole redemptive activity of Christ, the whole sweep of filial self-oblation that extends from his incarnation in the womb of Mary through his death on Calvary to his heavenly glorification. The Mass is therefore neither a new sacrifice nor a part of the one Sacrifice; it *is* the one Sacrifice in its totality, present under a sign.... It just *is* the sacrifice — sacramentally.[2]

A Musical Analogy

It may be asked how we can truly participate through the Mass in the threefold Offering of Christ. The most helpful analogy here is a musical one. Take a great symphony composed by Beethoven. The symphony originated as a series of thoughts in the mind of the composer, who then set it to paper using conventional notations. Subsequently, a symphony orchestra, using a variety of musical instruments, brings the scores to life. The thoughts that were in the mind of the composer and the notations with which he expressed them are "incarnated" every time a symphony orchestra performs the piece. As often as an orchestra performs it, the actual symphony, which embodies both the thoughts of the composer and their written expression, is "present" with us (the quality of the instruments and the capability of the musicians will obviously determine the nature of the performance).

Applying this analogy, we might say that at every Mass, the intention of Christ at the Paschal Meal, His sacrifice on Calvary, and His continuing intercession in Heaven are "incarnated" before us. The scores were written at the Passover Meal. The first performance by the Composer took place on Calvary. Thereafter, the Composer continues to play the same music in Heaven — and this Heavenly Music is incarnated here on earth in the Mass. A thousand Masses do not diminish the definitive nature of the actual historical sacrifice on Calvary — just as a thousand performances of a symphony by Beethoven do not signify that there was no original composition. Likewise every performance of the symphony has the same power (all other things being equal such as the quality of the instruments) as the original performance. We "participate" in the thoughts of Beethoven at every performance of the symphony. So it is with the Mass: the Sacrifice of Calvary becomes present in all its Power and Glory when the bread and the wine become the Body and Blood of Christ and are then offered up to the Father. Just as a song played at a radio station can be heard from thousands of transistor radios, so the One Sacrifice on Calvary becomes "present" at thousands of Masses.

Like all analogies about the supernatural, these examples fall far short of the original. Beethoven's music or the song on the radio are not "alive" unlike the Passion and its incarnation in the Mass. And whereas the symphony depends for its quality on instruments and musicians, the Sacrifice of the Mass is ultimately a Sacrifice offered by Christ of Himself — albeit in the person of His priest.

The Mass as Sacrifice

We speak of the Mass as a sacrifice, and this clearly needs further elaboration. On the concept of sacrifice, no Christian can disagree with the idea that we are all called to offer everything we are and have to God. Sacrifice is foundational to our relationship to God: It is praise, thanksgiving, surrender to the divine will. "Sacrifice" in this sense — and it is certainly a part of the Sacrifice of the Mass — is uncontroversial. But the Mass is not simply an offering of ourselves. It is an offering united with the Offering made by Christ of Himself on Calvary. Again the teaching that Jesus today continues to intercede for us in Heaven is not controversial — since this is clearly laid out in scriptural texts. The question before us is this: what kind of sacrifice are we talking about when we talk of the Sacrifice of the Mass and why is it necessary?

The historical answer is threefold. First, the Mass is a real participation in

Christ's offering of Himself in Calvary — but where graces were acquired at Calvary, these same graces are dispensed at every Mass.

Secondly, whereas those present at Calvary were *eyewitnesses* to Christ's immolation of Himself, at the Mass we are *witnesses* to this oblation in its present reality. For the Passover Supper and Calvary form one reality with the everlasting offering of the Son to the Father — and it is this reality that is "made present" before us here and now. Just as the Host retains the appearance of bread while being transformed in its essential reality during the consecration, the Mass contains within itself the essential reality of the threefold Offering of Christ while retaining the appearance of a man saying prayers over a piece of bread and a cup of wine. The actions of the priest celebrating the Mass are, on the one hand, acts of thanksgiving from the Christian community. But during the actual consecration they are acts of Christ — and the words of consecration are uttered in the first person — Who is present as Priest and Who offers up His Body and Blood to the Father in union with the Holy Spirit. We know that the bread and the wine become the Body and the Blood of Christ and we know that These are offered up to the Father as a sacrifice of praise, propitiation, and petition. The propitiation here is not the Atonement for Original Sin, which was made once for all at Calvary, but propitiation for the continuing sins of humanity.

The Need for Sacrifice

Finally, we unite ourselves and all that we have with Christ during the Mass. We offer ourselves in union with Christ's offering of Himself. We unite our sufferings, our minds and hearts, our intentions and acts with His. St. Paul (in Col. 1:24 but also in his other epistles) describes the life of a Christian as one of offering up our suffering to help complete the application of the effects of Christ's death on the cross: "If we are afflicted, it is for your encouragement and salvation" (2 Cor. 1:6). Moreover, we are to offer "spiritual sacrifices acceptable to God through Jesus Christ" (1 Pet. 2:5). To live as a Christian is to make all aspects of our life a sacrifice to God.

The culmination of this continuing sacrifice is the Sacrifice of the Mass where our sacrifices are directly united with the Sacrifice of Christ. The Church as the Body of Christ unites her offering with her head who is Christ. St. Augustine noted that the offering to the Father made by the human Christ on the Cross mirrors the Son's eternal self-offering to the Father just as the union of the Church's offering with that of Christ is analogous to the sacrifice of Christ on Calvary. The sacrifice of Calvary brought about the immediate conversion of two eyewitnesses: the thief on the cross and the centurion. Likewise, participation in the Mass brings about conversion, purification, sanctification for those who are witnesses.

Why do we need the Sacrifice of the Mass? Because, at the most basic level, both we and the world need it for our very survival. We need it to propitiate the wrath of God for the sins that we continue to commit against Him: Calvary was propitiation for Original Sin, the Mass is propitiation for actual sins. The code

The Holy Mass: Three in One

> The Self-Offering of the Passover Victim at the *Last Supper*
>
> > Consummation of the Passover Offering at the Sacrifice of *Calvary*
> >
> > > *Heavenly Intercession* (Heb. 9:23–24) of Christ, the true High Priest, the Lamb that was slain (Rev. 5:6) before the Father
> > >
> > > > *Holy Mass:* Earthly participation of the faithful in the one Offering Event constituted by the Passover Meal, the Sacrifice on Calvary, and the Intercession of the Lamb of God

of conduct in the universe is not restricted to the physical order but applies to the spiritual as well. Infringements of the laws and principles of the spiritual order bring about consequences as surely as attempts to defy the laws of nature (as when we knowingly place ourselves in front of a speeding bullet or a speeding truck). "Punishment" for actual sins did not cease with Calvary — this is amply evident in the New Testament, particularly in the Epistle to the Hebrews — and it is for this reason that we offer up the Mass as propitiation, an offering that is an earthly application of Christ's continual offering of Himself in Heaven. But it is not simply for propitiation: it is also for spiritual birth and growth and for the application to specific needs of the power of Christ's Sacrifice. The universal power of the Sacrifice of Calvary is localized, its effects made locally available.

Always a Victim

What is most striking about Revelation 5:6 ("A lamb that seemed to have been slain"), Romans 8:34 ("It is Christ...at the right hand of God who indeed intercedes for us"), Hebrews 9:24 (Christ has entered "heaven itself, that he might now appear before God on our behalf"), and Hebrews 7:25 ("He lives forever to make intercession for them.") is (1) the Victim Who was sacrificed on Calvary rose again and was glorified but will always remain a Victim, and (2) His continued intercession on our behalf is required and so He continues to intercede for us. In celebrating the Mass, we not only bring to mind but actually participate in the suffering of the Lamb who was slaughtered. This greatest imaginable tragedy is in its piercing poignancy the reverse image of the inexpressible sorrow of sin. The memory of His Passion is to be remembered and re-presented in its reality in the Sacrifice of the Mass through all of history. Calvary will never be a distant event in the past: it will be offered "from the rising of the sun to its setting" in "every place."

At the Passover He said that we must eat His Flesh to receive His Life. On Calvary, He gave up His Life in order that we might receive It. And now at the Sacrifice of the Mass, we both witness the offering up of His Life and partake of His Flesh that we might receive His Life.

Chapter 12

The Continual Coming: Miracles of the Eucharist in History

A miracle of the Eucharist refers to (1) any phenomenon involving a naturally inexplicable transformation in the physical and observable appearance of the consecrated Host or the consecrated "wine," and/or (2) a singularity in which the Host or the "wine" is observed to transcend a law of nature (for instance, the law of gravity).

It must be understood that a Eucharistic miracle understood in this sense neither detracts from nor should distract us from the fundamental mystery of the Eucharist, the transformation of the substance but not the appearance of bread and wine into the Body and Blood of Jesus Christ. Eucharistic miracles, in point of fact, draw our attention to this fundamental mystery. In certain Eucharistic miracles, the appearances of bread and wine are replaced with the appearances of flesh and blood. This does not imply that every consecrated Host has an underlying layer of flesh that we can reach given an appropriate level of slicing and dicing or that the consecrated "wine" will take on the properties of human blood given certain conditions. Eucharistic miracles are called miracles precisely because they are singular events. Like all divinely directed miracles, miracles of the Eucharist take place to achieve a divine purpose. The miracles of Jesus are ultimately important not in themselves but in drawing our attention to (1) His identity as the second Person of the Trinity united to a human nature, (2) His mission of redemption, and (3) the urgency of our response to His invitation. Likewise, the ultimate importance of miracles of the Eucharist is in drawing our attention to (1) the fact that bread and wine actually become the Body and Blood of Christ at every valid consecration, (2) the fact that the Eucharistic elements are vehicles of the divine Life offered to us, and (3) the urgency of our receiving the Eucharist precisely in order to partake of this Life. Every consecrated Host is as worthy of our adoration as a Host that changes into human flesh.

The famous miracles of the Eucharist have been described in several narrative works. Appropriately enough, most of these were written as works of piety. A few others are exhaustive documentaries chronicling the background and circumstances in which the miracles took place. In the present work, we will seek to (1) separate the "hard facts" from the anecdotal evidence and (2) focus on the comprehensive pattern that seems to emerge in and through these miracles. In gathering information on these miracles, the present author has visited several of the sites of the Eucharistic miracles.

Eucharistic miracles may be classified under the following categories:

• Transformation of the Host into flesh
• Appearance of blood on the Host
• Transformation of the consecrated "wine" into blood
• Preservation of the Host or Hosts over centuries
• Host or Hosts that transcend gravity or other laws of nature
• Visions of Jesus witnessed by the congregation during the consecration of the Host
• Lifetime subsistence on the Host

Eucharistic miracles of a "negative" kind include the ability of Satanists to discern the difference between consecrated and unconsecrated hosts.

Scientific Issues

Drilling deeper, the "hard facts," facts that may be deemed indisputable, in the historical miracles are the following:

• Continued preservation of Hosts that have turned to flesh
• Continued preservation of Hosts with streaks of blood
• Continued preservation of Hosts involved in other supernatural phenomena

Clearly, claims of miracles of the Eucharist cannot be dismissed as hallucinations because the subjects of some of these miracles — Hosts that have turned to flesh — are even today available for tangible observation.

A skeptic could very well admit that the Hosts do indeed continue to mysteriously perdure over such a long period of time but deny that anything else extraordinary took place. It is true that we cannot today prove to the skeptic that the piece of flesh on display today was once a piece of bread. But what is important here is that there is at least one hard and indisputable fact that defies natural explanation: the continued preservation of the Host or of the flesh (or the blood as the case may be). And, while we cannot, by the very nature of the case, replicate the transformation of the Host into flesh, we can point to the continued occurrence of the same kind of phenomenon in the present day. To take two prominent examples: in the case of Julia Kim of Naju, South Korea, the Host has on numerous occasions turned into bloody flesh when given to her during communion, and in the case of Little Audrey of Worcester, Massachusetts, Hosts brought near her bedside have started to bleed, a phenomenon recorded by skeptical inquirers from the mass media.

Like it or not, then, even the skeptics have to go along with two starting points: (1) various Hosts and fragments of flesh have been preserved over long periods of time, and (2) reliable reports of the conversion of Hosts into flesh and blood continue to this very day, and in certain cases these conversions have been accurately recorded.

That there is something extraordinary about (1), the preservation of Hosts and particles of flesh and blood over centuries, cannot be denied for the following reasons:

- In the case of the flesh, scientific analysis in the main instances has shown that the object in question is human flesh. How this flesh could retain its original characteristics over hundreds of years despite exposure to physical, biological, and atmospheric contaminants is inexplicable on a purely natural level.

- In the case of the blood, again scientific analysis has confirmed that we are dealing with human blood — in fact, blood with the sero-proteic make-up of fresh blood and containing all the minerals present in normal blood. It is well known that blood loses its chemical properties within an hour of being shed, and blood from a dead body decays almost immediately. In the cases of Lanciano, Trani, Santarem, Florence, and others, the samples of blood have been preserved for literally hundreds of years — without any preservatives present. This pattern of retaining the external and chemical characteristics of blood is true not just of the drops of blood preserved in their original state but also in those instances — like Daroca and Bolsena — where bloodstains continue to remain on corporals (the cloth on which the Host and the chalice are placed during Mass).

- The preservation of the Hosts is noteworthy because these Hosts are made from unleavened bread which can at best retain its original properties over a period of five to ten years. But the Hosts on display from the various miracles have maintained their original color and remained fresh over centuries — this without being kept in sterile conditions or in an airtight environment. Those that have been chemically analyzed were found to be edible and to retain the same starchy composition as bread. Dr. Siro Grimaldi, a professor of chemistry at the University of Siena and director of the Municipal Chemical Laboratory, noted that the preservation of the Hosts in Siena represents "a singular phenomenon that inverts the natural law of the conservation of organic material."

With this overview of the relevant categories and criteria, we can now consider the actual miracles themselves in their historical reality. The most famous Eucharistic miracles, it must be remembered, have been judged "worthy of belief" by ecclesiastical authorities after the requisite investigation. In most cases, the evidence for the miracle is still available for the public to observe or study. In studying the miracles, we have first divided them into four tables:

- Ancient Eucharistic Miracles with Continuous Contemporary Evidence
- Modern Eucharistic Miracles with Continuous Contemporary Evidence
- Hosts that Transcended the Laws of Nature
- Visions of Jesus during the Mass

The tables are followed by a brief historical review of the great miracles of the Eucharist for which there is evidence today.

Ancient Miracles of the Eucharist with Continuing Contemporary Evidence

c. 700   LANCIANO, ITALY. Host turns to flesh, wine to blood during the celebration of the Mass. *Reason:* Sign for priest celebrating the Mass who doubted the Real Presence of Christ in the Eucharist. *Contemporary Evidence:* Flesh and five pellets of blood from the miracle still on display after thirteen hundred years. Lanciano was named after Longinus, the soldier who pierced the side of Christ with a lance and became a convert after a drop of the Blood of Christ cured him of blindness. Upon examination, the flesh in the Lanciano miracle was found to come from the muscle tissue of the heart. Appropriately the Flesh and Blood of Christ manifested Itself first in a city named after the person who actually pierced Christ's body. The blood divided into five pellets that are said to symbolize the five wounds of Christ.

1000   TRANI, ITALY. Host boiled in oil by sorceress turns to flesh and begins to bleed profusely. *Reason:* Sacrilegious treatment of the Eucharist. *Contemporary Evidence:* Two fragments of the Host with bloodstains still preserved.

1171   FERRARA, ITALY. Host becomes flesh when broken after Consecration; blood spurts from It and sprays the dome behind the altar. *Reason:* A sign for citizens of the town who professed heretical views of the Eucharist. *Contemporary Evidence:* Blood from the Host is still seen on the ceiling of the church.

1194   AUGSBURG, GERMANY. Host that had been stolen by a woman and kept in her house changes into flesh with red streaks. *Reason:* Sacrilegious treatment of the Eucharist. *Contemporary Evidence:* Host still preserved in the church where the miracle took place.

1228   ALATRI, ITALY. Host stolen by a woman in order to prepare a "love potion" turns to flesh. *Reason:* Sacrilegious treatment of the Eucharist. *Contemporary Evidence:* Miraculous Host still on display.

1200s SANTAREM, PORTUGAL. Host taken to sorceress begins to drip blood. *Reason:* Sacrilege. *Contemporary Evidence:* Host with veins and blood at the bottom still on display (the blood sometimes appears to be fresh and at other times dried).

1230 FLORENCE, ITALY. Consecrated "wine" turns to Blood. *Reason:* Negligence of celebrant in cleansing the sacred vessels. *Contemporary Evidence:* Blood still preserved in chalice.

1239 DAROCA, SPAIN. Hosts left outside disappear and are replaced with bloodstains on corporals. (A corporal is the cloth on which the Host and the Chalice are placed during the Mass). *Reason:* God's protection of those who turn to Him especially at Mass. *Contemporary Evidence:* Corporals with bloodstains still on display. Blood subjected to clinical analysis and found to be of human origin.

1263 BOLSENA-ORVIETO, ITALY. Blood seeps from Host onto altar, corporal, and hands of celebrant after consecration. *Reason:* Priest's doubt about the Real Presence of Christ in the Eucharist. *Contemporary Evidence:* Corporal with bloodstains on display.

1273 OFFIDA, ITALY. Host heated over a tile (at the instructions of a sorceress) turns to flesh and begins to bleed. The Host along with the tile is wrapped in a tablecloth and buried under garbage in the stable where the animals show the burial spot reverence. When dug out after seven years, the Host is found to be incorrupt. *Reason:* Sacrilegious treatment of the Eucharist. *Contemporary Evidence:* Miraculous Host still on display along with tile and tablecloth with bloodstains.

1300 CEBRERO, SPAIN. Host turns to flesh, consecrated "wine" to blood in the presence of a skeptical priest and a devout believer. *Reason:* Priest's doubt. *Contemporary Evidence:* Flesh and Blood on display.

1317 HASSELT, BELGIUM. Host touched by man in mortal sin begins to bleed. *Reason:* Importance of being in a state of grace when handling the Eucharist. *Contemporary Evidence:* Host with bloodstains on display.

1330 SIENA, ITALY. Host between pages of breviary begins to bleed. *Reason:* Care and veneration of Eucharist. *Contemporary Evidence:* Bloodstained pages on display.

1331 BLANOT, FRANCE. Host that falls from lips of communicant onto cloth turns to blood. *Reason:* Care and veneration of Eucharist. *Contemporary Evidence:* Bloodstained cloth on display.

1356 MACERATA, ITALY. Blood seeps from particles of Host and falls on corporal. *Reason:* Priest's doubt about the Real Presence of Christ in the Eucharist. *Contemporary Evidence:* Corporal with bloodstains on display.

1374   MIDDLEBURG-LOUVAIN, BELGIUM. Host turns to flesh and bleeds when man in mortal sin bites into It. *Reason:* Importance of being in a state of grace when receiving the Eucharist. *Contemporary Evidence:* Miraculous Flesh and corporal with bloodstains on display.

1384   SEEFELD, AUSTRIA. Host turns blood red and knight who receives It unworthily sinks into the ground. *Reason:* Importance of receiving Eucharist worthily and humbly. *Contemporary Evidence:* Original Host on display and handprints of knight on altar still visible.

1412   BAGNA DI ROMAGNA, ITALY. Consecrated "wine" turns into blood and falls onto corporal. *Reason:* Priest's doubt about the Real Presence of Christ in the Eucharist. *Contemporary Evidence:* Corporal with bloodstains on display.

1608   FAVERNEY, FRANCE. Monstrance with two Hosts remains suspended in the air for thirty-three hours during and after fire in church. *Reason:* Power of the Eucharist over natural laws. *Contemporary Evidence:* Host on display.

1730   SIENA, ITALY. Stolen hosts remain miraculously preserved. *Reason:* Divine response to theft. *Contemporary Evidence:* Hosts on display after more than 250 years.

MODERN MIRACLES OF THE EUCHARIST WITH CONTINUING CONTEMPORARY EVIDENCE

1970   STICH, GERMANY. Bloodstains appear on cloth under chalice. *Contemporary Evidence:* Bloodstains on display. The samples were analyzed by medical experts and found to be instances of human blood.

Dec. 8, 1991   BETANIA, VENEZUELA. Consecrated Host starts bleeding. *Contemporary Evidence:* Material extruding from the Host was subjected to medical evaluation and found to be human blood.

From 1988   NAJU, KOREA. Host turns to flesh. Host descends from above. *Contemporary Evidence:* Transformations witnessed by numerous observers. Flesh and blood medically analyzed.

HOSTS THAT TRANSCENDED THE LAWS OF NATURE

1274   PARIS, FRANCE. A thief stole a golden case containing a consecrated Host. When he threw away the Host, It rose in the air and stayed above his head. A crowd along with various dignitaries gathered around him. Only when the priest who consecrated the Host arrived did the Host descend.

It was taken in a procession to a church and was preserved there until the French Revolution.

1280 SLAVONICE, CZECHOSLOVAKIA. A Host stolen from a local church was seen hovering unharmed in a fire above a pile of rocks into which It had been thrown. A church was built on this spot and commemoration of the event continues to this day.

1290 PARIS, FRANCE. A woman "exchanged" a consecrated Host for a dress she had left with a pawnbroker. The pawnbroker stabbed the Host before his family, and It started bleeding profusely. He then threw It in a fire only to find the Host rise untouched above the fire. Next he threw It in boiling water, at which point the water became bloody and started streaming out into the street. A woman who came in saw the figure of Jesus in front of the boiling pot. When the vision disappeared, she saw a Host in the air. The Host settled into a vessel she held and was solemnly taken to a church. After civil and ecclesiastical investigation, the house in which the incident took place was converted into a chapel.

1345 AMSTERDAM, HOLLAND. A fisherman on his deathbed was given the Eucharist by the parish priest. After the priest left, the man threw up everything he had eaten including the Host. Anxious to clean the room, his wife threw the Host into the fire in their fireplace. The next day she found that the Host had not been affected in any way by the fire. Awestruck, she took the Host to the priest. Their house was soon turned into a chapel. During the great fire of 1452 the entire city of Amsterdam was consumed by flames. The chapel with the miraculous Host also burned down. After searching through the ruins, both the Host and the monstrance in which It was kept were found to be unscathed. The celebration of this miracle became an annual event. The apparitions of Our Lady of All Nations of Amsterdam, which had a strong Eucharistic component, began in March 1945, six hundred years after the miracle.

1370 BRUSSELS, BELGIUM. Sixteen Hosts were stolen from a tabernacle and handed to a group of enemies of the Church, who proceeded to stab Them on Good Friday. The Hosts began bleeding. This alarmed the perpetrators, who now sought to get rid of the Hosts. Eventually the matter came to the attention of the authorities, who recovered most of the Hosts. For many years, until They were lost during the Reformation, the faithful came in pilgrimage to adore the Hosts.

1433 AVIGNON, FRANCE. When heavy rains all but submerged the city of Avignon, a group of monks set out on a boat to save the Hosts reserved at a chapel for the perpetual adoration of the Eucharist. On entering the chapel, they were amazed to find that it had been flooded but that the water had separated into two walls four feet high on either side so that the Altar with the Hosts was left dry.

1453   TURIN, ITALY. Two thieves stole various costly articles, including a case
       with a Host, from a church in Exilles and traveled with these to Turin.
       When the mule carrying the stolen goods collapsed, the Host, instead
       of falling to the ground with everything else, soared in the air and was
       surrounded by brilliant rays of light. A crowd soon assembled. When the
       bishop of the city arrived with a chalice, the Host came down into it.
       This miraculous Host was preserved for over one hundred years but was
       later consumed on the orders of the ecclesiastical authorities.

1560   MORROVALLE, ITALY. The local church was burnt to the ground. The hor-
       rified monks found that even the tabernacle had been reduced to ashes
       but were then amazed to find a Host in the ruins that was entirely un-
       harmed. This Host was the object of worship for nearly three hundred
       years until It was lost during the clashes between the Italian states.

1601   LA VILUENA, SPAIN. A fire destroyed the local church but left the
       tabernacle and the Hosts inside untouched.

1640   TURIN, ITALY. Flames enveloped a soldier who kicked in the tabernacle
       door to steal the Eucharist. Remnants of the attack are on display.

1772   PATERNO, ITALY. Two containers of consecrated Hosts were stolen from
       a church in this town. Despite fervent efforts, the faithful had no success
       in locating the Hosts. A few weeks later, strange lights were seen over
       a nearby field. After an intense search, the townspeople came to a tree
       before which there was a ball of light with a dove in the center. The dove
       flew into the ground. The observers dug up the area near the tree and
       found the Hosts buried there.

VISIONS OF JESUS DURING THE MASS

1153   BRAINE, FRANCE. During Mass, at the moment of consecration, the Host
       disappeared and the congregation saw a young child. This created a sen-
       sation, and the non-Christians present requested baptism. According to
       historical records, the miraculous Host was preserved for at least five
       hundred years, and annual processions were held in honor of the event.

1257   REGENSBURG, GERMANY. While celebrating Mass, the priest began to
       doubt the Real Presence of Jesus in the sacrament. Suddenly, the figure
       of Christ on the crucifix came to life, and its hand reached out and took
       the chalice away from the priest. When the priest repented of his lack of
       faith, the chalice was returned to him.

1822   BORDEAUX, FRANCE. The Eucharist was exposed to a community of nuns
       by a visiting priest. Both the priest and the congregation noticed that the
       face of Jesus appeared instead of the Eucharist. In his testimony, the
       priest wrote, "Instead of the Holy Species, I saw our Savior, head, chest

and arms, in the middle of the circle that served Him as a frame like a painting, but with this difference, that the painting looked alive. His figure was very white and represented a young man about thirty years old, extraordinarily beautiful. He was dressed with a dark red scarf draped over His shoulder and chest."

1867　Dubna, Poland (now Russia). During a Forty Hour devotion before the Eucharist, rays of light shone from the Host. Then the face of Jesus appeared in the Host and remained there throughout the forty hours. This happened in a village in Poland at a time when the Russian rulers forbade all such devotions.

Overview

Eucharistic miracles have been reported from the days of the catacombs. Tarsicius, a Christian of the third century, was martyred for protecting the Eucharist from desecration; the Eucharist he was carrying is said to have disappeared when he was beaten to death by his persecutors. Referring to other such miracles, St. Cyprian, writing circa 258 A.D., states:

If you do not fear future punishment, at least fear those of the present. How many apostates do we behold who have met an unhappy end? One is struck dumb, another possessed by a demon becomes his own executioner. This one, attempting to communicate [i.e., receive communion] amongst the faithful, is seized by horrible convulsions. That one, striving to open the tabernacle in which the body of the Lord was preserved, sees flames issuing forth.

Eucharistic miracles were also described by Church Fathers like St. John Chrysostom (d. 407), who reported that the Eucharist turned to stone when it was consumed by a heretic, St. Gregory of Nazianzus (d. 389), and St. Gregory the Great (d. 604).

Starting with the miracle of Lanciano in the eighth century, Italy became the single most prominent location for Eucharistic miracles, with miracles reported in every century from the eleventh through the eighteenth. Most of these miracles left tangible footprints available for contemporary inspection. The miracles were not, of course, restricted to Italy. Other significant sites of Eucharistic miracles in the second Christian millennium included France, Germany, Austria, Belgium, Holland, Portugal, Spain, Czechoslovakia, and Poland. In the twentieth century, Eucharistic miracles have been reported in Korea, Venezuela, Ecuador, Japan, Germany, and the United States.

Lanciano

The most famous Eucharistic miracle in history — and the first of the miracles that left us with continuing tangible evidence — was the miracle of Lanciano. At the turn of the century, around 700 A.D., a priest of the Order of St. Basil (the Basilians) had begun to doubt the Christian doctrine of the Eucharist, particularly the teaching that during the consecration at Mass the bread and the wine are converted into the Body and Blood of Christ. He had been influenced by then-popular heretical views of the Eucharist but nevertheless prayed for divine assistance in sustaining his faith. Then one day, as he celebrated Mass, the bread and wine turned to actual human flesh and blood during the consecration. On witnessing this marvel, he turned to the congregation and said, "O fortunate witnesses to whom the Blessed God, to confound my disbelief, has wished to reveal Himself in this Most Blessed Sacrament and to render Himself visible to our eyes. Come, brethren, and marvel at our God so close to us. Behold the Flesh and Blood of our most Beloved Christ."

News of the miracle spread all over Italy and Lanciano became the principal site of Eucharistic adoration and pilgrimages. The miracle took place in the Church of St. Legontian and St. Domitian. The church was run successively by the Basilians, the Benedictines, and the Franciscans. The original church building had to be torn down after an earthquake. The church rebuilt on the same site and in which the Flesh and the Blood are still kept was named the Church of St. Francis. The Flesh is preserved in an ivory reliquary and the Blood (now hardened into pellets) in a chalice believed to have been the very chalice in which the miracle took place.

Notable features of the miracle include the following:

- Lanciano is named after St. Longinus, the Roman centurion who thrust his lance into the side of Christ on the cross. The centurion is believed to have become a Christian, and later a martyr, after the Blood of Christ dripped on Him from the Cross and cured him of an eye ailment. Thus the city named after the man known for piercing the Heart of Christ to expose His flesh and blood became the site of the greatest miracle of the Flesh and Blood of the Lord, Flesh, in fact, Which was later found to be tissue from the Heart. The Blood from the miracle has divided into five pellets, which are believed to symbolize the five wounds of Christ.

- Samples of the Flesh and Blood were subjected to clinical studies in 1970 by two Italian scientists, Professor Odoardo Linoli, a specialist in anatomy and pathological histology and in chemistry and clinical microscopy, and Dr. Ruggero Bertelli, a specialist in human anatomy. Their March 4, 1971, report (copies of which are kept at the Santuario Del Miracolo Eucaristico in Lanciano) detailed the following conclusions:

   The Flesh is real Flesh. The Blood is real Blood.

   The Flesh and the Blood belong to the human species.

   The Flesh consists of the muscular tissue of the heart.

In the Flesh we see present in sections: the myocardium, the endocardium, the vagus nerve, and also the left ventricle of the heart for the large thickness of the myocardium.

The Flesh is a "HEART" complete in its essential structure.

The Flesh and the Blood have the same blood type: AB.

In the Blood there were found proteins in the same normal proportions (in terms of percentage) as are found in the sero-proteic make-up of fresh, normal blood.

In the Blood, there were also found these minerals: chlorides, phosphorus, magnesium, potassium, sodium, and calcium.

The preservation of the Flesh and the Blood, which were left in their natural state [i.e., without any chemical preservatives] for twelve centuries and exposed to the action of atmospheric and biological agents, remains an extraordinary phenomenon.

The Eucharistic miracles that came after Lanciano included transformation miracles (Host changes to flesh, "wine" changes to blood), miracles of transcendence over the laws of nature, visions of Jesus during or after consecration, and miracles of sustenance strictly on the Eucharist. The transformation miracles may be further classified under the following categories that specify their most likely causes: (1) unbelief, (2) negligence, (3) sacrilege, and (4) manifestation of divine power.

Unbelief

Lanciano is the classic instance of a transformation miracle that took place in response to unbelief. The other miracles occasioned by unbelief include Ferrara, Bolsena, Macerata, and Bagna di Romagna in Italy and Cebrero in Spain.

The miracle of Ferrara took place on March 28, 1171, an Easter Sunday, in the Church of Santa Maria del Vado, a church with one of the many images of the Blessed Virgin believed to have been painted by St. Luke. The circumstances surrounding the miracle are succinctly presented in an 1197 A.D. document authored by a Gerald Cambrense and now kept in the Library Lamberthiana of Canterbury: "In Ferrara, Italy, in these our times, the Host on Easter Day, was transformed into a small piece of meat. The bishop of Ferrara was called, and having verified the miracle, the citizens of that city who had been Patrarini and had professed heretical ideas on the Eucharist, the Body of Christ, returned to the Truth." The pastor of the parish was breaking the Host after the consecration when blood spurted from It and sprayed the vaulted dome behind the altar. The Host Itself turned to flesh. On hearing about the miracle, the bishop of the region came to the church and saw the bloodstains for himself. Numerous pilgrims and ecclesiastical authorities came to see the dome, and a papal bull was issued by Pope Eugene IV in 1442 affirming the authenticity of the miracle. A new church was built in the area in 1518 and the dome with the bloodstains was moved to a chapel in this church. The bloodstains on the dome are visible even today, and the ancient image of the Virgin still hangs in the church.

The next miracle in this category, Bolsena-Orvieto, is unique because of the context in which it took place and its impact on history. Consider this:

- Blessed Juliana of Liège, Belgium (1192–1258), abbess of the Augustinian Sisters of the Assumption, had a vision in 1208 in which "she saw a lunar disk surrounded by rays of dazzling white light; on one side of the disk, however, there was a dark spot that spoiled the beauty of the whole. The Lord explained to her that the dark spot meant that the Church still lacked a solemn feast in honor of the Blessed Sacrament." At that time Europe in general, and Liège in particular, was under pressure from anti-sacramentalists who rejected the traditional doctrine of the Eucharist.

- After her vision, Blessed Juliana began a campaign for the institution of a feast of the Body and Blood of Christ. Her claims were investigated by the archbishop of Liège, Robert of Turotte, and his archdeacon James (Jacques) Pantaleon. The vision of Juliana was finally accepted as authentic by Archbishop Robert, and in 1246 he celebrated a feast in honor of the Body and Blood of Christ in his archdiocese.

- Archdeacon James Pantaleon was later elected Pope and became Pope Urban IV in 1261. Disputes about the Eucharist continued to rage under his papacy, and St. Thomas Aquinas emerged as the most articulate defender of the orthodox position on the Eucharist.

- In 1263, Pope Urban IV was residing in the town of Orvieto, Italy. In the same year, a priest named Peter of Prague was making a pilgrimage to Rome to bolster his wavering faith in both Christ and the Eucharist. On his way he spent the night at the town of Bolsena, adjacent to Orvieto, and celebrated Mass the next morning at the Church of St. Christina. During the consecration, blood began to drip from the Host, falling on the altar and the corporal. Confused by this event, the priest left immediately to see the Pope. The Pope asked to see both the Host and the corporal, which were brought to him in a solemn procession. The linen corporal with the bloodstains is today displayed in the Cathedral of Orvieto. While the Host was being taken to Orvieto, blood from it also fell on the marble floor of the Church of St. Christina. Pieces of the bloodstained marble are on display in Bolsena.

- So impressed was the Pope by this miracle that he asked St. Thomas Aquinas to write the text for a special Mass to be said on a new feast, the Feast of Corpus Christi. This feast was decreed by the Pope a year later, on August 11, 1264. The two famous Eucharistic hymns, "O Salutaris" and "Tantum Ergo," were written by St. Thomas for the feast of Corpus Christi.

Three other miracles to allay doubt are noteworthy from a historical standpoint. The first took place in the year 1300 in Cebrero, Spain, a mountain village on the way to the shrine of St. James the Apostle in Spain (Santiago de Compostela). The miracle took place during an early morning Mass celebrated by a skeptical priest. The only other person present was a faithful peasant, Juan Santin, who had made his way there through the snow. Both priest and peasant were astounded to see the Host turn to flesh and the consecrated "wine" to blood. After ecclesiastical investigation, the miracle was approved by Pope Innocent III, and the day on which it took place was celebrated as a feast day. Both the Flesh and the Blood from the miracle are still preserved.

The miracle of Macerata, Italy, took place in 1356. A priest who doubted Christ's presence in every particle of the Eucharist was breaking the Host after consecration when blood began to ooze out of It. So startled was the priest that he let some of the blood fall onto the corporal. The bloodstained corporal is still preserved along with a fourteenth-century account of the event.

The miracle of Bagna di Romagna, Italy, took place in 1412. Again, a priest who doubted the Real Presence was celebrating Mass. This time, after consecration, the consecrated "wine" turned to blood and, welling up in the chalice, It gushed out onto the corporal. This was called the miracle of the Living Blood because the Blood was in visible motion. The corporal with the bloodstains is on exhibit in the village.

Negligence

The next category of miracles concerns those that sprang from negligence. Belief is best reflected in action. Belief that Jesus is present in the Eucharist requires us to revere His Body and Blood, clothed though They are in the appearance of bread and wine. Although negligence in treating the Eucharist with due reverence is not nearly as serious a fault as the crime of sacrilege, it is nevertheless serious enough to occasion divine intervention. In Old Testament times, irreverent treatment of the Holy of Holies was punished by death. In the New Testament era such treatment has brought forth miracles that shame us into doing what is right.

Three such miracles are mentioned here. The first took place in Florence, Italy, in 1230. After saying Mass on December 29, Uguccionne, the Benedictine parish priest of the church of St. Ambrose, forgot to clean the chalice, leaving in it some of the consecrated "wine." The next morning he was both amazed and horrified to find that the "wine" had turned into human blood. This miracle was investigated by both civil and ecclesiastical authorities and approved as authentic by Popes Clement IV (in 1266) and Boniface IX (in 1399). The Blood from the miracle can still be seen today and retains the appearance of blood. Numerous miracles, including protection from a plague and an earthquake, have been attributed to Its power.

The next miracle in this category took place a hundred years later in Siena, Italy. A priest had been asked to bring communion to a sick peasant. Although in such situations the Host is supposed to be kept in a secure container called a pyx, this particular priest threw the Host between the pages of his breviary. On reaching his parishioner, the priest found that the Host had melted. Only bloodstains remained on the two pages between which It had been kept. The startled priest set out to see a famed confessor (since beatified), Simone Fidati of the Monastery of St. Augustine. Blessed Simone listened to his confession and gave absolution. The two bloodstained pages were left with Blessed Simone. One page was lost in the nineteenth century. The second is now kept in the town of Cascia. Scientific studies in 1962 confirmed the presence of particles of blood on this page. It has also been confirmed in photographs that an image of the sorrowful face of a man can be seen in the bloodstain.

Another miracle, occasioned by similar circumstances, took place a year later on Easter Sunday in the town of Blanot, France. It was the custom at the time to hold a long piece of cloth in front of the communicants in case the Host were to slip down. On this particular day, the Host accidentally fell from the mouth of one of those receiving communion, a widow d'Effours. The parish priest, Hugo de Baulmes, sought to retrieve the fallen Host and found that It had been replaced by a stain of blood on the cloth. The priest tried to wash the cloth but found that the blood would not come off. He was then convinced that a miracle had taken place. The claim was investigated and then approved by the archbishop of Autun and a year later by Pope John XXII. The cloth with the bloodstain continues to be preserved and revered in the parish of Blanot.

Sacrilege

Miracles of another class owe their origin to the most shocking circumstances. They were divine responses to hideous acts of sacrilege. Lest it be thought that these deeds as described never took place and that their alleged perpetrators were simply innocent victims of witch-hunts and Inquisition-type excesses, let it be said that desecrations of the Eucharist have never been as widespread as they are today. Moreover, for every desecration of the Eucharist that became known through a miracle, numerous other such sacrileges remained hidden, for the practice of the "black mass" has had a long and sordid history. The sacrilege-related miracles mentioned here are simply those for which there is still tangible evidence.

Miracles in this category can be further classified in terms of the central character behind the sacrilege: in some cases it is a "sorceress" or a Satanist who entices one of the faithful to secure the Host; in others the principal responsible party is the recipient of communion.

The first sacrilege involving a sorceress took place in Trani, Italy, in 1000 A.D. On Holy Thursday of that year, a sorceress paid a Christian woman to bring her a consecrated Host. She dropped the Host into a pot of boiling oil. At once the Host turned to flesh and began to bleed. Soon the blood was pouring out onto the floor. These events apparently led to a change of heart in the sorceress, who repented of her sin. The Host with the bloodstains is still preserved in the Cathedral of Trani. Pope Urban VI accepted the authenticity of the miracle in 1384.

The next such incident took place in Alatri, Italy, in 1228. A love-smitten young woman sought the help of an older lady known for preparing love potions. This lady asked her to bring a consecrated Host in order to prepare the requisite potion. Although the girl secured a Host, she regretted her action and kept the Host in her house. A few days later, she found that the Host had turned to living flesh. Repentant by now, she took the miraculous flesh to her parish priest. After investigating the incident, Bishop Giovanni of Alatri affirmed that a miracle had taken place. The reigning Pope, Gregory IX, also gave his approval. The flesh from the miracle, slightly brown in color, is still kept in Alatri.

Satan's surest path to the human soul is desire. How many souls have literally been sold to fulfill a desire that has become an obsession. This is the most common theme in the incidents involving the procurement of Hosts for a sorceress. Such was the case in early thirteenth-century Santarem in Portugal. A woman frustrated by her husband's infidelity sought the help of a sorceress. In return for her services, the sorceress demanded a consecrated Host. The woman secured the Host and wrapped it in a veil. She was taking it to the sorceress when the Host started bleeding profusely. When her attempts to hide the bleeding Host failed, she finally brought It to the attention of the parish priest. The Host with veins running through It and a pool of liquid blood below is available for observation to this day in the Church of the Miracle.

The most dramatic sorceress miracle of all is perhaps the miracle of Offida, Italy, in 1273 (the actual miracle took place in Lanciano but the relics from the miracle are kept in Offida). Again it was desire that brought about this terrible event. Ricciarella's problem was not an unfaithful husband but a husband who alternately mistreated and ignored her. Seeking relief from this state of affairs, she requested the assistance of a witch. The witch advised her to fry a consecrated Host and add Its ashes to her husband's food. But when Ricciarella started heating the Host on a tile, she found to her horror that It had turned to flesh and was bleeding. In a panic, she wrapped the tile and the flesh in a tablecloth and buried It under a garbage heap in their stable. When her husband returned, he was surprised to see that his horse for some reason did not want to go into its stable. When finally forced inside, the animal prostrated itself before the garbage heap. The Host remained under the garbage for the next seven years. During all this time the animals entering the stable would act strangely, walking sideways when near the garbage heap. Ricciarella, meanwhile, was in agony. Finally she confessed her sin to Giacomo Diotallevi, an Augustinian. The priest came with her to the stable. They dug through the garbage and found that the bloody Host, the tile, and the tablecloth retained their original form. The priest took them to his hometown of Offida. Today the Host, the tablecloth, and the tile are displayed in the Sanctuary of St. Augustine in Offida.

Other sacrileges involved only the person who received the Host in communion. In 1194, a lady in Augsburg, Germany, wished to keep a consecrated Host in her house, a practice prohibited by the Church. She kept the Host in a wax reliquary she had assembled. After five years, her conscience compelled her to confess this sacrilege to her pastor. The Host was then transferred by the pastor to her church, the Church of the Holy Cross. When the priests of the parish took the Host out of the reliquary they noticed that It had turned to flesh streaked with red marks. They notified their bishop, who confirmed the authenticity of the miracle and declared a special feast in his diocese in honor of the miracle. The Host is still on display for the faithful and the feast in Its honor is held every year on May 11.

Miracles in this subset have also transpired when a person in mortal sin touched the Host or received communion. In 1317 in Hasselt, Belgium, a priest was taking communion to a sick parishioner. While talking to the parishioner, he left a container of consecrated Hosts in an adjoining room. Meanwhile, a neighbor walked in and started rummaging through the Hosts. As he did so, the Hosts began to bleed and he fled in terror. When the priest saw the bleeding Hosts he was just as startled and took Them back to his church. The bloody Hosts are now kept in the Cathedral of Hasselt.

Yet another miracle in this genre took place in the same century and the same country. A man in a state of mortal sin received communion in the first Sunday of Lent in 1374 in the city of Middleburg in Belgium. When the Host was put in his mouth, It turned to flesh, and when he bit into It, the flesh started bleeding. Thereupon the presiding priest extracted the flesh from his mouth. Both the flesh and a cloth with bloodstains from the flesh are reverently exhibited in the Church of St. Jacques in Louvain, Belgium.

Humility before the Eucharist seems an obvious response to believers. But it is not always easy for those in positions of power. On Holy Thursday in 1384 in the village of Seefeld, Austria, a certain knight who was the local administrator attended Mass at the Church of St. Oswald. Following consecration, he surrounded the altar with his soldiers and demanded that he be given the large Host usually consumed by the priest. When this Host was put in his mouth, the ground started sinking under his feet. Somehow, he managed to hold on to the stone altar. Responding to his desperate gestures, the priest removed the Host from his mouth and everything returned to normal. The Host, however, was found to be blood-red. The handprints of the knight on the stone altar are still visible. The Host too is on display. The knight at the center of the story underwent a complete conversion after the event.

Surprisingly, the history of the Eucharist is full of stories about theft. Most of these thefts concerned the expensive containers and reliquaries holding the Hosts, not the Hosts Themselves (although the class of thefts involving Satanists focused strictly on the Eucharist). Sadly, the thieves who purloined the containers often simply threw away the priceless Treasures they held. One of the most famous Eucharistic miracles concerns the Hosts recovered after such theft. On August 14, 1730, thieves broke into the Church of St. Francis in Siena and stole a golden ciborium containing over two hundred Hosts. The Hosts were found on August 17 in the collection box of another local church. It was soon established that these were the missing Hosts. Several scientific studies were carried out on these Hosts in subsequent years. Over two and a half centuries later, the Hosts continue to retain the appearance and smell of fresh bread and are available for public observation.

Among the great preservation miracles is the miracle of Alcala de Henares in Spain. An enemy of the church, remorseful for his past actions, came to a clergyman in this town in 1597 with twenty-four consecrated Hosts that he said had been stolen from various churches. Since the church authorities had no way of knowing whether the Hosts had been consecrated, they stored them in the pantry. After the passage of a decade, the Hosts remained as fresh as ever as verified in various tests performed by academics of the time. It was observed that unconsecrated hosts placed next to these Hosts decomposed after a short time. The preservation of the Hosts was declared miraculous in 1619. The Hosts were put on display for public adoration for centuries but then disappeared during the Spanish Civil War in the 1930s.

Power over Nature

Another major category of Eucharistic miracles simply concerns God's power over the laws of nature. Notable miracles in this group are described in the chronology titled "Hosts That Transcended the Laws of Nature" (see above p. 188). One such miracle bears special mention because the Hosts involved continue to be preserved. On Pentecost Sunday in 1608 in the Church of Notre Dame de la Blanche in Faverney, France, the Eucharist was placed for public adoration in a monstrance on the altar (a monstrance is a vessel with a glass opening through which the Eucharist can be viewed). During the night a fire broke out in the church, and the altar in particular was burnt down. The monks who were putting out the fire soon noticed that the monstrance with the Eucharist was floating in the air above the location of the altar. It continued in this position for thirty-three hours, as witnessed by numerous observers. Various priests celebrated Mass during this period. When a new altar was constructed and brought inside, the monstrance came back down and rested on it. One of the two Hosts that was in the monstrance is still preserved in Faverney. After investigation, the authenticity of the miracle was accepted both by the local archbishop and other church authorities.

A Note on the Satanists

The infamous Black Mass and other rituals of Satanists may be considered as a negative witness to the Real Presence of Jesus in the Eucharist. The *Dictionary of the Occult* notes:

> It is a fact that consecrated Hosts are occasionally abstracted from Roman Catholic Cathedrals, which goes far to suggest that diabolism is practiced, for the desecration of the Host is part of its ritual; also, the circumstances of the thefts prove that in each case the wafers and not the vessels containing

them had been the object of the miscreants.... The ritual of Devil-worship consists of the complete inversion of the Roman Catholic rites. The Black Mass of St. Secoine, as the diabolic ceremony is called, is carried out at midnight in a ruined church with a renegade priest officiating. His assistants must be public prostitutes, and the Holy Eucharist befouled with human excrement.[1]

Eucharistic Miracles in the Lives of the Saints

Eucharistic miracles of different kinds have been reported in the lives of some of the canonized saints and other holy men and women. Several saints have been known to levitate during the celebration of the Mass, in particular St. Teresa of Avila, St. Alphonsus Ligouri (d. 1787), and, most notably, St. Joseph of Cupertino (d. 1663). Others have miraculously received the Eucharist from an invisible source — St. Catherine of Siena (d. 1380), St. Mary Magdalen de Pazzi (d. 1607), St. Mary Frances of the Five Wounds (d. 1791), and, in this century, the three visionaries of Fatima. Perhaps the most dramatic category, in terms of duration, are those miracles involving individuals who lived only on the Eucharist for many years without any other means of nourishment and without any loss of weight or energy. In most such cases, the saint could not eat anything else without getting sick to the stomach. Two holy women of the twentieth century, Alexandrina da Costa and Theresa Neumann, who lived entirely on the Eucharist, were placed under continuous medical observation and found to have no other means of sustenance.

St. Catherine of Siena, who died in 1380, lived only on the Eucharist for the last seven years of her life. Blessed Angela of Foligno, Italy (d. 1309), lived on just the Eucharist for twelve years. St. Nicholas of Flue of Switzerland became a hermit at the age of fifty, in 1467, and for the next twenty years took no food or drink. Once a month he received the Eucharist. Since he was quite prominent in his time, his life has been chronicled in some detail. St. Lidwina of Holland, who died in 1433, had an accident at a young age that left her physically disabled. All through the rest of her life she underwent all kinds of physical agony that she offered up to God. She was well known for her many mystical gifts. For the last nineteen years of her life her only physical nourishment was the reception of the Eucharist twice a month.

In the twentieth century, Alexandrina da Costa (1904–1955) lived for thirteen years on the Eucharist alone. She was paralyzed at the age of fourteen, and from that time she entered into a state of continuous suffering. On Fridays and during Holy Week she shared in the Passion of Christ. She was also the recipient of various locutions from the Lord. From 1942 to 1955 she lived only on the Eucharist. At the beginning of this period, she received this message from Jesus: "You will not take food again on earth. Your food will be my Flesh; your blood will be my Divine Blood, your life will be my Life." After placing her under twenty-four-hour surveillance in a hospital, Dr. Gomez de Araujo of the Royal Academy of Medicine, Madrid, issued a formal report, which said,

It is absolutely certain that during forty days of being bedridden in hospital, the sick woman did not eat or drink...and we believe such phenomenon could have happened during the past months, perhaps the past 13 months...leaving us perplexed.

The certificate attached to the report stated,

Her abstinence from solids and liquids was absolute during all that time. We testify also that she retained her weight, and her temperature, breathing, blood pressure, pulse and blood were normal while her mental faculties were constant and lucid and she had not, during these forty days, any natural necessities. The examination of the blood, made three weeks after her arrival in the hospital, is attached to this certificate and from it one sees how, considering the aforesaid abstinence from solids and liquids, science naturally has no explanation. The laws of physiology and biochemistry cannot account for the survival of this sick woman for forty days of absolute fast in the hospital, more so in that she replied daily to many interrogations and sustained very many conversations, showing an excellent disposition and a perfect lucidity of spirit.

Also famous in the last century was Theresa Neumann of Konnersreuth, Germany, who lived from 1926 to 1962 on the Eucharist alone. As a young girl, she had an accident that damaged her spine and left her paralyzed. She was healed of all her ailments on May 17, 1925, the date of the canonization of St. Therese of Lisieux, whose intercession she had sought. Although healed, she offered to suffer for the sake of sinners. In March 1926 she was privileged to receive the Stigmata, the five wounds of Christ, and by Christmas of that year she was living simply on the Eucharist and water. From September 1927, she stopped taking even water, and for the remaining thirty-five years of her life she lived only on the Eucharist. As with Alexandrina, she was placed under round-the-clock medical surveillance, during which her physiological activities were monitored. At the end of a fifteen-day period of observation, it was found that her weight remained the same.

A contemporary counterpart to these two remarkable women is Little Audrey Santo of Worcester, Massachusetts, who, after a swimming accident at the age of three, has been in a coma for over a decade. Consecrated Hosts have turned bloody and statues have wept oil and blood near her bedside. These phenomena have been captured on popular television shows. To preclude the possibility of fraud, some reporters brought their own statues to the site and found that these too were exuding oil or blood.

Modern Eucharistic Miracles

In modern times, the sites and recipients of Marian apparitions have sometimes been involved with Eucharistic miracles as well. The three visionaries of Fatima, Portugal, were given the Eucharist by an angel and taught the importance of

Eucharistic adoration. The apparition of Our Lady of All Nations in Amsterdam, Holland, in 1945 began exactly six hundred years after the Eucharistic miracle of Amsterdam. The apparitions of Betania, Venezuela, to Maria Esperanza, and Naju, Korea, to Julia Kim, have involved Eucharistic miracles.

The Betania apparitions began in 1976. On December 8, 1991, the feast of the Immaculate Conception, a consecrated Host at the apparition site began to bleed. On being analyzed in Caracas, It was found to have human blood.

The most remarkable Eucharistic miracles in the history of Marian apparitions seem clearly to be those associated with Naju. The apparitions began in 1985 and the Eucharistic miracles began in 1988. The information below on these miracles was provided by *Mary's Touch*, an organization distributing information on the Naju phenomenon.

1. *The external appearance of bread in the Holy Eucharist changed. It was transformed into visible flesh and blood on Julia's tongue* (twelve times between May 1988 and October 1996). The miracle on October 31, 1995, was witnessed by Pope John Paul II during a Mass in the Pope's private chapel in the Vatican. Bishop Roman Danylak from Toronto, Canada, and Bishop Dominic Su of Sibu, Malaysia, also witnessed the miracles in Naju and Sibu, respectively, and wrote their testimonies expressing their belief in the authenticity of these miracles.

2. *The Sacred Host descended from above to the chapel in Naju* (seven times between November 24, 1994, and August 27, 1997). The first two miracles were witnessed by the Apostolic Pro-Nuncio in Korea during his visit to Naju. On July 1, 1995, seven Sacred Hosts descended. They were consumed by two priests and five lay people, including Julia, according to the local Archbishop's instruction. The external appearance of the Sacred Host that Julia received changed into visible Flesh and Blood on her tongue. A sample of this Blood was tested in the medical laboratory at Seoul National University and was found to be human blood. The descent of the Eucharist on June 12, 1997, was witnessed by Bishop Paul Kim of the Cheju Diocese in Korea. The Eucharist again descended on August 27, 1997, during Father Raymond Spies's visit to Naju. An intense fragrance is continuing (as of May 1998) from the spot on the floor in the chapel where the Eucharist came to rest.

Conclusion

The preceding study of the Eucharistic miracles of the past and the present indicates the following:

1. The miracles have taken place over vast stretches of history and geography, and it would be imprudent therefore to dismiss them as mere products of cultural conditioning or parochial delusion.

2. Despite the diverse nature of the miracles, all of them are in one way or another compatible with the teaching that the bread and the wine become

the Body and the Blood of Christ at consecration. In fact, it might well be said that these miracles testify to the truth of this teaching.

3. The miracles with continuing contemporary evidence (for instance, human flesh preserved for well over a thousand years) present us with a set of "hard facts" that demand an adequate explanation. The Christian doctrine of the Eucharist seems to be the most comprehensive and coherent explanation of these facts and of the many other events associated with the history of the Eucharist.[2]

Conclusion

Alpha and Omega

The teaching that Jesus Christ is the Alpha and the Omega has often been lost in the tumult of theological controversies on the millennium and the Second Coming. We have been so focused on the end of the world in the sense of its demise that we have barely paid attention to the question of its "end" in the sense of purpose. But it is focus on "end" in this second and more ultimate sense that can better help us understand "end" in the first sense. Jesus Christ, Who is the Alpha, our uncreated Source, is also the Omega, our everlasting End.

Three passages from Scripture are of cardinal importance here:

> In the beginning was the Word, and the Word was with God, and the Word was God. He was in the beginning with God, and without him nothing came to be. What came to be through him was life, and this life was the light of the human race. (John 1:1–4)

> He is the image of the invisible God, the firstborn of all creation. For in him were created all things in heaven and on earth, the visible and the invisible, whether thrones or dominions or principalities or powers; all things were created through him and for him. He is before all things, and in him all things hold together. (Col. 1:15–17)

> "I am the Alpha and the Omega," says the Lord God, "the one who is and who was and who is to come, the almighty...." Then I saw a new heaven and a new earth. The former heaven and the former earth had passed away, and the sea was no more. I also saw the holy city, a new Jerusalem, coming down out of heaven from God, prepared as a bride adorned for her husband. I heard a loud voice from the throne saying, "Behold, God's dwelling is with the human race. He will dwell with them and they will be his people and God himself will always be with them [as their God]. He will wipe every tear

from their eyes, and there shall be no more death or mourning, wailing or pain, [for] the old order has passed away." The one who sat on the throne said, "Behold, I make all things new." Then he said, "Write these words down, for they are trustworthy and true." He said to me, "They are accomplished. I [am] the Alpha and the Omega, the beginning and the end. . . . Behold, I am coming soon. I bring with me the recompense I will give to each according to his deeds. I am the Alpha and the Omega, the first and the last, the beginning and the end. Blessed are they who wash their robes so as to have the right to the tree of life and enter the city through its gates." (Rev. 21:1–6, 22:12–14)

The greatest mystery of all is, of course, God. The greatest mystery in the natural world is its origin and ultimate fate — and, of course, both origin and fate are inseparably linked to purpose. What will happen to the world is related to why it is. Genesis and Revelation are the two books of the Bible that deal with origin and destiny. Both are deliberately ambiguous in their language and can and have been interpreted in many different ways. But certain truths are all but indisputable from these texts:

1. The world had a beginning.

2. The world will not come to an end but will be supernaturally transformed. The Bible begins with the creation of heaven and earth and ends with the revelation of the new heaven and the new earth that is to come.

3. The world is "good" because it is a creation of God, but evil is a real and powerful force that exists because it is possible to abuse the freedom with which all free beings are endowed.

4. There will be a climax to the conflict between good and evil before the ultimate transformation of the world.

5. Jesus Christ, the Alpha through Whom all things were created, is also the Omega Who has overcome evil and will reign over the transformed world. The world that began as a Paradise will end its pilgrimage to the Promised Land in a new and everlasting Eden.

The true end, the consummation and crowning glory, of the material creation was the Incarnation of the Son of God. The Incarnation was "fitting" even if there was no Original Sin because "all things were created through him and for him." No event analogous to the Incarnation was required in the spiritual universe of the angels, because as pure spirits they could be drawn to, transformed, and fulfilled in their Creator purely in their own realm since God is Pure Spirit. But in the case of the human person, a union of flesh and spirit, its destiny of sharing in the divine nature required a transformation at both levels of its being. We know and love through the cooperation of flesh and spirit, and the consummation of these powers in the knowing and loving of Infinite Truth and Infinite Good can come about only through the joint elevation of both the material and the spiritual. Only when the Word became Flesh could our flesh participate in the

Life of the Word. The event that made the ultimate union of the divine and the human possible was material and spiritual: He had to shed His Blood and give up His Body. It is this same Body and Blood that we now receive at His great wedding feast, for the vehicle through which the God-Fleshed gives us His Life is Itself material. Through the Resurrection, we realize that Life in God for human beings is a Life that transforms both matter and spirit. And just as Christ underwent suffering and death because of the sin of humanity but then rose in glory, so too will the world have to "die" before it rises again in the glory of a new heaven and a new earth.

The revelation of Jesus as Alpha and Omega shows that there is a progression of themes moving to a climax in Scripture:

1. Jesus came to announce and inaugurate the Kingdom of God. It is this Kingdom that reaches fulfillment at the "end," it is this Kingdom that is the end of all creation.

2. Through His Resurrection from the dead, Jesus has begun a transformation of material creation that will reach consummation when He comes again in glory.

3. Through His institution of the Eucharist, Jesus has begun the process of distributing the divine Life that will energize us for all eternity: "On either side of the river grew the tree of life that produces fruit twelve times a year, once each month; the leaves of the tree serve as medicine for the nations" (Rev. 22:2).

Given this frame of reference, many of the debates over Apocalypse and the end-times are seen to be superfluous.

We know that each one of us lives in this world for an instant but that we are destined to live forever in union with God or in separation from Him. What happens in this instant is infinitely important because how we choose and what we do will determine our eternal destiny. Thus the primary focus of our choices and actions should be God and His will for us. Whether or not there is an Antichrist or a Millennium, a Chastisement or a Cleansing, is of secondary importance to the primary task of doing God's will. Only this matters in and for eternity.

We know that Jesus came to bring about the Kingdom of God: the reign of God over the world and over history, a reign that begins in the present but continues for all eternity. The Lord's Prayer tells us that the Kingdom exists wherever God's will is done whether on Heaven or on earth. Christ is the center of this Kingdom which is everlasting: "He will rule over the house of Jacob forever, and of his kingdom there will be no end" (Luke 1:33); "The eternal kingdom of our Lord and savior Jesus Christ" (2 Pet. 1:11). "To him who loves us and has freed us from our sins by his blood, who has made us into a kingdom, priests for his God and Father, to him be glory and power forever [and ever]. Amen" (Rev. 1:5–6). It is open to all nations: "Many will come from the east and the west, and will recline with Abraham, Isaac, and Jacob, at the banquet in the kingdom of heaven" (Matt. 8:11).

The Kingdom will reach its culmination in the universal acknowledgement of the reign of Christ, the reward of the righteous, and the punishment of those who reject God:

> "He who sows good seed is the Son of Man, the field is the world, the good seed the children of the kingdom. The weeds are the children of the evil one, and the enemy who sows them is the devil. The harvest is the end of the age, and the harvesters are angels. Just as weeds are collected and burned [up] with fire, so will it be at the end of the age. The Son of Man will send his angels, and they will collect out of his kingdom all who cause others to sin and all evildoers. They will throw them in to the fiery furnace, where there will be wailing and grinding of teeth. Then the righteous will shine like the sun in the kingdom of their Father." (Matt. 13:37–43)

> "Let us rejoice and be glad and give him glory. For the wedding day of the Lamb has come, his bride has made herself ready. She was allowed to wear a bright, clean linen garment." [The linen represents the righteous deeds of the holy ones.] Then the angel said to me, "Write this. Blessed are those who have been called to the wedding feast of the Lamb." (Rev. 19:7–10)

Instead of speculating about the millennium, our immediate and continuing duty is to announce and live the Kingdom so that we may be called to the great wedding feast.

Given that we know the ultimate destiny of the world, we are still, however, left with the question of what happens at the conclusion of human history. What about the Antichrist or the Millennial Reign of Christ?

In interpreting the so-called end-time texts of the Bible we must beware of both literalism and reductionism. These texts deal with mysterious themes and literalism and reductionism are the two equal and opposite errors in responding to mystery. Let us first confess our ignorance: We do not know the precise details of what will happen at the end of history either through our natural knowledge or from the ambiguous descriptions in Scripture. But we do know that three truths have been consistently taught and believed by the Fathers:

1. There will be a climactic confrontation between good and evil at the end of history (with an era of peace before the confrontation). The forces of evil will be led by a historical person referred to as the Antichrist in both Scripture and the Fathers. Who the Antichrist is and when the confrontation will take place we do not know. It would be a waste of our time to speculate on these matters because our mission remains the same whether we live in the "end-times" or at any other period of history — to do the will of God in preparation for eternity — and our focus should be on this mission.

2. There will be a Second Coming of Christ at the end of history when evil has been vanquished forever. Again we do not know when this will take place or what it will be like, and Scripture tells us we cannot know. Our focus must be on our mission: "Seek first the kingdom [of God] and his righteousness and all these things will be given you besides. Do not worry about tomorrow; tomor-

row will take care of itself" (Matt. 6:33–34). Reductionists deny the Second Coming and literalists speak of even four comings of Christ (the rapture, followed by a millennial reign, followed by a final battle with Satan). Neither position is compatible with Scripture and consistent Christian teaching over two millennia.

3. The "end" of the world is its total transformation and the emergence of a new heaven and a new earth. Here again we know nothing about the nature of this transformation beyond the first manifestations of it in the Risen Body of Christ and the Eucharist.

With all this, we are still left with the texts referring to the "millennium" in which Christ physically reigns in the world:

> Then I saw an angel come down from heaven, holding in his hand the key to the abyss and a heavy chain. He seized the dragon, the ancient serpent, which is the Devil or Satan, and tied it up for a thousand years...I also saw the souls of those who had been beheaded for their witness to Jesus and for the word of God.... They came to life and they reigned with Christ for a thousand years. The rest of the dead did not come to life until the thousand years were over. This is the first resurrection. Blessed and holy is the one who shares in the first resurrection. The second death has no power over these; they will be priests of God and of Christ, and they will reign with him for [the] thousand years. When the thousand years are completed, Satan will be released from his prison. He will go out to deceive the nations at the four corners of the earth.... But fire came down from heaven and consumed them. The Devil who had led them astray was thrown into a pool of fire and sulphur where the beast and false prophet were. There they will be tormented day and night forever and ever. (Rev. 20:1–2, 4–10)

This mysterious passage has been the inspiration for a wide variety of "end-time" scenarios and even movements in which Christians have sold their material possessions in anticipation of the "end of the world." The parables of Christ in all their mysterious profundity could not have been rightly interpreted without the assistance of the Narrator Himself, who explained their hidden significance. We do not have the benefit of such direct divine assistance in interpreting these particular texts. We do know, however, that those who have interpreted these texts in carnal and materialistic terms have been consistently condemned throughout Christian history — and all too often such interpretations disproved themselves when predictions associated with them failed to materialize. The only interpretation that both explains the texts as they stand and has stood the test of time in terms of being consistently and widely accepted is the exegesis of St. Augustine.

The thousand-year reign is the reign of Christ through His Church: it is His Kingdom and He reigns as King. The number one thousand symbolizes the Church in its triumph: seven the number of Christ plus three the number of the Trinity is ten and ten cubed is one thousand. The first resurrection refers to those who are resurrected from spiritual death by receiving the life of God through baptism and other vehicles such as the Eucharist. Those who receive and retain the divine Life in this world will not suffer the second death in the next: they will not be separated forever from God. While in this world they will reign with Christ, sharing in His Sonship and Priesthood (the priesthood open to all believers as distinct from the sacramental priesthood).[1]

The Church on earth is also the Church that suffers persecution, and the 1260 days of persecution spoken about in the Book of Revelation could refer to the persecution of the Jews by Antiochus from June 168 to December 165 B.C. After the coming of Christ and His Church, Satan is chained: he will not have as much power as he did in the past because of the victory of the Cross and the ministry of exorcism and healing initiated by Jesus Himself and continued in His Church: "Jesus said, 'I have observed Satan fall like lightning from the sky. Behold I have given you the power to tread upon serpents and scorpions and upon the full force of the enemy and nothing will harm you' " (Luke 10:18–9). Although Satan has been chained by the Cross, he will continue his attacks until the Final Judgment when he and his followers will be separated forever from those who enter Heaven (it is believed that the Satanic war will reach its peak at the end of history just before the Judgment). This exposition of Revelation 20 accords also with Jesus' own account of His Kingdom in the Parable of the Sower (Matt. 13) and the attacks on it from Satan that will cease with the Final Judgment.

With respect to the climactic confrontation between good and evil, these excerpts from St. Faustina's accounts of her conversations with Jesus are of particular interest:

"Write this: before I come as the Judge, I am coming first as the King of Mercy. Before the day of justice arrives, there will be given to people a sign in the heavens of this sort: All light in the heavens will be extinguished, and there will be great darkness over the whole earth. Then the sign of the cross will be seen in the sky, and from the openings where the hands and the feet of the Savior were nailed will come forth great lights which will light up the earth for a period of time. This will take place shortly before the last day."[2]

"Oh, what great graces I will grant to souls who say this chaplet; the very depths of My tender mercy are stirred for the sake of those who say the chaplet. Write down these words, My daughter. Speak to the world about My mercy; let all mankind recognize My unfathomable mercy. It is a sign for the end times; after it will come the day of justice. While there is still time, let them have recourse to the fount of My mercy; let them profit from the Blood and Water which gushed forth for them."[3]

"In the Old Covenant I sent prophets wielding thunderbolts to My people. Today I am sending you with My mercy to the people of the whole world. I do not want to punish aching mankind, but I desire to heal it, pressing it to My Merciful Heart. I use punishment when they themselves force Me to do so; My hand is reluctant to take hold of the sword of justice. Before the Day of Justice I am sending the Day of Mercy."[4]

But discussion of the end-times should not distract us from the more fundamental question of what comes after, for the end of time is the beginning of eternity (at least for mortals), and the end of the world signals the beginning of a new heaven and a new earth. Matter obscures the activity of spirit in this world, but in the new world it is spirit that will be preeminent. The immanence of God will be as apparent as His transcendence ("Behold, God's dwelling is with the human race. He will dwell with them and they will be his people and God himself will always be with them [as their God]").

Even in this world we recognize that God's creation is inescapably hierarchical. At the natural level, we find pure matter at one end and pure spirit at the other. On the supernatural level, there is also a hierarchy: God Incarnate is at the head of creation. Next there is His Mother, the Mother of God and also the Mother of humanity, who intercedes for all her children. She is "next," but where He is infinite, she is finite. And yet she is the highest of the finite because her obedience brought forth the Redeemer and the sword that pierced her heart was her consent to the Sacrifice of her Son. Below the Virgin Mother are the angelic hosts, the pure spirits who ceaselessly serve their Creator, then the saints, those men and women who died with their wills united with the divine Will, then the souls in purgatory, those who have said "Yes" to their Maker but who still need to be cleansed and purified of their earthly imperfections, and finally those of us here on earth who tread a path toward or away from God. If there is one message shared by all religions it is the need for humility in the face of God. And such humility demands that we respect the hierarchy that He instituted by recognizing and cooperating with the God-given role of each of its members. If we seek the intercession of the Virgin or the Archangel Michael or St. Anthony of Padua, we have nothing to lose and everything to gain. The God of Scripture works through prophets, apostles, angels, and the Mother of the Redeemer to accomplish His Plan, and so must we.

All the great premonitions of the past, the Prajapathi of the Vedas who is the Sacrificer at his own Sacrifice and the Messiah of Judaic prophecy whose "chastisement makes us whole," all the central events of the Incarnation, ranging from the Passion and Death of Christ to His institution of the new and everlasting covenant, all the poignant revelations of the Sacred Heart and the Divine Mercy reach final fulfillment in that meeting of time and eternity, Heaven and earth, that lies ahead of us. At the center of it all is Jesus Christ. "In my beginning is my end. In my end is my beginning," wrote T. S. Eliot in his famous poem *Four Quartets*.[5] In the Alpha of the world is its Omega, and in its Omega is its Alpha: "all things were created through him and for him." The joy of the world to come is not a distant event, with no bearing on our life here and now. On the contrary, for those who have consecrated their lives to Jesus Christ through His Holy Mother, the echo of everlasting joy is heard at every horizon of human experience. We hear it in the splendor of every sunset, in melodies that rush us out of space and time, in fairy tales and folklore, in the pursuit of truth by way of every form of thought and study, in carnivals and the pleasures of sport, in laughter and kindly humor, in thunderstorms spent indoors, in sun-specked lakes, in the roar of ocean waves. Goodness, beauty, and love are droplets from an everlasting fountain, sunbeams from a sun that shines forever, breath from the nostrils of God.

Appendix

Reductionism

Consider this: why do many intellectuals, including even learned theologians, not believe in the divinity of Jesus Christ or in the Real Presence of Christ in the Eucharist? Some of them, in fact, reject other such fundamental affirmations as the existence of God and the soul. On the other hand, there are thinkers who expound and defend these beliefs. So why is there such a radical difference of perspective? Why do the same facts and data leave some cold and others inspired? It is our contention here that the widespread disbelief of our day is above all to be attributed to a destructive disease of the mind, one which requires a cure before it turns out to be fatal.

It has often been said that the modern world has lost a sense of wonder. Wonder, however, is neither a poetic nor mystical phenomenon. It is as natural and necessary for human beings as the capacity to think and to feel. To lose the capacity of wonder, in fact, is to lose one avenue of knowledge — for certain truths can be known only if we have a minimal comprehension of their grandeur. Thus, the realization that anything exists at all is an apprehension wrapped in the most incredible sense of mystery. Let us say that the universe was always here. But *how* could it thus be here and be here in its present form (no matter how it came to take its present form)? If it had no beginning, we still want to know how an entity with such properties came to exist. The normal mind cannot be satisfied with the universe — especially one that contains beings with consciousness and intelligence — as simply a brute fact. Only brutes take refuge in brute facts. The fact that anything exists points ineluctably to a need for an explanation of the existence of all that exists, and such an explanation can ultimately be found only in the existence of a Being that explains both its own existence and that of everything else, a Being Who exists necessarily and has all the perfections of existence. But then we wonder how it came to be that there is such a Being. Conceptually we know that there has to be such a Being to explain the existence

of anything at all. But to know *that* is not to know *how*. To think about this
Being Whom we call God is to be struck by wonder in the face of overwhelming
Mystery — the fact that God always existed and that all of time and the citizens
of time are "seen" by Him from all eternity. This is a Mystery that confronts us
at every instant, for every time we realize that we or anything around us exists
we are moved to wonder how this was and is possible and how it all began.

Again, take the intricate design and order manifested in nature. We can in
knee-jerk fashion repeat that these originated from blind and random forces in
the distant past. Nonetheless, we have to admit that these processes that manifest design and order are currently neither blind nor random. What the skeptic
is saying, of course, is that at some point in the past there was a transition from
randomness to order. But let us focus on this very claim. Even the most determined skeptic has to admit that the so-called "blind" forces were not really
blind. They were governed by fundamental physical laws even at the time when
there was a "transition" from "random" to "ordered." In fact these laws applied
from the very birth of the universe. No scientist denies that laws of mass-energy
applied as long as you had mass-energy. So then it becomes a question of how
did these laws — which are manifestations of intelligence and rationality — originate. The more science advances, the more it becomes clear that intelligence is
imprinted in matter. In Darwin's time, it was easy to say that "blind forces" and
natural selection did the job (although here they ignored the fact that laws of
nature operated on these "blind" forces even in their scenario). But the discovery
of the genetic code made them retreat from "random forces" to "random mutations." The point they keep missing is that every "random" scenario involves
the operation of certain laws of nature. And sometimes the flight to "randomness" as an explanation is clearly desperate — as desperate as the claim that the
universe is a "brute fact."

The cells of a human being contain twenty-three pairs of chromosomes consisting of seventy to eighty thousand genes. In humans and in other organisms,
chromosomes and genes contain the instructions — written in DNA — that
"run" the chemical processes in all of biological life. This is an observed "law
of nature." Confronted with this, the skeptic turns to gene mutations to explain
the origin of new species. Clearly genetic mutations do take place. But the issue
here is not whether or not such mutations took place in a random fashion over
hundreds of millions of years and miraculously produced all the different forms
of life we have today. The issue is the origin of the genetic code as such. Mutations take place only if there already exists genes that can mutate. And when
mutations take place, the genes still follow fundamental laws of genetics. How
did these laws that govern all biological life originate? The discovery of the genetic blueprint of a being is the discovery of the chemical instructions that direct
its life and growth. Where did the instructions come from? Every code (and all
languages are code structures) contains intelligent information which implies rationality, and the genetic code is no different. Moreover, new insights in quantum
or chaos theory show laws operating at other levels of nature.

In ancient times, the beauty of a flower or the majesty of the "heavens" led the average person to postulate the existence of a Creator. Later skeptics scoffed at such "superstitions" by postulating blind forces that actually "created" the flower and the sky. In modern times, the superstitions of these skeptics have been swept aside as we have been confronted by the undeniable fact of majestic and beautiful (adjectives used by famous scientists) laws that underlie all of physical reality. Intelligence is imprinted in all of nature directing it at every instant — an intelligence implanted by an infinite Intelligence.

Turning to yet another undeniable datum of experience: we are conscious and aware that we are conscious. The data of our consciousness range from sensations that reach us through one or more of the five senses; memories that "relive" sensory experiences of the past; images that we form in our imagination by extrapolating from our sensory experience; concepts that do not have any correlation with our sensory experience such as the notion of liberty or mathematical entities and theories; intentions that we form and execute such as planning to go for a walk or a vacation; and choices that we make ranging from giving up our lives for our country to telling the truth in a conversation. Some of the data of our consciousness are directly related to the physical world, for instance, the objects perceived by the five senses or objects that we imagine from our previous sensory experience, whereas others are simply pure acts of the intellect, for instance the acts of understanding, judging, and reasoning. To reflect on the act of thinking is to know that our thinking is radically different from all physical reality (our thought of justice has no size or shape); and it is again obvious that this activity of thinking that we experience every day could not have arisen out of mindless matter or blind physical forces, just as a rock cannot give rise to a thought, even over an infinite period of time. As noted earlier, we cannot take seriously the idea that a certain bundle of mass-energy just happened to exist (without beginning or end) and then evolved without any direction or guidance over time into *thought*. "Conscious thinking" could originate only from Something that is Itself Conscious and Thinking.

This discourse on the origins of the physical universe and its laws and of the human mind is not a digression. It illustrates the blind spots of what we shall call the reductionist mind-set. As definitions go, reductionism is the tendency to reduce one reality to another, for instance, describing the mind as merely a complex form of matter or human nature as simply and solely a product of genetics. "Brute facts" and "blind forces" are typical terms of the reductionist. The problems with Reductionism are numerous but a few of the more obvious ones may be mentioned:

- It denies obvious facts of our experience (it tells us that our consciousness of being conscious thinking persons is an illusion).

- It explains away these obvious facts with implausible and even absurd narratives that are accepted only because the explainers are often learned people using complex, technical arguments. The idea that consciousness is an illusion has been defended using abstruse materialist arguments over the years; interestingly, each argument, for instance, behaviorism, lasts only for a short period before its defenders drop it in embarrassment and move on to an entirely different train of thought, which too will sooner or later be repudiated.

- Its main argument tends to be abuse: condescension, flippancy, sarcasm are the main weapons used against opposing views. Terms such as "dated," "old-fashioned," "naïve," "fundamentalist," "puritanical," "extremist," "sexist," "intolerant," and "obscurantist" are commonly thrown around.

- Its thesis is often self-contradictory: if our thoughts are material in nature they cannot be true — since truth and falsehood do not belong to the realm of physical law — and therefore the idea that thoughts are material cannot be true.

Despite its obvious weaknesses, reductionism has triumphed. The modern mind is incapable of thinking: it denies and it explains away but it has no trust in its ability to come to grips with the foundational facts of experience. When you read the newspapers or the best-selling books of our time, there is no discussion at all about the most obvious and the most fundamental mystery of all: that we exist! Likewise the mysteries of mind and intelligence are ignored — although any rational reflection worthy of the name would show their indisputable reality. It is not just a question of being brainwashed but of being brain-dead. And there is only one cure for this terrible disease of the mind: some form of shock treatment that will put us back in touch with our everyday experience and give us the courage to form convictions grounded in obvious facts of experience.

The first step in this treatment is the recovery of a sense of awe and wonder as we contemplate the intelligence imprinted in nature and our own existence as conscious, thinking beings. The second step, which is the theme of this book, is to consider God's actions in human history.

Now there is a certain sense in which access to the data of divine Revelation requires some form of initiation: we have to believe that there is a personal God Who can intervene in history and that He can and has revealed great truths to us and that these truths have been reliably preserved and handed down. But many of today's theologians have replaced these logically sound ground rules with their own reductionist dogmas. Reductionism has taken a toll not just in philosophy but in theology.

In the present study of the Incarnation and the Eucharist, we have seen that those who deny these truths inevitably resort to the stratagems of the reductionists:

- "Hard facts" are evaded or explained away. The transformation of the Apostles is a hard fact that must be addressed by those who reject the Resurrection. The writings of the Fathers and the texts of the ancient liturgies affirm a "literal" reading of Christ's institution of the Eucharist. The great Eucharistic miracles continue their silent testimony to the truth of traditional Eucharistic doctrine.

- Attempts to explain away these hard facts are almost always exercises in elaborate and credulity-straining speculation. The rapidity with which such speculative theories replace each other is a measure of their inherent implausibility.

- Condescension and abuse are tools in trade of theological reductionists.

If we can leave the theological reductionists with one message it is this: return to the hard facts and in examining them obey the maxim prescribed by Shakespeare: "to thine own self be true."

Notes

Introduction

1. Sr. M. Faustina Kowalska, *Diary: Divine Mercy in My Soul* (Stockbridge, Mass.: Marians of the Immaculate Conception, 1999), 301.

2. Ibid., 378.

3. Ibid., 1146.

4. Ibid., 1446.

5. Sr. Josefa Menéndez, *The Way of Divine Love* (Rockford, Ill.: TAN, 1973), 104, 214.

6. Ibid., 237–38.

7. Ibid., 353.

8. Kowalska, *Diary,* 80.

9. Ibid., 1146

10. Ibid., 1488.

Chapter 1: The Search for the Jesus of History

1. Rudolf Bultmann, *Jesus and the Word* (New York: Scribner's Sons, 1934), 16.

2. Ibid., 9.

3. N. T. Wright, *Who Was Jesus?* (Grand Rapids, Michigan: William B. Eerdmans, 1992).

4. In Bruce Chilton and Craig A. Evans, eds., *Studying the Historical Jesus* (Leiden: Brill, 1994), 554.

5. James D. G. Dunn, *The Parting of the Ways* (Philadelphia: Trinity, 1991), 9.

6. Michael Cahill, "An Uncertain Jesus: Theological and Scholarly Ambiguities," *Irish Theological Quarterly* 1 (1998): 28.

7. Ibid., 22.

8. Ibid., 28

9. N. T. Wright, "Five Gospels but No Gospel: Jesus and the Seminar," in *Crisis in Christology,* ed. William R. Farmer, Great Modern Debates 3, gen. ed. Roy Abraham Varghese (Livonia, Mich.: Dove, 1995), 118–19.

10. Ibid., 123.

11. Ibid., 124.

12. Ibid., 126

13. Ibid., 128.

14. Ibid., 144.

15. *Biblical Archaeology Review* (July/August 2000).

16. Howard Clark Kee, "A Century of Quests for the Culturally Compatible Jesus," *Theology Today* 52, no. 1 (1995): 28.

17. William P. Loewe, "From the Humanity of Christ to the Historical Jesus," *Theological Studies* 61 (2000): 318.

18. Ibid., 329.

19. E. P. Sanders, *Jesus and Judaism* (Philadelphia: Fortress, 1985), 2.

20. *Time,* August 15, 1988, 41.

21. Neil Asher Silberman, "Searching for Jesus," *Archaeology* (November/December 1994), 31–40.

22. Cited in Ben F. Meyer, "Appointed Deed, Appointed Doer: Jesus and the Scriptures," in *Crisis in Christology,* 311.

23. Ibid., 326.

24. Marcus J. Borg and N. T. Wright, *The Meaning of Jesus: Two Visions* (San Francisco: HarperCollins, 1999), 66.

25. Craig A. Evans, "Life-of-Jesus Research and the Eclipse of Mythology," *Theological Studies* 54 (1993): 19.

26. Ibid., 3–36.

27. Borg and Wright, *The Meaning of Jesus: Two Visions,* 122.

28. Interview with the author.

29. Pinchas Lapide, *The Resurrection of Jesus: A Jewish Perspective* (Minneapolis: Augsburg, 1983), 125–26.

30. Ibid., 129–30.

31. Ibid., 130.

32. William Lane Craig, *Truth: A Journal of Modern Thought* 1 (1985).

Chapter 2: The Identity of Jesus

1. Martin Hengel, "Jesus, the Messiah of Israel," in *Crisis in Christology,* ed. William R. Farmer, Great Modern Debates 3, gen. ed. Roy Abraham Varghese (Livonia, Mich.: Dove, 1995), 237–38.

2. Jean Galot, *Who Is Christ? A Theology of Incarnation* (Chicago: Franciscan Herald Press, 1981), 114.

3. Ibid., 115–16.

4. Peter Stuhlmacher, "Jesus of Nazareth — the Christ of Our Faith," in *Crisis in Christology,* 273, 288.

5. Marcus J. Borg and N. T. Wright, *The Meaning of Jesus: Two Visions* (San Francisco: HarperCollins, 1999), 165–66.

6. Wright, "Five Gospels But No Gospel," in *Crisis in Christology,* 130.

7. Walter Kasper, *Jesus the Christ* (London: Burns and Oates, 1976), 238.

8. Ibid., 249.

9. Interview with the author.

10. Brian Hebblethwaite, "Jesus Christ — God and Man: The Myth and Truth Debate," in *Crisis in Christology,* 1–12.

11. Josef Seifert, "The Uninventable Glory of God as the Deepest Reason for Our Faith in Jesus Christ," in *Theos, Anthropos, Christos,* American University Studies, ed. Roy Abraham Varghese (New York: Peter Lang, 2000).

12. William M. Thompson, " 'Distinct but Not Separate': Historical Research in the Study of Jesus and Christian Faith," *Horizons* 21, no. 1 (1994): 132.

13. D. Moody Smith, "When Did the Gospels Become Scripture?" *Journal of Biblical Literature* 119, no. 1 (2000): 19.

Chapter 3: The Witness of Mythology and the World Religions

1. Timothy Freke and Peter Gandy, *The Jesus Mysteries* (London: Thorsons, 1999).
2. C. S. Lewis, *God in the Dock* (Grand Rapids, Mich.: William B. Eerdmans, 1970), 66–67.
3. Hugo Rahner, *Greek Myths and Christian Mystery* (London: Burns and Oates, 1963), 31.
4. Ibid., 32.
5. Ibid., 34.
6. Ibid., 34–35.
7. Ibid., 42–43.
8. Ibid., 15.
9. Odo Casel, *The Mystery of Christian Worship* (New York: Crossroad, 1999), 32, 33.
10. Ibid., 35.
11. Ibid., 60–61.
12. Eric Mascall, *Corpus Christi* (London: Longmans, 1965), 70–71.
13. Leon McKenzie, *Pagan Resurrection Myths and the Resurrection of Jesus* (Charlottesville, Va.: Bookwrights Press, 1997), 53, 54, 68–69.
14. The citations here are taken from Aravindaksha Menon, *Divine Harmony* (Muringoor, India: Divine Publishers, 1997), *Verses from the Holy Scriptures of Sanathana Dharma* (Muringoor, India: Divine Publishers, 1997), Koshy Abraham, *Prajapathi, the Cosmic Christ* (Delhi: ISPCK, 1997), and Martin P. Joseph, *The Vedas in the Light of the Bible* (Nagercoil, India: Nanjil, 1995).
15. McKenzie, *Pagan Resurrection Myths and the Resurrection of Jesus,* 70–71.
16. Gavin D'Costa, "Taking Other Religions Seriously," *The Thomist* (July 1990): 525.
17. Terrence Merrigan, "For Us and for Our Salvation," *Irish Theological Quarterly* 64 (1999): 347–48.
18. Bertram Stubenrauch, "Controversy about the Incarnation," *Irish Theological Quarterly* 64 (1999): 354.

Chapter 4: "Saul, Saul, why are you persecuting me?"

1. Martin Luther, *Luther's Works,* ed. Jaroslav Pelikan (St. Louis: Concordia Publishing House, 1958–67), 6:329.
2. E. C. Brewer, *Dictionary of Miracles,* and cited in Phillip Wiebe, *Visions of Jesus* (New York and Oxford: Oxford University Press, 1997).

Chapter 5: The Sacred Heart

1. John Croiset, *The Devotion to the Sacred Heart of Jesus* (Rockford, Ill.: Tan, 1988), 36–37.
2. Vincent Kerns, ed. and trans., *The Autobiography of St. Margaret Mary* (London: Darton, Longman and Todd, 1976), 44–45.
3. Ibid., 46–47.
4. Croiset, *The Devotion to the Sacred Heart,* 59.
5. Timothy O'Donnell, *Heart of the Redeemer* (San Francisco: Ignatius Press, 1989).
6. Karl Rahner, *Heart of the Savior* (New York: Herder, 1958), 32.
7. O'Donnell, *Heart of the Redeemer,* 80.
8. Ibid., 82.
9. Ibid.
10. Ibid., 83.
11. Ibid., 84.
12. Rahner, *Heart of the Savior,* 155.
13. Croiset, *The Devotion of the Sacred Heart,* 242ff.
14. Ibid.

15. Ibid.
16. Ibid.
17. Ibid.
18. Ibid., 243.
19. *Thoughts and Sayings of Margaret Mary,* ed. the Sisters of the Visitation of Paray-le-Monial (Rockford, Ill.: Tan, 1986), 100–101.
20. Ibid., 102–3.
21. Ibid., 60.
22. *Life and Writings of St. Margaret Mary,* ed. the Sisters of the Visitation of Paray-Le-Monial, 3 vols. (1920), 2:67.
23. Ibid., 2:73.
24. Ibid., 2:65.
25. Ibid., 2:139.
26. Ibid., 2:70.
27. Ibid., 2:190.
28. Ibid., 2:152.
29. Ibid., 2:193.
30. Ibid., 2:167.

Chapter 6: The Divine Mercy

1. Sr. M. Faustina Kowalska, *Diary: Divine Mercy in My Soul* (Stockbridge, Mass.: Marians of the Immaculate Conception, 1999).

Chapter 7: Other Accredited Visions and Messages

1. Sr. Consolata, *Jesus Appeals to the World* (Rockford, Ill.: Tan, 1975), 155.
2. Ibid., 42–44.
3. Ibid., 98.
4. Ibid., 40–41.
5. Ibid., 49.
6. Ibid., 137.
7. Ibid., 52.
8. Ibid., 164.
9. *The Spiritual Legacy of Sr. Mary of the Holy Trinity,* ed. Silvere Van Den Broek (Rockford, Ill., Tan), 90.
10. Ibid., 349.
11. Ibid., 608.
12. Ibid., 313.
13. Ibid., 178.
14. Ibid., 84.
15. Ibid., 215.
16. Ibid., 237.
17. Ibid., 594.
18. Ibid., 299.
19. Ibid., 270.
20. Ibid., 582.
21. Ibid., 55.
22. Ibid., 208.
23. Ibid., 5.
24. Ibid., 177.
25. Ibid., 96.
26. Ibid., 425.
27. Ibid., 247.

28. Ibid., 37.
29. Ibid., 414.
30. Ibid., 273.
31. Ibid., 562.
32. Ibid., 628.
33. Ibid., 483.
34. Ibid., 186.
35. Ibid., 164.
36. Ibid., 79.
37. Ibid., 328.
38. Ibid., 159.
39. Sr. Conchita, *Aut.* I:216/218, in *A Mother's Spiritual Diary,* ed. M. M. Philipon, trans. Aloysius J. Owen (New York: Alba House, 1978), 33.
40. Sr. Conchita, *Diary,* April 1898, in ibid.
41. *Diary,* February 25, 1897.
42. *Diary,* September 25, 1894.
43. *Diary,* June 7, 1916.
44. Josefa Menéndez, *The Way of Divine Love* (Rockford, Ill.: Tan, 1975), 343.
45. Ibid., 86.
46. Ibid., 327.
47. Ibid., 244.
48. Ibid., 377.
49. Ibid., 201.
50. Ibid., 104.
51. Ibid., 112.
52. Ibid., 218–19.
53. Ibid., 201–2.
54. Ibid., 305.
55. Ibid., 104.
56. Ibid., 343.
57. Ibid., 422.
58. Ibid., 26.
59. Ibid., 214.
60. Ibid., 237.
61. Ibid., 289.
62. Ibid., 237–38.
63. Ibid., 377.
64. Ibid., 174.
65. Ibid., 259.
66. Ibid., 263.
67. Dorothy Scallan, ed., *The Golden Arrow* (Rockford, Ill.: Tan, 1990), 76–77.
68. Ibid., 92.
69. Ibid., 109–10.
70. Ibid., 112–13.
71. Ibid., 124.
72. Ibid., 129–30.
73. Ibid., 131–32.
74. Ibid., 134–35.
75. Ibid., 136.
76. Ibid., 141.
77. Ibid., 145.
78. Ibid., 153–54.
79. Ibid., 156.

80. Ibid., 158.

81. Solh B. Saez, *True Devotion to the Holy Face of Jesus,* booklet (Manila, Philippines: Holy Face Center, 1990).

Chapter 8: Bible Code

1. Robert Sungenis, *Not by Bread Alone: The Biblical and Historical Evidence for the Eucharistic Sacrifice* (Goleta, Calif.: Queenship Publishing, 2000), 133.

2. Eric Mascall, *Corpus Christi* (London: Longmans, 1965), 189.

3. As cited in ibid., 158.

4. Rudolf Bultmann, *The Gospel of John,* trans. G. R. Beasley-Murray (Philadelphia: Westminster Press, 1971), 236.

5. Cited in Sungenis, *Not by Bread Alone,* 175, 193.

6. Elizabeth Anscombe, *On Transubstantiation,* pamphlet (London, 1974), 111.

7. Edward Holloway, *Catholicism: A New Synthesis* (Surrey: Faith Keyway, 1970), 326.

8. Eugene La Verdiere, *The Eucharist in the New Testament and the Early Church* (Collegeville, Minn.: Liturgical Press, 1996), 7–9.

9. Scott Hahn, *The Lamb's Supper* (New York: Doubleday, 1999), 119.

10. Sungenis, *Not by Bread Alone,* 89–92.

11. Cited in Mascall, *Corpus Christi,* 161–62.

12. Ibid., 73–74.

13. Cited in ibid., 170–71.

14. *The Eucharist* (Lausanne: Lutheran World Federation, 1978), I, 3.

15. *Anglican-Roman Catholic International Commission: The Final Report* (London: CTS-SPCK, 1982), III.

Chapter 9: Heaven Here and Now

1. J. N. D. Kelly, *Early Christian Doctrines* (San Francisco: Harper and Row, 1978), 214.

2. Adolf Von Harnack, *Lehrbuch der Dogmengeschichte* (Freiburg, 1886–1889; Tübingen, 1903; ET, of the third German edition, London, 1894–1899), II, 144; IV, 189.

3. Aidan Nichols, *The Holy Eucharist* (Dublin: Veritas, 1991), 35.

4. Eric Mascall, *Corpus Christi* (London: Longmans, 1965), 72–73.

5. Cited in Michael Gaudoin-Parker, ed., *The Real Presence through the Ages* (New York: Alba House, 1993), 12.

6. Ibid., 13.

7. Ibid.

8. Ibid., 15.

9. Ibid., 19.

10. Ibid., 20.

11. Ibid., 23.

12. Ibid., 24.

13. Ibid.

14. Ibid., 27.

15. Ibid., 29.

16. Ibid., 30.

17. Ibid., 31.

18. *To the Newly Baptized* (PG 26), 1325.

19. Cited in Gaudoin-Parker, *The Real Presence through the Ages,* 33.

20. Ibid., 35.

21. Ibid.

22. Ibid., 37.

23. Ibid., 39.

24. Ibid., 40.

25. Cited in James T. O'Connor, *The Hidden Manna* (San Francisco: Ignatius Press, 1988), 57.

26. Ibid., 59.

27. Ibid., 15.

28. Ibid., 22.

29. Ibid., 25.

30. Ibid., 32.

31. Ibid., 148.

32. Ibid., 32.

33. Canon XVIII, NPNF IL, v.14, 38, cited in *Not by Bread Alone*, 249.

34. Address by Ephiphanius, cited in Nichols, *The Holy Eucharist*, 41.

35. Quoted in Johannes H. Emminghaus, *The Eucharist* (Collegeville, Minn.: Liturgical Press, 1997), 44–45.

Chapter 10: The Progressive Elevation of Matter

1. George Gaylord Simpson, *Science* (1964): 143, 771.

2. W. Ford Doolittle, "Uprooting the Tree of Life," *Scientific American* (February 2000): 90–95.

3. Werner Arber, in *Cosmos, Bios, Theos,* ed. Henry Margenau and Roy Abraham Varghese (Chicago: Open Court, 1992), 142.

4. John Maddox, *What Remains to Be Discovered* (New York: Free Press, 1999).

5. Sir John Eccles, in *Cosmos, Bios, Theos,* 164.

6. Sir Nevill Mott, in *Cosmos, Bios, Theos,* 66.

7. Albert Einstein, in *The World Treasury of Physics, Astronomy and Mathematics,* ed. Timothy Ferris (Boston: Little, Brown and Company, 1991), 58.

8. Cited in Michael Gaudoin-Parker, ed., *The Real Presence through the Ages* (New York: Alba House, 1993), 100.

9. Faustina Kowalska, *Diary: Divine Mercy in My Soul* (Stockbridge, Mass. Marians of the Immaculate Conception, 1999), 1420.

10. Ibid., 1407.

11. The relevance of quantum theory may be briefly noted here. Amazing advances were made in the last century in understanding the fundamental structure of matter. But these advances have been accompanied by an awareness that our ability to describe activities in the microstructure of matter and the laws governing these activities is inherently limited (for instance, the impossibility of simultaneously measuring momentum and position). From the standpoint of the present issue, the distinction drawn in the doctrine of Transubstantiation between a reality and its appearance curiously parallels the debates about the distinction between classical and the quantum descriptions of a physical reality. Transubstantiation, of course, says that the bread and wine change at both a macro and a micro level to the Body and Blood of Christ, and so quantum physics sheds no new light on the doctrine. But the quantum debates are relevant to the extent that we cannot confidently claim to know everything there is to know even about the "appearances" (at the subatomic level) of a physical object, let alone that which makes it the kind of object that it is (its "substance").

12. Two recent books that are relevant to some of the themes touched on here are to be highly commended for their original and important contributions. The first, *What Is Life?* (Amsterdam: Rodopi, 1997), by Professor Josef Seifert, winner of the European Medal of Philosophy, is an incisive critique of reductionist accounts of life. The second is *Substance: Its Nature and Existence,* by Joshua Hoffman and Gary S. Rosenkrantz (London: Routledge, 1997), a powerful exposition of the concept of substance in the context of modern science and philosophy. I would like to thank Fr. James T. O'Connor, author of *The Hidden Manna,* for kindly reviewing the contents of this chapter. Finally, I want to note that the primary themes here arose out of a discussion I had with my son Michael.

13. Kowalska, *Diary: Divine Mercy in My Soul,* 156.

14. Ibid., 1385.

15. Ibid., 1447.

16. Ibid., 1489.

Chapter 11: How the Paschal Supper, Calvary, and the Heavenly Intercession Become Present Here and Now in the Holy Mass

1. *Homilies on Hebrews* 11, 2–3; *On the Priesthood* 3,4.

2. Eric Mascall, *Corpus Christi* (London: Longmans, 1965), 132–35.

Chapter 12: The Continual Coming

1. Julian Franklyn, ed., *The Dictionary of the Occult* (Detroit: Gale Research Company, 1981), 79.

2. Works that have been consulted for this chapter include: *Immaculata* magazine (Marytown Press, 1600 W. Park Ave., Libertyville, IL 60048; 1984–85); Stefano Manelli, *Jesus Our Eucharistic Love* (New Bedford, Mass.: Franciscan Friars of the Immaculate, 1996); Joan Carroll Cruz, *Eucharistic Miracles* (Rockford, Ill.: Tan, 1987); Bob and Penny Lord, *Miracles of the Eucharist* (Fair Oaks, Calif.: Journeys of Faith, 1986); Bryan and Susan Thatcher, *Eucharistic Apostles of the Divine Mercy* (Stockbridge, Mass.: Eucharistic Apostles of the Divine Mercy, 1999); Francis Johnston, *Alexandrina: The Agony and the Glory* (Dublin: Veritas, 1979); Michael H. Brown, *Secrets of the Eucharist* (Milford, Ohio: Faith Publishing, 1996); and numerous others. Dr. Bryan Thatcher and Mr. Dan Gallo of *Immaculata* have been of invaluable assistance in generously providing documentation for this essay.

Conclusion: Alpha and Omega

1. For an interpretation that stays close to both Scripture and the Fathers, see Alfred Joseph Mary Shamon's *Apocalypse* (Milford, Oh.: Faith Publishing Company, 1991).

2. Faustina Kowalska, *Diary: Divine Mercy in My Soul* (Stockbridge, Mass.: Marians of the Immaculate Conception, 1999), 83.

3. Ibid., 848.

4. Ibid., 1588.

5. T. S. Eliot, *Four Quartets* (New York: Harcourt, Brace and World, 1943), 11, 17.